THE AESTHETICS OF SOLIDARITY

The AESTHETICS of SOLIDARITY

Our Lady of Guadalupe and American Democracy

Nichole M. Flores

GEORGETOWN UNIVERSITY PRESS / WASHINGTON, DC

The publisher is not responsible for third-party websites or their content. URL links were active at time of publication.

Library of Congress Cataloging-in-Publication Data

Names: Flores, Nichole M., author.
Title: The aesthetics of solidarity : Our Lady of Guadalupe and American democracy / Nichole M. Flores.
Other titles: Moral traditions series.
Description: Washington, DC : Georgetown University Press, 2021. | Series: Moral traditions | Includes bibliographical references and index.
Identifiers: LCCN 2020034787 | ISBN 9781647120900 (hardcover) | ISBN 9781647120917 (paperback) | ISBN 9781647120924 (ebook)
Subjects: LCSH: Religion and politics—United States. | Hispanic Americans—Religion. | Hispanic Americans—Politics and government. | Solidarity—Political aspects—United States. | Solidarity—Religious aspects. | Guadalupe, Our Lady of. | Christian sociology—Catholic Church. | Political theology—United States.
Classification: LCC BL65.P7 F54 2021 | DDC 322/.10973—dc23
LC record available at https://lccn.loc.gov/2020034787

22 21   9 8 7 6 5 4 3 2 First printing

Printed in the United States of America

Cover design by Nathan Putens
Interior design by BookComp, Inc.

The image on the cover is of a National Farm Workers Association march during the California Grape Strike in 1966. Jon Lewis photograph, Beinecke Rare Book & Manuscript Library © Yale University. All rights reserved.

In memory of María Guadalupe García Flores

CONTENTS

ACKNOWLEDGMENTS

In March of 2011 I journeyed with my spouse and in-laws to the Basilica of Our Lady of Guadalupe located on the outskirts of Mexico City. A second-year doctoral student at the time, I arrived at Tepeyac with a notebook and a Nikon, prepared to observe popular worship at the basilica. I was certain that what we would see, hear, and experience that day would inform my research on a budding dissertation. As soon as I crossed the threshold of the basilica, however, I burst into tears. I had come to Tepeyac as a researcher but was experiencing it as a pilgrim. In many ways the writing of this book has been an extension of that experience and that journey. I wish to acknowledge those who have accompanied me on the pilgrimage over the past decade.

My thanks especially go to Al Bertrand and the editors of Georgetown University Press's Moral Traditions series, David Cloutier, Andrea Vicini, and Darlene Fozard Weaver, for their confidence in this project and their crucial support in shepherding it to completion. I am also indebted to Kristin Heyer and Richard Brown for recognizing the promise of this work in its earliest stages. Since 2017 the editorial team at *America: The Jesuit Review of Faith and Culture* has welcomed me and shaped me as a writer. Thank you for allowing me to share in the pages of the magazine some of the stories that inspired this book.

I remain grateful to the members of my doctoral committee, Lisa Sowle Cahill, Nancy Pineda Madrid, and David Hollenbach, for their continued enthusiasm and support for the project as it matured from dissertation into book. There is a cloud of witnesses—teachers and mentors—who inspired me during the formative years of my doctoral studies at Boston College, especially Roberto Goizueta, M. Shawn Copeland, James Keenan, Stephen Pope, Richard Gaillardetz, James Bretzke, Mary Jo Iozzio, and Hosffman Ospino. I am also appreciative of the time I spent working at the Boisi Center for Religion and American Public Life alongside Erik Owens and Alan Wolfe; much of my initial reflection about this work took place behind the French doors of the graduate assistant's office, and the finished work reflects the spirit of the Boisi Center in those days.

I have been fortunate to write this book surrounded by colleagues in the Department of Religious Studies at the University of Virginia, who care about me both as a scholar and a person. Willis Jenkins, Charles Mathewes, Paul Dafydd Jones, and James Childress have supported me and advocated for me since my earliest days at UVA. Many colleagues in the department also helped me to hone this work over the past five years: Jalane Schmidt, Jennifer Geddes, Larry Bouchard, Charles Marsh, Asher Biemann, Matthew Hedstrom, Heather Warren, Kathleen Flake, Ashon Crawley, Karl Shuve, Janet Spittler, Martien Halvorson-Taylor, Elizabeth Alexander, Cynthia Hoehler-Fatton, John Nemec, Sonam Kachru, Shankar Nair, and Kurtis Schaeffer.

To the untrained eye it may appear somewhat unseemly for a *Guadalupana* to teach about religion at Mr. Jefferson's University. And yet the relationships and collaborations I have built at UVA have been essential to this project. I am especially grateful for my collaboration with Bruce Williams, my teaching partner of the course Do We Have Faith in Democracy?; teaching alongside him has enriched me as a teacher, a scholar, and a human. The Institute for Humanities and Global Cultures, the Institute for Advanced Studies of Culture, and the Project on Lived Theology have offered various forms of support during my time at UVA. Conversations with Larycia Hawkins, Tony Lin, Garnette Cadogan, Chad Wellmon, Shilpa Davé, Tamika Carey, Kwame Otu, Laurie Balfour, Rebecca Stangle, Ricardo Padron, Emily Ogden, and Andrew Hayashi have immensely strengthened this work.

Let me also thank my UVA students—graduate and undergraduate— who have read and commented on drafts of this book's manuscript, recommended sources for consideration, and gifted me with reading and learning from their own work: Charles Gillespie, Shifa Amina Noor, Lucila Crena, Erik Hilker, Elizabeth Cable, Creighton Coleman, Kyle Nicholas, Blair Wilner, Jason Evans, Michelle Bostic, William Boyce, Caleb Hendrickson, Evan Sandsmark, Luke Beck Kreider, Mae Speight, Timothy Shriver, Olivia August, Grey O'Neil, Elizabeth Woods, Sarah Katherine Doyle, Robert McCarthy, Grant Tabler, and Zyahna Bryant. It is an honor to be your teacher.

Friends and colleagues from across my field and countless others have helped to enhance this book: Christina McRorie, Michael Jaycox, Ruben Rosario Rodríguez, María Teresa Dávila, Victor Carmona, Rámon Luzárraga, Jeremy Cruz, Miguel De La Torre, Bryan Massingale, Shawnie Daniels-Sykes, Vincent Lloyd, Grace Kao, Kevin Ahern, Meghan Clark, Rebecca Espstein-Levi, Brandy Daniels, Jeremy Sabella, Frederick Simmons, Cecilia González-Andrieu, Carmen Nanko-Fernández, Tony Alonzo, Susan Reynolds, Robert J. Rivera, R. Ward Holder, Erik Cleven, Daniel Daly, Bede Bidlack, Nicole Reibe, Elizabeth Klein, Amanda Osheim, Stephen Okey, Christopher Conway, Timothy Matovina, Peter Cassarella, Natalia Marandiuc, Ryan McAnnally-Linz, Drew Collins, and Angela Gorrell.

A number of institutions invited me to present and discuss portions of the manuscript, for which I am grateful: the Yale Center for Faith and Culture, the Political Theology Project at Villanova University, College of the Holy Cross, Candler School of Theology at Emory University, the Augustine Institute, Colorado College, Santa Clara University, and Saint John's University. The feedback from each of these workshops was truly beneficial to the development of this book. I am fortunate to participate in several academic groups in which my ideas are able to flourish: the Academy of Catholic Hispanic Theologians of the United States, the Latino/a Working and Interest Group of the Society of Christian Ethics, the Ethics Section of the American Academy of Religion, the Consultation on Hispanic Latino/a Theology of the Catholic Theological Society of America, and the Project on Race, Faith, and Culture of the Institute for Advanced Studies in Culture.

This work is anchored by the dedication of artists, organizers, and activists located in Denver, Colorado, and Charlottesville, Virginia. I am humbled by the opportunity I have had to listen to and learn from community leaders along the way, including Federico Peña, Micaela Garcia de Benevides, Seth Wispelwey, Tracy Howe Wispelwey, Osagyefo Sekou, Eric Martin, Isaac Collins, Zyahna Bryant, and Christen Yates. Several church communities in Charlottesville have nourished me, including the Church of the Incarnation, St. Thomas Aquinas University Parish, All Souls Charlottesville, and Casa Alma Catholic Worker Community. I am particularly thankful for the spiritual guidance of Fr. Gregory Kandt, Deacon Chris Morash, Pastor Winn Collier, and Pastor Brendan Jamieson.

Many Charlottesville community partners made the completion of this work possible by caring for my family and our essential needs so that I could dedicate time and attention to writing: Ixchel Freed, Linda Crennan, Vicki Briggs, Alyson Quillon, Stephanie Clevenger, Christy Rexrode, Jackie Draper, Amanda Baber, Tonya Henderson, Sara Albrecht, Crystal Shelton, Brittainy Stevens, Patricia Masias, Michael Williams, Kimberly Dowdell, Diane Rozycki, Ken Horne, Liz Reynolds, Toni Halkos, Katie Wade, Rachel Shockley, Sarah Wightman, Anita Johnson, Brenda Michie, Corey Tyler, Doug Burgess, Jean Blackwell, Jessica Aquilina, Jennifer Via, and Erin Bruce Garcia. I remain grateful to a host of other friends and neighbors who care for my family through their abundant hard work, talent, and commitment to the shalom of our community!

I would like to express profound affection for my friends Tanya Skypeck, Kori Pacyniac, Nicole Galio, and Sandra Valdes Lopez, who have accompanied me over the course of many seasons of my life. Thank you for your support in ways both large and small. This project simply could not have been as rich and multidimensional as it has become without the help of my best friend, Rebecca Lipman, who is more like a sister to me. To my friends Jes Kast, Nadia Bolz-Weber, Austin Channing, Mihee Kim-Kort, Kerlin Richter, Emily Scott, Neichelle Guidry, Winnie Varghees, Theresa Tames, Lanecia Rouse, Jeff Chu, and Rachel Kurtz: thank you for your daily love, support, and solidarity over the years. To three special families who have accompanied ours over many years—John and Lauren Boyles, Rob and Tessa Snider, and Jon and Ann Ungerland—thank you for shining Christ's love into our lives.

Thank you to my beloved *familia* for their constant love and support, especially my parents, Denise and Ramiro Flores, for always encouraging my *fides quaerens intellectum* (faith seeking understanding). My father-in-law, Bill Henry, and late mother-in-law, Nancy Henry, stimulated my thinking on this project in many ways. *Gracias a Carla Anguiano Vargas por su amor y apoyo.* To my siblings by birth and marriage, Nina-Christine Meadows, Noelle Flores, Jeremie Meadows, Chris Henry, and Carolyn Junkins: in accord with their duties as siblings they have kept me from taking myself too seriously and on occasion have let me win at Settlers of Catan. Each one of them has asked incisive questions and debated various aspects of this work. I am very blessed, as well, to have constant love and support from my Flores, Henry, and Rose extended families.

Roberto Emmanuel Flores Henry read his first Guadalupe picture book— a gift from his Tía Jes Kast—when he was just three months old. Watching my son begin his own journey of *fides quaerens intellectum* has been the greatest joy of my life. Thank you, Ro, for reminding me everyday that Guadalupe is "Jesus' mama!"

To my spouse, James Daryn Henry: I would never have completed this book without your love, dedication, editorial pen, and good cooking. You are my partner in all things and my great love.

INTRODUCTION

Sound bursts forth from the *quiquiztli* (conch shell), filling the theater with a low, resonant hum. The scent of *copal* (incense) fills the air. Aztec dancers dressed in traditional *Mexica* costumes enter from the back of the theater, accompanied by dancers with shakers and drums. All are covered in ornate beading that jangles as they dance. Behind the dancers enters a procession of actors wearing costumes ranging from peasant clothing to clerics to contemporary street attire. The dancers and actors lead the audience in a dance honoring the Four Winds. This ritual begins the performance of *The Miracle at Tepeyac*, a play that recounts the narrative of Our Lady of Guadalupe's appearance to Juan Diego intermingled with the story of a Hispanic Catholic parish in a fictional Colorado tourist town. The once-thriving and beautiful parish is fighting to survive but also struggling to meet the immense spiritual, economic, social, and political needs of its members and the broader community with few resources or support from their bishop.

The play interlaces the story of the parish with a retelling of the story of Guadalupe's appearance to Juan Diego on Tepeyac, a hill on the outskirts of modern-day Mexico City. By weaving Guadalupe's symbol into its portrayal of the multidimensional experiences of marginalization and suffering experienced by the fictional parish members, the play draws a connection between Juan Diego's struggle for recognition in colonial society and the ongoing struggles for justice among Denver's Chicanx community.[1] Guadalupe appears as a tender yet powerful vision to Juan Diego. She speaks to him in his native language, Nahuatl, and appears before him on the sacred site dedicated to Tonatzin, the Aztec mother goddess whose temple was destroyed by colonial forces.

The performers are members of Su Teatro, Denver's Chicano community theater. Founded in 1972 as a student theater group at the University of Colorado Denver, Su Teatro performed its earliest works at protests and on picket lines during the Chicano civil rights movement in the 1970s.[2] The company is led by playwright and activist Tony Garcia, who writes or cowrites the majority of the company's works. Su Teatro owns a theater located on

Santa Fe Drive in Denver's rapidly gentrifying Westside neighborhood, where it performs plays about Chicanx and Latine experience in Denver (see Note on Terminology later in this chapter).

The Miracle at Tepeyac is Garcia's lament for the loss of the Auraria neighborhood, one of Denver's first Hispanic neighborhoods. In 1969 the city of Denver called a special bond issue vote to raise funds for the Auraria Higher Education Center.[3] Passage of the bond would have forced Auraria's residents to move from their neighborhood to make way for the campus. The move also would have resulted in the closure of the neighborhood's institutions, including predominantly Hispanic Saint Cajetan's Catholic Church.

Saint Cajetan's was the heart of Auraria, orienting life in the neighborhood for the Hispanic and Chicano people. In addition to weekly liturgies, the parish hosted fiestas and cultural events (plays, concerts) and even founded a credit union.[4] "The lives of the Hispanic people in Auraria revolved around their church," writes Magdalena Gallegos, director of Auraria Remembered, an oral history project about the neighborhood. "The Hispanic people did not have much at that time; they did not have a public institution where they could mingle and feel important. St. Cajetan's became that place."[5] Led by Fr. Pete Garcia of Saint Cajetan's, residents formed the Auraria Resident's Organization (ARO) to save their neighborhood and their parish. Hoping for support for their cause from other area Catholics, the ARO visited every other Catholic church in Denver to distribute leaflets and make its case for voting against the bond issue. Despite the ARO's efforts, Archbishop James Casey wrote a letter in support of the bond issue to be read from every pulpit in Denver before the election. The bond passed in 1972, the same year as Su Teatro's founding. Auraria's residents were forced to relocate, scattering across communities on Colorado's Front Range. The Archdiocese of Denver closed Saint Cajetan's, consolidating the parish with a nearby parish, St. Elizabeth of Hungary. Don Vigil, a former Auraria resident, remarked, "It was funny, most Hispanics went to Saint Cajetan's and most of the Anglos went to St. Elizabeth's."[6] And despite Saint Cajetan's vibrant parish life and cultural significance for Auraria's Chicanos, it was Saint Elizabeth's that survived. The former Auraria Higher Education Center is now home to three institutions: Community College of Denver, Metropolitan State University of Denver, and University of Colorado Denver. Saint Cajetan's was converted into a multipurpose community center at the Auraria Higher Education Center; Su Teatro returned to its community's deconsecrated sanctuary to perform *The Miracle at Tepeyac* in 1995, which it called the "Saint Cajetan's Reunification Project."[7]

Garcia, who grew up in the Auraria neighborhood and later attended the University of Colorado Denver, uses the relationship between Guadalupe and Juan Diego to explore the various emotional, spiritual, and political dimensions of the removal of Chicanos from Auraria. In his interview for *Auraria Remembered*, Garcia reflected on growing up in the neighborhood: "I remember a real sense of community. . . . The community was a safe harbor and the outside world harbored racism and economic oppression and was not safe for man or beast." The loss of Auraria was a loss for the Chicanos who had found consolation from the harsh realities of racism in the neighborhood and at the parish. The play expresses the community's desolation and explores its abandonment by both civic and ecclesial powers through the portrayal of a fictional Hispanic parish that has been ignored and dismissed by its archbishop. Each character meets opposition to their desire for community from the powers that be, whether the law, the culture, the archdiocese, or the parish itself. At the same time, Garcia's play portrays the relationship between Guadalupe and Juan Diego as a source of hope for justice and restoration in the community. This is not a facile hope for reconciliation with oppressors, most of whom remain offstage even though their actions affect the lives of each character. Rather, Garcia illustrates the birth of solidarity among the church members, who come to realize their responsibility and commitment to one another over the course of the play.

Garcia's play also illuminates a broader issue facing US Latines: marginalization within supposedly democratic structures that determine many aspects about their lives. Some would point to muted voter turnout numbers among Latines, relative to White and African American voters, as the root of this problem. "Latinos punch below their weight electorally," remarked former Pew Forum on Religion and Public Life director Luis Lugo in 2012.[8] While Lugo does not address voter suppression among Latines (an issue that has received broader public attention during the 2020 election season), he argues that there is reason to believe that Latino turnout could be much higher in coming national elections.[9] Responding to various factors curtailing turnout, Latines in politics have turned to grassroots organizing practices to increase participation among their communities in both formal and informal ways. This approach has yielded increased participation in various aspects of a modern democracy. What often remains unexamined, however, is the role the very structures of liberal democracy itself plays in hindering robust participation among Latines and other marginalized groups. Understanding why this is the case invites an exploration of the relationship involving political liberalism, Latine theological aesthetics, Catholic social teaching, and Our Lady of Guadalupe.

GENTRIFICATION AND THE
"THROWAWAY CULTURE"

The removal of the Auraria residents from their neighborhood in the 1970s foreshadowed the role of gentrification—defined here as the displacement of a community's less wealthy residents by residents with more wealth—in Denver's political and cultural climate in the early twenty-first century.[10] The city experienced a population boom after a period of economic and cultural growth beginning in the 1980s. This growth, along with associated demographic shifts, spurred Denver's ascent as a major US city and a regional economic, cultural, and political center. The city now draws White middle- and upper-class residents attracted to the region's promise of sunshine, skiing, and substances. But this growth has destabilized Denver's communities of color and resulted in unsustainable surges in housing prices as well as the displacement of long-standing institutions in neighborhoods of color (churches, restaurants, and social clubs, for example). Like the Auraria neighborhood in the early 1970s, Denver's Black and Brown neighborhoods in the early 2020s are struggling to survive against the gentrification driven by rhetoric that advocates for an Enlightenment-inflected ideal of the "highest and best" use of land without accounting for the consequences of this pursuit for poor and marginalized communities.[11]

In his 2015 environmental encyclical, *Laudato si'*, Pope Francis decries the "throwaway culture" that diminishes all people and all things to "rubbish."[12] The throwaway culture leads to "the globalization of indifference," a condition in which human beings have little regard for the intrinsic value of all created things or for our responsibility to care for all.[13] The mentality that people are disposable has shaped the politics of movement for Latine people in the United States and the Americas. Beginning with practices of enslavement and genocide of their African and Indigenous ancestors, Latine people have experienced a pattern of displacement and removal that pulsates throughout their history. This still-continuing pattern reduces modern Latine life to a disposable commodity within global capitalism, where the same bodies are exploited for cheap labor to perform essential tasks before being "thrown away" via economic, political, or legal means.

The disposability of Latine and Black lives rose to the forefront of public consideration in March 2020 as the COVID-19 pandemic took hold of lives and economies across the globe. Scores of Black and Brown workers were deemed "essential workers" whose labor was necessary for society's continued functioning, while others sheltered in place. Essential workers were required to continue working in agricultural fields, meatpacking facilities, warehouses, nursing homes, grocery stores, and other occupations that placed them at higher risk for contracting the virus. Predictably, the virus ravaged through communities of these workers, who also were more likely to have dangerous comorbidities but less likely to have access to quality health care due to other inequalities in society's basic structure. "The COVID-19 pandemic showed that while all might be vulnerable, we are not equally vulnerable," writes Bryan Massingale:

> The contributing factors for this vulnerability have been documented for decades: lack of insurance, less access to healthcare, negligent treatment from and by healthcare professionals, overcrowded housing, unsafe and unsanitary working conditions. All of this compounded by how the least paid and protected workers are now considered "essential" and must be exposed to the virus' hazards. As a young black grocery clerk told me, "Essential is just a nice word for sacrificial."[14]

As the virus raged across the United States from sea to shining sea, people began to identify and acknowledge the structures of oppression that shaped life for Black and Brown people in the Americas long before the time of the coronavirus.

Solidarity is an essential response to the throwaway culture and the globalization of indifference, argues Francis. While he calls for participation in practical actions that foster solidarity, he also exhorts sharing stories that allow us to cultivate a shared identity: "Around these community actions, relationships develop or are recovered and a new social fabric emerges. Thus a community can break out of the indifference induced by consumerism. These actions cultivate a shared identity, with a story which can be remembered and handed on."[15] It is in these stories, or what Alejandro García-Rivera calls the "little stories," where a solidarity that rejects a mentality of disposability operates in patterns of displacement and shape Chicanx culture, religion, and politics.

THE WESTSIDE'S "LITTLE STORIES"

In his writing on St. Martín de Porres, García-Rivera contrasts the little stories of Latin American popular religion with the "Big Story" told by the institutional powers of Catholicism. "The 'Big Story,'" he explains, "tells a story of universal principles believed to be responsible for human being, giving it locus and meaning in the cosmos."[16] These principles can seem opaque and inaccessible to those who have not been "trained in the art of disclosing the universals" like theologians and philosophers have. Nevertheless, we ask and attempt to answer challenging questions about our existence: What does it mean to be human? How should we relate to one another? How should we relate to other creatures? Does God exist and what is God's nature? How ought we relate to God?

Discourse about the Big Story is thus vital to education and the ongoing pursuit of truth. García-Rivera argues that the work of experts is essential to the pursuit of truth in society, but he is wary of the Big Story being told in a manner that is comprehensible only by other specialists. Retreating into an echo chamber of communication by and for elites, the account of the Big Story is actually a particular insider's account of reality: "As it turns out, the 'Big Story' account of reality turns out to be not so much a universal tale of human being, but merely a skewed or specialized story, an insider's story that makes sense only to those who tell it."[17]

García-Rivera contrasts this kind of trumped-up Big Story with the little stories that animate Latin American popular religion. A little story does not attempt to explain theological or philosophical principles, at least not directly. Rather, little stories attend to the particular rather than the universal. García-Rivera uses the example of St. Martín de Porres's healing ministry. He cared for people who were sick, but he also cared for dogs, cats, and mice. He made friends with these creatures, caring for them with tenderness equal to what he showed to humans. He even invited the animals to eat from the same bowl of soup despite their animosities. The other friars in his priory were astounded to witness the dog, the cat, and the mouse drinking soup from the same bowl while sitting at Saint Martín's feet.[18]

To some the minutiae of this story can seem insignificant to larger questions related to the Big Story of our common humanity. But García-Rivera contends that attention to small particular stories is necessary for understanding the big stories. "Hidden in the simplicity of the 'little stories' of St. Martín de Porres is a 'Big Story' about human being."[19] The story about the dog, the cat, and the mouse, he argues, reveals a bigger story about the nature of difference among humans: "These differences . . . do not necessarily make us natural enemies of one another. We are bound in common fellowship. . . . Our creatureliness becomes the basis for sharing our resources. We all can drink from the same bowl of soup, for we are creatures not of some universal humanity but of one Creator."

Writing as a Catholic theologian, García-Rivera rejects the modern notion of a homogenized human identity in favor of plurality and particularity. His insistence on human plurality allows space for little stories to weave together a common good that does not rely on adherence to just one religious faith. Instead, it gestures to the possibility that telling little stories allows us to understand our common humanity in a nuanced way and does not demand reduction of all that is human to a single conception of rationality. It denies modernity's pseudoscientific tendency to bifurcate—mind from body, male from female, White from Black—to create hierarchies that maintain systems of oppression. Indeed, attending to the little stories suggests a response to monological reasoning that perpetuates conceptions of "disposable" or "sacrificial" humans while also suggesting the possibility of cultivating an aesthetic solidarity that can envision a common good based on a just solidarity.

Su Teatro uses performances of *The Miracle at Tepeyac* to tell the little stories that interlace stories of the past with the present realities of gentrification in Denver's Chicano neighborhoods. In so doing Garcia uses the little stories of the Westside's *Guadalupanos* to articulate a political critique of the laws, policies, institutions, and structures that devastate Black and Brown communities. While his play explores Guadalupe's religious and cultural significance, Garcia also invokes Guadalupe as an explicitly political symbol, employing both her image and her relationship with Juan Diego to interrogate the treatment of the Chicanx community and other marginalized people for the sake of economic and political progress. Inhabiting the genre of the Guadalupe play, Su Teatro celebrates Chicanx religion and culture in Denver while rejecting the neocolonial political and economic arrangements that displace and erase marginalized communities there.[20]

The Miracle at Tepeyac demonstrates the capacity of the story of Guadalupe to inform substantive critiques of laws, policies, and institutions. From the United Farm Workers in the fields of Delano, California, to the *comités Guadalupanos* (Guadalupe committees) in New York City, Latine social justice activists use Guadalupan grammar to articulate their critiques of unjust political and economic arrangements. Simultaneously these justice movements marshal the aesthetic dimensions of Guadalupan images, narratives, and liturgies to invite society at large to join them in their campaign. Guadalupe's bright image invites the cultivation of a solidarity committed to changing the laws, policies, and institutions that treat Latine people and communities as disposable implements in local, national, and global economies.

Judith Dupré, who photographs and writes about Marian images in religion and culture, explains Guadalupe's ability to unite people from different backgrounds around a common cause: "Guadalupe has gone global, mirroring back to everyone their own dreams and priorities, and in the process binding together unlikely bedfellows."[21] Dupré emphasizes the political power of the image, noting its use by advocates for the confirmation of Sonia Sotomayor, the first Latina nominated and confirmed to the US Supreme Court in 2009. Citing the importance of the image to mediate contradictions and build bridges between different social groups in society, Dupré offers a prayer for Guadalupe's intervention into the politics of immigration justice: "That Guadalupe's image is found on bottle caps as well as in basilicas is evidence of the wide faith in her perennial power to build bridges between people with different values. Let's hope she makes an appearance soon on the Senate floor."[22] Dupré gestures to Guadalupe's potential to mediate differences between enormous religious, cultural, and political rifts. She does not assert that Guadalupe's image will on its own persuade opponents to change their minds about particular proposals for just immigration reform. Nevertheless, she does express hope in Guadalupe's capacity to cultivate solidarity across unexpected religious, cultural, economic, and political boundaries to form bonds of affection necessary for changing minds and changing hearts.

Liberal orthodoxy relegates the use of "thick" religious symbols—whether Big Story or little story—to what John Rawls calls the "background culture." It is clear, nonetheless, that the justice claims pursued through religious language can bear directly on society's basic structures. Beyond assertion of justice claims, however, Guadalupe inspires a vigorously participatory vision of democracy, one that reflects a conception of cultural citizenship that emphasizes the practices of democracy available to all members of society even as they are barred from pursuing legal status and a full schedule of rights associated with a juridical conception of citizenship (e.g., voting).[23] In examining Guadalupe as a public symbol that makes substantive claims about democracy and the common good, a crucial question for the life of democracy in the twenty-first century arises: To what extent can the little stories be engaged on matters pertaining to society's basic structure in a pluralistic society? This question invites us to consider anew the framework through which we evaluate religious and cultural particularity in the life of democracy today.

RELIGION, AESTHETICS, AND SOLIDARITY

As Philip Quinn has noted, "Politics and religion are a dangerous mixture; combining them, even in academic discussion, risks generating more heat than light."[24] The "danger" and "heat" of thinking about religion and politics together emanates from a conception of religion (along with ideas about emotions and the body) as a destabilizing force. Funded by Enlightenment-era tendencies to bifurcate reality into higher and lower categories, political liberalism labors to curtail religion's destabilizing influence on laws and institutions. Certainly liberalism's commitment to maintaining a legal separation between our common governmental institutions and particular religious traditions remains necessary and crucial in the context of twenty-first-century democracy. The commitment seems particularly relevant when religious discrimination is leveraged to undermine democratic equality. Nonetheless, the expression of religious perspectives on issues that influence the development of laws, policies, and institutions to form society's basic structure is a reality of our common democratic life. Failure to grapple with that reality renders us unable to respond to threats to common life posed by individuals, laws, policies, and institutions that undermine authentic pluralism. At the same time, an inadequate framework for engaging substantive justice claims expressed by marginalized people also hinders the possibility of cultivating a robust, participatory democracy.

In response to this problem, religious ethicists have argued for an expansion of the liberal framework to make religious language and arguments legible within a pluralistic society without capitulating to antidemocratic modes of governance that undermine this pluralism.[25] This expression allows ethicists to acknowledge not only the reality of religious perspectives within the common life of democracy but also the potential for the forthright expression of these perspectives to cultivate a culture of civic trust.[26] Ethicists have also reflected on the potential role of religious practices in generating a civic culture in which religion can be engaged while pursuing a society ever more amenable to authentic religious pluralism.[27] What remains in need of elaboration is the way that the aesthetic dimensions of particular religious traditions can be engaged in cultivating a more participatory democracy that invites substantive contributions to society's common life from religious people and communities.

Aesthetics presents itself as a particularly beneficial category for navigating the tensions among and between religious particularity, democratic participation, and authentic pluralism. While aesthetic discourse has often referred to the study of the beautiful (especially in theology and philosophy), I am interested specifically in the aesthetic dimensions of the human experience, which need not be limited to experiences of beauty per se. Aesthetic experience is concerned with the sensory dimensions, or the *felt* qualities, of everyday encounters and how such encounters shape human actions.[28] Christopher Tirres describes aesthetic meaning as emerging organically within everyday experience. Interlacing John Dewey's argument for the everyday character of the aesthetic with Ada María Isasi-Díaz's *mujerista* (a theological discourse that prioritizes the voices of grassroots Latinas working for justice) account of the ethical significance of *lo cotidiano* (everyday experiences), Tirres argues for the essential role of aesthetic experience in the struggle for justice: the aesthetic quality of everyday experiences, Tirres argues, can empower communities that are striving for political and social change by allowing them to express their desire for liberation.[29] Denver's burgeoning antigentrification movement, for example, engages the "every-dayness" of aesthetic experience—stories, music, poetry, dance, art, religious iconography—to both console and empower those who live amid conditions of social, political, and economic erasure while also cultivating a rich imaginative space for articulating a vision of the good life in the midst of social upheaval and indeterminacy.

Despite his well-earned reputation for exaltation of abstraction and lack of interest in aesthetics, I argue that Rawls's political philosophy expresses an anonymous aesthetics that is predicated on the role of imagination as manifest in his articulation of the original position, the sense of justice, and public reason. Rawls's liberal aesthetics has immense implications for the practice of democracy, especially as it pertains to the engagement of religion and culture in the context of society's basic structures. Specifically, the Rawlsian aesthetic has shaped the aesthetics of public life to exclude the histories, experiences, and concerns of Black and Brown people who have been subjected to profound communal and personal injury by the same basic structures—including law enforcement agencies such as local police departments and federal immigrations authorities—that Rawls's philosophies seek to construct and protect.

As Polemarchus is heir to Cephalus's argument, so Martha Nussbaum inherits Rawls's argument about political stability and provides a "reasonable moral psychology" that can support the adjustments to Rawls's theory.[30] Nussbaum articulates her own liberal aesthetics, based on her cognitivist account of emotions, in arguing that political emotions such as love and compassion are actually crucial for generating political stability. (Significantly, she rejects other emotions, such as anger and shame, as candidates for providing stability to public life.) Although Nussbaum advocates for greater engagement of cultural particularity through the arts, she severely curtails the permissibility of public engagement with religious and cultural particularity. For instance, she argues that Martin Luther King Jr.'s sermons ought to be treated as civic poetry, sundering his Christian beliefs—indeed, his prophetic indictment—from the public dimension of his message. One struggles to imagine how Nussbaum might conceive of acceptable engagement of Our Lady of Guadalupe and associated justice claims within a liberal framework. Nussbaum's liberal aesthetics thus struggle to provide an adequate framework for constructive engagement of religious and cultural particularity in a democratic society constituted by robust pluralism.

Latine theological aesthetics can help generate a framework for thinking about pluralism and participation within a democracy that uses a more
nuanced approach to religion and culture in the context of our common
life. For some, stereotypes about social insularity and cultural insufficiency
might render Latine theology an illegitimate source for reflection on difference. Similarly, shallow thinking about the relationship between religion and
public life have hindered our society's ability to think about religious beliefs
and practices—both our own and those of others—in sophisticated and generative ways.[31] Nonetheless, Latine theologians have engaged in sustained
thought about what it means to form community amid differences. Alejandro
García-Rivera's proposal that aesthetic encounters can be crucial to the formation of communities across difference presents itself as a crucial resource
for elaborating a framework for aesthetic solidarity in a pluralistic and democratic context.

Latine theological aesthetics, like Latine theology more broadly, contains
an implicit conception of justice. But neither aesthetic experience nor the
communities that are formed across difference through shared experiences
are self-evidently just. For example, the August 2017 Unite the Right Rally in
Charlottesville, Virginia, illustrated the power of shared aesthetic experiences
to sow a solidarity of hatred among diverse groups of White supremacists
(through the shared aesthetic symbols of Nazi salutes, the haze of tiki torches,
and the vibrations of hate chants echoing across The Lawn at the University
of Virginia). Theirs is a solidarity untethered from adequate norms of justice.
Latine theological aesthetics obviously does not wish to promote this kind of
hate-filled solidarity. Nonetheless, this example demonstrates the need for an
explicit ethical account of the norms of solidarity, justice, and the common
good to act as an anchor for the constructive contributions of religion and
aesthetics in the life of democracy.

Catholic theological ethics provides a uniquely beneficial discourse for
understanding the role of aesthetic engagement in responding to injustice in
the life of democracy in the twenty-first-century United States. Responding
to prominent-yet-underdeveloped expressions of solidarity within Catholic
social teaching (the teachings from the Catholic Church's official teaching
office, also known as the Magisterium), Catholic ethicists have argued for the
mutual constitution of solidarity, justice, and the common good. David Hollenbach situates solidarity as an essential aspect of the pursuit of justice and
the common good in a pluralistic society. "From a common good perspective," he argues, "justice calls for the minimal level of solidarity required to
enable all of society's members to live with basic dignity." Linking solidarity
to his definition of justice allows Hollenbach to articulate a conception of

the common good that prioritizes the flourishing of each individual member of society even as it seeks to augment the good of society as a whole: "No one can be left out or excluded from larger society without being unjustly harmed."[32] His definition of justice provides a helpful standard for assessing the adequacy of common good claims. These claims are empty if they do not promote the flourishing of all members of society while also seeking the aggregate benefit of all.

Meghan J. Clark similarly links solidarity with justice. Building on Catholic feminist theological anthropologies, she identifies mutuality, equality, and participation as essential characteristics of solidarity. The *imago Dei*, she argues, is in fact an *imago Trinitatis*. While acknowledging that all language about the Trinity is analogical, she asserts the ethical significance of humankind's creation in the image of the Trinity: "Equality, mutuality, and reciprocity of the persons of the Trinity are revelatory for the participation and community to which humanity is called."[33] Clark's basic criteria for just and unjust relationships allow for an adjudication between solidarity claims: White supremacist solidarity is unjust because it seeks to foster inequality and domination rather than equality and mutuality, for example. The distinction between just and unjust relationships clarifies solidarity's scope and allows for the fruitful interaction between aesthetics and ethics in constructing a framework for engaging religious and cultural particularity and forging a democratic culture characterized by equality, mutuality, and participation.

At this juncture, it is helpful to explicate the method I use to bring the sources that inform this work into conversation with one another. This work is primarily one of practical ethics, engaging in the distinct-but-related conversations of Catholic theological ethics, Christian ethics, and religious ethics. I aim to develop a framework to inform practical action within communities pursuing justice and solidarity. At the same time this project is steeped in Latine theology, meaning that it is a work of *teologia en conjunto*. Concretely this means that the work is informed by other Latine theologians, both their published scholarship and their accompaniment through conversations over many years about Guadalupe, aesthetics, popular religion, *lo cotidiano*, justice, emotion, politics, and democracy. I cite many Latine theologians and see their work as foundational to my own. *Teologia en conjunto* is itself a work of solidarity, one that requires conversations with theologians, activists, and artists beyond one's own intellectual *familia*. This pursuit of solidarity is evident in the range of interlocutors employed. For this reason it would be a hermeneutical mistake to read this book as a project that seeks to place Latine theology in opposition to other theological discourses, especially given the profound influence of the many theological and religious scholars and discourses on my thinking about this topic. Latine theology and ethics are essential to our common discourses about religion and democracy in the United States and should thus be engaged in the broader conversations pertaining to our common life.

As a project in Latine theology, this book also attends to the voices of the communities discussed in the text, in both their synchronic and their diachronic dimensions. The historical accounts of Denver's Our Lady of Guadalupe Parish, Chicano Crusade for Justice, Su Teatro, and The SOURCE Theater Company are shaped by archival research in the Denver Public Library's Western History Collection, including scripts, photographs, poems, playbills, bulletins, letters, and other documents. I also attended live performances of Su Teatro's *The Miracle at Tepeyac* (December 2017) and The SOURCE's *The Five Points/ Wrapped Around My Soul* (May 2015). My description of Federico Peña's faith and public life is based on archival research of his electoral campaigns as documented in the Western History Collection (some of which I began as an undergraduate in 2003) and three personal conversations with him over the course of two years. Finally, my remarks on the events of #Charlottesville are informed by conversations with local organizers, including Eric Martin, Seth Wispelwey, and Jalane Schmidt, in their capacities as grassroots community activists whose commitments are animated, in part or in whole, by Christian traditions of justice and solidarity. These sources help describe the theological, religious, social, economic, and political contexts that inform the practical ethical work of the project.

PLAN OF THE BOOK

Beginning with historical analysis of the formation of Guadalupan devotional practices, chapter 1 reflects on *The Miracle at Tepeyac* to construct a political theology of Guadalupe and Juan Diego. This political theology is predicated on the solidarity expressed in their encounter, where Juan Diego's realization of his fundamental dignity, autonomy, and relationality is essential to his empowerment in colonial society. The relationship between Guadalupe and Juan Diego is crucial to the symbol's theological, political, and ethical signification in the context of twenty-first-century US democracy. The chapter concludes by posing a crucial question for the life of democracy in the twenty-first century: How ought particular religious and cultural symbols be engaged in a pluralistic society?

Chapter 2 unveils John Rawls's liberal aesthetics. Beginning with an exploration of the theme of imagination in Federico Peña's 1983 campaign

for mayor of Denver, I trace the role of imagination in Rawls's political philosophy to disclose aesthetic elements of his notions of the original position,
the sense of justice, and public reason. Exposing these aesthetic aspects of
Rawls's thought unveils his discomfort with religion and the negative effects
of his exclusion of difference—including religious difference—on democratic participation among marginalized people in the United States.

Chapter 3 outlines Martha Nussbaum's liberal aesthetics, which aim to
articulate the relationship between cultural particularity and Rawls's account
of political stability. Nussbaum advocates for engagement with literature and
other narrative-based art forms (film and opera, for example) to form political
emotions that sustain the project of identifying a common good within a liberal and pluralistic society. Taking on various philosophical critiques of emotions as simply destabilizing and destructive forces, Nussbaum argues that
affective and aesthetic engagement can in fact promote political stability as
Rawls defines it. Although Nussbaum aims to offer a more permissive framework for acknowledging cultural differences in public life, her requirement
that religious narratives and symbols be translated as "civic poetry" serves as
the aesthetic equivalent of Rawls's requirement for "public reason": both lead
to the excision of religious and cultural signification of justice claims that are
vital to comprehending their meaning. Similar to Rawls's philosophy, Nussbaum's liberal aesthetics fails to comprehend the specificity of justice claims
made by marginalized communities in the life of a democracy.

Responding to liberalism's aesthetics, chapter 4 engages Alejandro García-
Rivera's Latine theological aesthetics to construct a more adequate framework for engaging religious and cultural difference in the life of a democracy.
García-Rivera's framework comprehends religious and cultural differences
without capitulating to the demand for evacuating substantive particularities
that can benefit the larger democratic goals of engendering participation, stability, and equality within society's basic structures. The aesthetic encounter
ignites "the will to interpret a mind other than one's own" and catalyzes the
energy to attend to particularity across difference. Identifying foregrounding
as an aesthetic norm, García-Rivera's framework highlights the potential of
aesthetic experience to "[bring] down the powerful from their thrones, and
[lift] up the lowly" (Lk 1:52 NRSV). This aesthetic norm is essential to an
ethical framework for solidarity that prioritizes the formation of relationships
predicated on mutuality, equality, and participation.

Having outlined García-Rivera's aesthetic framework for forming a community of interpretation, the final chapter demonstrates the significance of
social solidarity in generating a participatory democracy that is capable of
comprehending and responding to justice claims made from diverse religious

and cultural communities, especially communities that have existed on the margins of US democratic life. The chapter adopts a multidimensional approach to solidarity and builds on ethical discourses of intellectual solidarity (dialogue that seeks to cultivate relationship across difference and is oriented toward the common good) and practical solidarity (collective action taken toward fostering communities that are characterized by mutuality, equality, and participation). The chapter augments these with a framework for aesthetic solidarity, or the engagement of sensory experience in cultivating communities characterized by mutuality, equality, and participation. The chapter concludes with illustrations of the enactment of a political theology of Guadalupe and Juan Diego that makes Guadalupe's people visible as actors in US democracy.

A NOTE ON TERMINOLOGY

One challenge of writing about the theology and ethics of Guadalupe and Juan Diego is the ever-shifting terminology employed to identify Latine communities. In this book the challenge is compounded by the use of cross-cultural, historical, and intergenerational sources that do not necessarily utilize a common vocabulary. My preference is already evident even in this introduction. Latine, in my opinion, conveys the broad scope of Latinx/o/a identity while still being able to be readily incorporated into both spoken Spanish and English.

While the polyphony of terms used to identify Latine communities can be overwhelming for those unacquainted with the profound complexity and diversity of Latinidad, the same breadth of language allows for rich intersectional analysis but may be elusive when working within a singular linguistic structure. As Carmen Nanko-Fernandez has argued, playing with terminology allows for critique of racial, gender, and sexual hierarchies latent in both English and Spanish that have been used to marginalize, oppress, and artificially delineate *la comunidad*.[34] Further, Jacques Derrida's conception of iteration helps conceptualize how much of the terminology has developed, if only incrementally, in response to changes in the social, political, and economic realities of the community.[35] Seyla Benhabib extends Derrida's conception to identify a process of *democratic* iteration through "linguistic, legal, cultural, and political repetitions-in-transformation, invocations that also are revocations. They not only change established understandings but also transform what passes as the valid or established view of an authoritative precedent."[36] Benhabib shows that a community is not only subject but also the author of these constructs. Communal description thus evolves alongside a community's own self-understanding even as the community draws from the authority of previous iterations. Various iterations thus allow for an ongoing project of critique and (re)construction of *la comunidad* across diverse contexts and over the course of generations.

I categorize terminology used in the text into three clusters. The first cluster consists of terms that are less commonly used today due to their inherent racial or gender exclusions, including Hispanic, Latino, and Chicano. I employ these terms only when used in reference to specific institutions, events, or people who identified (or continue to identify) with them. For example, I use "Chicano" to refer to the Chicano movement, particularly in its manifestation in the second half of the twentieth century. Similarly, I use the term "Hispanic" only in cases when it has been used by a specific source (e.g., when quoting a specific news or governmental source that uses the term) or where it has been used for self-identification (e.g., when someone self-identifies as Hispanic).

The second cluster consists of the terminological constructions of "Latina/o," "Latinx," and "Latine," along with "Chicanx" and "Xicanx." These terms are used in theology and ethics to interrogate gender essentialism in the Spanish language (and in Romance languages in general). I find these iterations satisfying for their capacity to indicate the complexity of gender identity, with each one foregrounding a marginalized group within the community: women-identified people in the former (both trans- and cis-) and trans-identified folx in the latter. I use Latinx, Latina, and Latino to signal specific gender identification of individuals or groups only as necessary. Otherwise, I use Latine in reference to the broader community as an iteration of terminology that attempts to describe *la comunidad* in our racial, cultural, linguistic, sexual, and gender diversity. I use Chicanx to refer specifically to individuals and communities identifying with the Chicano movement in the present day who seek to expand gender inclusivity of the movement's language.

NOTES

1. Young, *Justice and the Politics of Difference*, 39. Young identifies the five faces of oppression as exploitation, marginalization, powerlessness, cultural imperialism, and violence. I employ these facets to help articulate a multidimensional account of oppression.
2. Su Teatro, "History."
3. Auraria Higher Education Center website.
4. Gallegos, *Auraria Remembered*, 52, 68.
5. Gallegos, 1.
6. Gallegos, 68.

7. Flores, "Heart of the Neighborhood."
8. Lugo, *Latinos and the 2012 Elections*, 3.
9. Lugo, 3.
10. Clark, "Order and Simplicity of Gentrification," 25.
11. Clark, 27.
12. Pope Francis, *Laudato Si'*, no. 22.
13. Pope Francis, no. 52.
14. Massingale, "Assumptions of White Privilege."
15. Pope Francis, *Laudato Si'*, no. 232.
16. García-Rivera, *St. Martín de Porres*, 1.
17. García-Rivera, 1.
18. García-Rivera, 4.
19. García-Rivera, 5.
20. González-Andrieu, "Our Lady's Final Appearance," 36. Gonzalez-Andireu's theological reflection on "La Virgen de Tepeyac" shows how another Guadalupe play highlights both the cultural and political dimensions of the symbol: "What Valdez builds," she says in reference to the playwright, "embodies the story by adding the inescapable context of a bloody history, mixing the verses of two poetic languages, Spanish and Nahuatl, and weaving Indigenous symbols, songs, and dances with Catholic images, prayers, and hymns."
21. Dupré, "Virgin Mary Becomes Pop Symbol."
22. Dupré.
23. Gálvez, *Guadalupe in New York*.
24. Quinn, "Political Liberalisms and Their Exclusions of the Religious," 35.
25. See Stout, *Democracy and Tradition*; Mathewes, *Theology of Public Life*; Gregory, *Politics and the Order of Love*; and Kaveny, *Prophecy without Contempt*.
26. Kaveny, *Prophecy without Contempt*.
27. See Cahill, *Theological Bioethics*; Cahill, *Global Justice, Christology and Christian Ethics*; and Bretherton, *Resurrecting Democracy*.
28. Tirres, *Aesthetics and Ethics of Faith*, 57; Brown, *Religious Aesthetics*, 22. Frank Burch Brown highlights the sensory dimension of religious aesthetics: "In point of fact, aesthetics should perhaps be nothing less than basic theoretical reflection regarding all aesthetic phenomena, including modes of significant interrelation with, and mediation of, what is not inherently aesthetic: abstract ideas, useful objects, moral convictions, class conflicts, religious doctrines and so forth. The coherence of the field of aesthetics so conceived would derive its central interest in *aesthetica*—a term we can use technically to denote not perceptibles (as in Greek) or beautiful objects alone, *but all those things employing a medium in such a way that its perceptible form and 'felt' qualities become essential to what is appreciable and meaningful*" (emphasis added).
29. Tirres, *Aesthetics and Ethics of Faith*, 72, 76–77.
30. Nussbaum, *Political Emotions*, 9.
31. Flores, "In Jefferson's Shadow."
32. Hollenbach, *Common Good and Christian Ethics*, 192.
33. M. Clark, *Vision of Catholic Social Thought*, 60.
34. Nanko-Fernandez, *Theologizing in Espanglish*.
35. Derrida, "Signature, Event, Context [1971]," 90ff.
36. Benhabib, *Another Cosmopolitanism*, 48.

1

A Political Theology of Guadalupe and Juan Diego

Su Teatro first performed *The Miracle at Tepeyac* in 1975 in the basement of Our Lady of Guadalupe Parish, a largely Hispanic Catholic parish on Denver's north side.[1] The company was invited to perform by the parish's pastor, Fr. Jose Lara. Despite their mutual willingness to collaborate on the production, however, the relationship between Our Lady of Guadalupe Parish and Su Teatro exposed the enduring tensions between the religious and political significance of Guadalupe herself. The theater and the parish had divergent interpretations of Guadalupe's meaning. Anthony J. Garcia, playwright and director of *The Miracle on Tepeyac* who also portrayed Juan Diego in the play's initial run, wanted his script to move beyond a strictly religious rendering of the story of the Virgin of Guadalupe and Juan Diego to a critique of the ecclesial, political, and cultural forces that had caused and perpetuated the oppression of those on the underside of history. Garcia was concerned that the parish's influence on the production would blunt his play's political message. He was committed to telling the story of Guadalupe and Juan Diego but he wanted to show its relevance for the political and social struggles of the Chicano community.

Garcia's interpretation of the story did disturb some of the parishioners at Our Lady of Guadalupe, where practices of religious devotion to their patroness remain sacrosanct. During rehearsals in the church basement, for example, Garcia would often use what he calls "four letter words" to castigate the actors in his capacity as director. Some parishioners took issue with his language, especially since he was portraying the revered Juan Diego: "After one rehearsal, the church ladies were cooking, and I was in the basement/theater alone. They were being very nice to me and giving me samples of the food they were preparing. All seemed well until one of them instructed me, that as Juan Diego I shouldn't speak as I had been doing. I then explained

19

that I wasn't Juan Diego, so I should be able to say anything I wanted."[2] The parishioners emphasized the sacred dimensions of the story; Garcia, who was once an altar boy at Saint Cajetan's Parish but who saw himself as "divorced from organized religion," emphasized the narrative's cultural and political ramifications.[3]

The conflict between Garcia and the parishioners reflects some broader conflicts between the parish, the Archdiocese of Denver, and the Chicano movement. On one hand, Father Lara's church was the object of suspicion among Chicano movement leaders. Corky Gonzalez, who headed the Denver-based Chicano organization Crusade for Justice, viewed the parish with suspicion due to its ties to the institutional Catholic Church. This antagonism had resulted in verbal and even a physical confrontation between Our Lady of Guadalupe parishioners and Crusade for Justice.[4] On the other hand, the Archdiocese of Denver considered Father Lara to be a radical, with his allegiance to the Church corrupted by his association with the Chicano movement. The tension reached its climax when the archdiocese gave the Denver Police Department (DPD) permission to search the parish buildings for explosives following a DPD tip from a parishioner. The search, ordered and conducted without Lara's permission or foreknowledge, ended with the pastor handcuffed by the DPD. Lara responded to the raid by calling the incident evidence "that the Archdiocese of Denver and the CIA have something going together."[5] When asked whether his ongoing conflict with the archdiocese had broken his vow of obedience, Lara responded, "Oh, no. My vow of obedience is to Christ."[6] Given Lara's radical reputation, the production of Garcia's play represented a new opportunity for cooperation between Chicano activists and Our Lady of Guadalupe Parish. Nonetheless, friction persisted between Garcia and the parishioners even as they worked together to tell the story of Guadalupe and Juan Diego.

The conflict between Garcia and the parishioners reflects the contested interpretation of Guadalupe's symbol in the late twentieth- and early-twenty-first century. It is too simplistic to interpret the Virgin of Guadalupe as merely religious. She has been leveraged by groups representing various religious, political, and economic interests in their efforts to make public claims about justice. She was *la bandera* of Mexican revolutionaries led by Miguel Hidalgo y Costilla.[7] Her image was emblazoned on protest banners for the United Farm Workers (UFW) and in Latine social movements for immigration reform and cultural recognition. She has been commissioned by Latine Catholics fighting against the closure of their parishes by dioceses attempting to shore up their operating costs.[8] She has been deployed as a logo for Banamex, the second-largest bank in Mexico that sponsors a major installation of devotional art at the

Basilica of Our Lady of Guadalupe at Tepeyac, outside of Mexico City. Capitalizing on her appearance with a black band tied around her waist, Catholic pro-life groups marshal her image as an antiabortion symbol. The range of values and visions mapped onto her image underscore her contested meaning for both religion and politics.

Despite the many interpretive conflicts, however, the performance of Garcia's *The Miracle at Tepeyac* at Our Lady of Guadalupe Parish demonstrated that the story of Guadalupe and Juan Diego remains inextricably religious, cultural, *and* political. Su Teatro has performed the play for Denver's various Chicanx communities on multiple occasions since its initial run. While the script has remained largely the same over the course of four decades, Garcia's classic continues to illuminate the political and religious challenges the communities face in their city. The play represents a classic in David Tracy's sense of the word: it is an expression that arises within a tradition (in this case, Chicanx Catholicism) and discloses both an excess and a permanence of meaning.[9] By demonstrating the narrative's multivalent character, Garcia's play performs a political theology of Guadalupe in the context of twenty-first-century US democracy. Garcia does this by interlacing Guadalupe's synchronic and diachronic relationships: her synchronic relationship with Juan Diego and her diachronic relationship with the members of Padre Tomas's parish. Garcia uses these relationships to interrogate the social, economic, and political dynamics that perpetuate various forms of oppressions that Latines face today.

While many interpretations of Guadalupe's manifestation on Tepeyac focus on her image as it is said to have appeared on Juan Diego's *tilma* (cloak) in 1531, an examination of the relational interaction between Guadalupe and Juan Diego is essential for formulating a political theology of the symbol within a democratic context. A political theology of Guadalupe and Juan Diego helps formulate an ethical conception of solidarity that accounts for the need to eradicate systemic inequality. Attending to the relationship between Guadalupe and Juan Diego attempts to leverage Guadalupe as a symbol of solidarity that is severed from a corresponding call to justice. This relationship thus offers a substantive contribution to the pursuit of justice and solidarity within the context of modern US society.

This chapter begins with an examination of the historiographical controversies pertaining to the veracity of the Guadalupe apparition and origins. I employ the feminist axiom of the mutual constitution of the personal and the political to identify the religious, cultural, and political significance of Guadalupe's symbol. I then interpret the ethical dimensions of the relationship between Guadalupe and Juan Diego, arguing that Juan Diego's encounter with

Guadalupe demonstrated his fundamental dignity, including his capacity to exercise political power within the context of colonial ecclesial and civil structures. Returning to the case of *The Miracle at Tepeyac* performed among Chicanx communities in Denver, I conclude the chapter with an exposition of the political potential of the narrative of the Guadalupe–Juan Diego encounter to resist unjust social, economic, and political structures that hinder the survival and flourishing of Latine communities.

A GUADALUPAN CONTROVERSY

Articulating a political theology of the Virgin of Guadalupe is a fraught task, especially in light of ongoing historical debates about the event. Historians of Guadalupe debate the veracity of the apparition. Did the apparition actually take place as it is described within the various accounts? How might an answer to this question influence Guadalupan studies in theology and religion? For the purposes of this study, the debate about the veracity of the apparition influences how we interpret the significance of the Guadalupe event in the context of twenty-first century US democracy.

The encounter between the Virgin of Guadalupe and Juan Diego is said to have taken place in 1531, though the earliest known written account was recorded more than a century later, in 1648. Juan Diego, as the story goes, is drawn to the hill of Tepeyac, which he calls *xochitalpan* (in pre-Colombian Nahuatl it literally means "the place of flowers," but taken metaphorically it means "heaven").[10] Juan Diego finds Guadalupe on Tepeyac. Guadalupe asks Juan Diego to petition Bishop Juan de Zumárraga to build a basilica in her honor at Tepeyac. Juan Diego demurs, feeling unworthy to petition the bishop due to his marginal status in colonial society. Nevertheless, Guadalupe persists, convincing Juan Diego that it is he, not a person of higher social status nor one with more influence, who she wants to appear before the bishop on her behalf. Juan Diego, after unsuccessful attempts to persuade the bishop to build Guadalupe's basilica, appears before him a final time. This time Guadalupe sends Juan Diego with a tilma full of roses grown in the frozen December earth of Tepeyac. When Juan Diego unfurls his lapfold to present the flowers to the bishop, a brilliant image of the Virgin of Guadalupe appears embedded in the garment. Converted by the splendid image of Guadalupe on Juan Diego's cloak, Zumárraga believes his story and grants his request to build a basilica dedicated to Guadalupe.

This composite narrative echoes four central known accounts composed by the so-called Four Guadalupe Evangelists: Miguel Sánchez (1648), Luis

Laso de la Vega (1649), Luis Becerra Tanco (1666), and Francisco de Florencia (1688). Although Sánchez's narrative, *Imagen de la Virgen Maria*, was the first major account, it was gradually eclipsed by Laso de la Vega's *Nican mopahua* (Here it is told). Laso de la Vega's account was originally composed in Nahuatl and was first translated into Spanish in 1926. Whereas Sánchez's account was primarily directed toward the locally born Spaniards (*criollos*) of Mexico City, Laso de la Vega's account had the Nahua, as well as colonial religious authorities conversant in Nahuatl, as its primary audience.[11] This account has been the literary basis for modern theological interpretations of Guadalupe in liberation theology; the account's composition in Nahuatl is interpreted as evidence of its resonance with the plight of those on the underside of history and in accord with the preferential option for the poor.[12]

Stafford Poole contests the historical veracity of Guadalupe's appearance to Juan Diego. He asserts that interpretations of the Guadalupe event rely on an inadequate or erroneous historical foundation. He writes, "Hence the essential question is that of the historical reality of the apparition account and its message. Are these indeed factual events or are they legends and pious inventions? Is there an authentic tradition that connects the modern devotion with its manifold meanings to events that actually occurred in 1531?"[13] There is no documentation of the Guadalupe event during a time period when one would expect to find it; Poole argues that documentation should exist for an event as monumental in Mexican history as the alleged apparition. Typically an argument from silence is not persuasive, writes Poole, but "it is very strong when the sources would logically be expected to say something."[14]

Poole criticizes liberation theologians in particular for failing to wrestle with the historical debates surrounding the Guadalupe event: "These questions cannot be avoided as . . . some liberation theologians have attempted to do, by saying the symbolism and meaning of the devotion are independent of the objective reality of the traditional account. In Guadalupe history and symbolism are inextricably intertwined."[15] The implication of Poole's critique is that the historical veracity of the apparition is essential to the understanding of its religious, theological, and political significance. Without an objective historical basis for the apparition, interpretation merely refracts other ideological agendas. In the absence of an objective historical account of the apparition to anchor its meaning, Guadalupe becomes an ever more pliable symbol, manipulated to support the ends of those who invoke the story. Poole's critique reveals how Guadalupe's symbolism can be marshaled to support causes as divergent as the United Farm Workers movement and Banamex: the symbol becomes malleable without objective historical evidence to anchor its meaning.

Timothy Matovina argues that Poole does not appreciate the nature of the Guadalupe tradition's development, including its local and oral character. Matovina rejects Poole's requirement for documentation from the sixteenth and early seventeenth centuries: "Since the significance of Guadalupe for Mexican history was still in its nascent stages during the first century of devotion to her, it is inconsistent to expect that chroniclers and noted figures of the period would necessarily have written about her."[16] Citing the continual development of the tradition from the early sixteenth century forward, Matovina also rejects the demand for definitive proof of the apparition as a justification for its significance in US Latine theology. Poole's requirement for documentation overlooks the depth and complexity of contemporary Guadalupan studies, which "transcend debates about historical veracity in a rapidly expanding body of scholarly and artistic works."[17] Requiring the establishment of such objective proof of the apparition as a condition for studying the significance of Guadalupan devotion, writes Matovina, "eviscerates the theological task of critically examining faith as it is expressed and lived among believers who, in the case of Guadalupe, encompass millions of devotees."

Descriptive, normative, and constructive scholarship about the Guadalupe event ought to be informed by debates about the apparition's veracity. Nonetheless, Matovina's rejoinder to Poole is compelling in light of the oral development of the tradition. While indisputable evidence proving or disproving the event remains elusive, developments in the historiographical debate allow Guadalupe scholars to remain cognizant of the political, social, and economic context in which the tradition developed. The debate about the veracity of the apparition thus produces a generative tension in theologies of Guadalupe, chastening impulses to make definitive claims about Guadalupe's meaning while underscoring the necessity of studying the symbol's influence on devotees and, more broadly, on our common life in the context of American democracy.

These historical debates have proved themselves to be difficult to resolve but they illuminate some of the difficulties facing efforts to interpret Guadalupe in the twenty-first-century United States. As Alysha Gálvez observes in her ethnographic analysis of Guadalupe's political use among immigrant communities in New York City, there have been notable shifts in interpretation that influence Guadalupe's contemporary political significations. Resonant with Poole's concerns over the manipulation of Guadalupe's meaning, Gálvez argues that the interpretation of Guadalupe as an icon of social justice is the result of "strategic revindication by United States–based social movements such as the United Farm Workers mobilized by [César] Chavez, and Chicano theologians of liberation."[18] This interpretation results from an alliance between Guadalupan activists and liberation theologians in the decades following the Second Vatican Council.[19] She argues that this justice-oriented interpretation has migrated back to Mexico, where Guadalupe as a symbol of social justice has influenced *guadalupanismo* despite that country's theological conservatism and relative paucity of public theological expression. Pope Francis, on his pilgrimage to Tepeyac in February 2016, emphasized the social justice implications of Guadalupe's encounter with Juan Diego: "She managed to awaken something he did not know how to express, a veritable banner of love and justice."[20]

Gálvez's analysis affirms Matovina's assertion of the priority of studying the place of Guadalupe's symbol in the everyday lives of her devotees. In accord with the feminist axiom "the personal is political," a political theology of Guadalupe necessitates attention to the *lived* theology of Guadalupe as well as a method that attends to how theological beliefs shape the lives of believers in and among the realms of religion, culture, and politics.[21] This approach resonates with Hans-Georg Gadamer's conception of history of effects, where the significance of the narrative is constituted by "both the reality of history and the reality of historical understanding."[22] Accounting for both of Gadamer's dimensions of interpretation allows for a more comprehensive consideration of the symbol's influence on particular devotees along with society at large in the realms of religion, culture, and politics. The veracity of the Guadalupe event lacks definitive evidence from the sixteenth century, but what *is* historically demonstrable is that the Guadalupe devotional tradition has been a potent religious and political narrative for people and communities in Mexico, in the United States, and throughout the Americas and the rest of the world. The history of the effects of the Guadalupe event over the course of nearly five centuries suggests the need for sustained attention to Guadalupe across the range of subdisciplines in theology and religious studies.

Gálvez concludes that this debate does not invalidate the inquiry into the lived dimensions of Guadalupan devotion and its influence within various domestic and public spheres: "While many scholars may continue to struggle to prove or disprove the apparition story, the veracity of the apparition account is irrelevant. . . . Indeed, if the depth and ubiquity of devotion to the Virgin of Guadalupe among Mexicans through to the present day is any measure, her cause indeed needs no more support than itself."[23] Gálvez pivots from questions about apparitions and origins of devotion to the urgent questions of that value of Guadalupe's history and its effects on US democracy, particularly where the Latine community faces challenges to its survival and flourishing in the context of empire, colonization, and migration.

Matovina and Gálvez offer a compelling defense for the study of Guadalupe in lived religious and cultural experience. Still, the quest for the historical Guadalupe should continue, as these debates help us to better understand the context in which the tradition emerges and the consequences for contemporary Guadalupan interpretation. These deliberations should chasten the appropriation of Guadalupe in theology and ethics, mindful of contested meanings of the symbol and the narrative. That said, Matovina is right to caution against allowing these ongoing debates to stifle all contemporary inquiries into Guadalupe's influence on the lived theology of her devotees. As I will demonstrate, Guadalupe has functioned as a central symbol for justice among US Latine communities in the twentieth and twenty-first centuries, and these inquiries are essential to understanding the context of pluralistic and democratic society in the United States, Mexico, and beyond.

ELEMENTS OF A POLITICAL THEOLOGY OF GUADALUPE

Questions concerning Guadalupe's influence on the lived experience of devotees raises a crucial question for Guadalupan interpretation: What is Guadalupe's political significance for US democracy? In this political theology of Guadalupe and Juan Diego, I unpack the symbol's substantive contributions to the pursuit of justice within twenty-first-century United States.

Examining Guadalupe's influence in contemporary public life requires interdisciplinary engagement in theology, ethics, history, philosophy, sociology, and politics. Political theology is particularly amenable to investigating the multivalent significance of Guadalupe's symbol, which is simultaneously Catholic and Indigenous, personal and universal, ethical and political.[24] I argue that any useful political theology of Guadalupe ought to be shaped by her relationship with Juan Diego as a "humble commoner, a poor ordinary person" whom she selected to advocate for her before the colonial ecclesial authorities.[25] The encounter between Guadalupe and Juan Diego articulates a relational ethics in which Juan Diego is empowered by his encounter *in xochi in cuicatl* ("with flower and song") to recognize his dignity and personhood, which are constituted by both autonomy and relationality.[26] Beyond his personal experience of conversion, the aesthetic encounter with Guadalupe participates in Juan Diego's empowerment and change in status vis-à-vis colonial ecclesial power structures. In light of Juan Diego's experience of empowerment, I anchor this political theology of Guadalupe and Juan Diego in the Magnificat, showing how this relationship participates in "[bringing] down the powerful from their thrones" and "[lifting] up the lowly" (Lk 1:52 NRSV).

In the coming section I employ the feminist axiom of the personal as political to demonstrate Guadalupe's multivalent significance for her devotees: religious and cultural, personal and political. I then examine Roberto Goizueta's theological exegesis of the relationship between Guadalupe and Juan Diego, illustrating the implications of his work for conceptualizing an ethics of solidarity that accounts for the aesthetic dimensions of human experience. Finally I describe how aesthetic engagement of Guadalupe's symbol through the method of interlacing brings to the surface a political theology of Guadalupe and Juan Diego that emphasizes the empowerment of those who have been unjustly disempowered within political society. Guadalupe advocates for a vision of solidarity of relationships that are characterized by equality and mutuality, which are essential for fostering a just democracy.

The Personal Is Political

A recurring question in Guadalupan theological interpretation is whether the symbol is essentially one of private devotion (directing the devotee toward Jesus as the Son of God born of the Virgin Mary) or one of larger political and cultural significance (exerting power within various public realms). The question itself assumes a dichotomous view of the relationship between religion and public life that is characteristic of modernity.[27] It is this same dichotomous worldview that enforces a strict separation between the domestic and the public spheres, relegating religious devotion to the private and domestic. This is particularly prevalent in feminized aspects of religious and theological traditions, including Catholic Marian devotion. Devotion to Mary as Mother of God, including Guadalupe, is understood as a private matter carried out in a domestic context. But recent social scientific studies, particularly of the sociology of religions and through the use of ethnographic methods, have demonstrated the inextricably public and political dimensions of personal and ecclesial Marian devotions. The feminist axiom "the personal is political" helps illustrate the inherently public dimensions of Marian devotion.[28]

In her analysis of the Virgin of Charity (La Caridad del Cobre or La Cachita), the primary Marian devotion of Cuba, Jalane Schmidt highlights the significance of Marian piety in Cuban public life. Similar to other communities with local devotions to Mary, Cubans learn devotion within the domestic sphere.[29] Nonetheless, Schmidt argues, public performances of piety to La Cachita as carried out in the streets of Cuba are essential to the formation of a national identity. While over the course of centuries the politics of public piety have shifted depending on the political climate, Schmidt argues that public rituals have been essential to the development of political consciousness and national identity: "Cubans' planning of and participation in these events produced, in effect, a revolution in their streets."[30] Schmidt's analysis uncovers the connection between devotional practices of the domestic sphere and political practices of the public sphere, which are essential to shaping conceptions of national identity.

The connection between the domestic and public dimensions of Marian devotion is also evident among devotees of the Virgin of Guadalupe. Jeanette Rodriguez finds that Guadalupe has strong personal significance for women. In interviews these women describe Guadalupe as a reflection of both their faith in God and their Mexican American identity. The women who participated in Rodriguez's study are not involved in political activism, even in Mexican American social justice organizations; Rodriguez avers that this kind of activity might not be encouraged or supported among the young mothers with whom she spoke. Even so, the study participants describe how Guadalupe helps them respond to struggles in their social world, especially those that they experience as mothers. "Consider what happened to Mary," Rodriguez explains. "Her son was crucified, suffered, and died. But he rose from the dead! Therefore, things will be well, despite the torment, pain, alienation, loneliness, confusion, and suffering."[31] Guadalupe understands the pain they experience as mothers who are marginalized in society due to their ethnicity, culture, and gender. It is in this identification that Guadalupe's political significance becomes evident: "The image of Our Lady of Guadalupe is a symbol of power for a population in a seemingly powerless situation."[32] Guadalupe is a source of empowerment that helps women to survive amid astringent political circumstances. If the personal is political, then the empowerment of Mexican American women in the context of their everyday lives is already an act of political resistance to social, economic, and political structures that undermine their dignity.

María Del Socorro Castañeda-Liles's study on views of Guadalupe among Mexican women living in the United States yields similar findings. When she asks Esperanza, one study participant, whether Guadalupe is a Mexican cultural symbol or Catholic religious symbol, Esperanza's response grapples productively with Guadalupe's multivalent significance:

> In a firm but endearing tone, [Esperanza] asked: "Could you please do me a favor and remove the milk from the coffee you are drinking?" . . .
> I looked at her and told her that what she asked me was impossible, for the coffee and milk were mixed. She then proceeded to say:

Exactamente mija, México es como el café con leche. No se puede separar a la Virgen de Guadalupe de la religión y la cultura, todo esta mezclado. (Exactly *mija*, México is like coffee with milk. You cannot separate the Virgin of Guadalupe from religion and culture, it is all mixed.)[33]

Esperanza gives an apt illustration of Guadalupe's manifestation in both religion and culture. While it can be helpful, perhaps, to make analytical distinctions between religion and culture for the sake of conceptual clarity, the lived expression of religion and culture is mutually constitutive. Guadalupe is simultaneously sacred and secular, religious and cultural, personal and political.

Esperanza's insight also gestures to Guadalupe's multidimensional meaning in the context of twenty-first-century democracy. As I will explain in chapter 2, the attempt to distinguish between religious and cultural matters (which are typically relegated to what John Rawls calls the "background culture") and matters that are public and political (Rawls's "basic structure") is essential for establishing a freestanding conception of justice that protects religious and cultural pluralism while also establishing shared norms and institutions. Yet it is not the case that particular identities (or, in Rawlsian terms, "comprehensive doctrines") can be sloughed off when members of society participate in public and political life. Guadalupe's formative religious and cultural influence is not something that Mexican Americans simply abandon when they interact with matters of public significance. While Castañeda-Liles's study participants describe Guadalupe's personal and religious significance in their lives, their responses to the author's questions are inflected by their social, political, and economic context.

Demonstrating this point, Castañeda-Liles describes the political circumstances encountered by "Las Madres," a group of study participants who migrated to the United States in the midst of the economic turmoil generated by the signing of NAFTA. This trade agreement wreaked havoc on the Mexican economy, sending the value of the peso into a tailspin. These women were part of the "tsunami of migration" from Mexico to the United States in the aftermath of the agreement. "Most of those that came from México are undocumented," reports Castañeda-Liles. "Those that have kept in contact with me and are undocumented experience real fear of being separated from their US-born children, as a result of Trump administration's focus on the detainment and deportation of undocumented immigrants."[34] While these women approach Guadalupe through the lens of personal experience, their devotion to La Virgencita influences their responses to situations of political, social, and economic instability. Devotion to Our Lady of Everyday Life, as Castañeda-Liles calls her, is thus simultaneously personal and political. For her devotees, removing Guadalupe from the workings of democracy is like removing milk from coffee: an impossible task that is unhelpful for comprehending Guadalupe's importance in their personal lives or for understanding our common culture and political life, which together inform the practice of democracy in our contemporary context.

Whereas Rodriguez and Castañeda-Liles emphasize Guadalupe's personal significance for Mexican and Mexican American women, Gálvez's study links Guadalupan devotional practices that are carried out in the context of parishes and private homes with direct political action for immigration justice. Gálvez investigates the work of parish-based comités Guadalupanos in New York City that are united at the diocesan level in the Asociation de Tepeyac (Tepeyac association). Similar to Schmidt's observation of Cuban devotional practices to La Cachita, Gálvez reports that the parish-based committees help preserve domestic devotional practices, such as the display of Guadalupe's image in homes and in church sanctuaries and the maintenance of parish Guadalupe shrines.

The comités, however, still engage in public piety of Guadalupe through inherently political dimensions. For example, they organize an annual public procession in conjunction with Guadalupe's feast day celebration on December 12, making it an act of *both* religious devotion *and* political protest. The procession is rich with religious ritual but also serves an explicit political purpose: as a protest for immigrant justice. Gálvez describes the participants in the event as both pilgrims and protesters: "They kiss images of the Virgin, carry costumes associated with the story of the Virgin's apparition; and they also carry signs asking for immigration reform, chant "¡Si se puede!" [Yes, we can!] just like protesters do at marches, and display Mexican and U.S. flags."[35] Additionally, the Asociation de Tepeyac organizes La Antorcha Guadalupana (Guadalupe torch run) during which a flame is carried by relay runners from the Basilica of Our Lady of Guadalupe on the outskirts of Mexico City to Saint Patrick's Cathedral in New York City, arriving at the cathedral during the feast day procession.

Such acts of devotion aim to raise public awareness about the Guadalupanos' struggle for full citizenship rights. "While the devotional practices centered on Our Lady of Guadalupe engaged in by Mexican immigrants in New York City may seem familiar to some observers," writes Gálvez, "they occur in a unique historical moment of massive and accelerated migration, militarization of the border, stagnation of immigration laws, and worldwide struggles for rights by those displaced by globalization."[36] Hence these practices contain both devotional and political significance. For example, although the binational relay is a religious pilgrimage, it also possesses a politically transgressive quality, serving as a public demonstration against the separation of families and communities by unjust immigration policies. Guadalupan devotional practices thus enter the public square, articulating rights claims in the idiom of Latine popular religious devotion.

Gálvez's findings make explicit all that is implied by Rodriguez's and Castañeda-Liles's studies of the personal significance of Guadalupe for her devotees: that Guadalupe is inherently personal and political and influences interaction with the public sphere in both explicit and implicit ways. The multivalent expressions of public piety are crucial to both religious and devotional practice. A political theology of Guadalupe written in a US context should strive to explicate Guadalupe's political significance for a democracy in the twenty-first century as it is reflected in these ethnographic studies. Toward offering a framework for interpretation, the next section examines the ethical and political dimensions of Guadalupe's narrative, particularly her relationship with Juan Diego. While this relationship is often glossed over in interpretations of Guadalupe's symbol, it is essential to understanding the symbol's democratic significance.

A Relational Ethics of Guadalupe and Juan Diego

Guadalupe's religious, cultural, and political implications invite a specification of the symbol's significance for a modern democracy. What is the political significance of Guadalupe for US Latinx communities engaged in liberative political projects within the context of a twenty-first-century US democracy? Roberto Goizueta addresses this question by providing a theological framework for interpreting the relationship between Guadalupe and Juan Diego. Goizueta's theological interpretation of their encounter gestures to its ethical dimensions by demonstrating how Guadalupe empowered Juan Diego to recognize his own personhood in a society that attempted to deny his inherent dignity.

To some, Goizueta's interpretation may seem like an unlikely instrument for constructing a political theology of Guadalupe. His work is part of a larger "aesthetic turn" in US Catholic Latine theology that has been criticized for focusing too narrowly on issues of cultural marginalization at the expense of structural injustices such as poverty and violence.[37] Virgilio Elizondo initiated this turn through his introduction of *mestizaje* as a basis for theological reflection on the "origination of a new people from two ethnically disparate parent peoples."[38] This emphasis helped focus theological attention to cultural marginalization among Latine people and communities in the United States. Since then, US Latine theologians have utilized mestizaje as a response to the religious and cultural challenges facing Latine communities living in the heart of empire.[39] The centrality of mestizaje in Latine theological reflection gave rise to interest in Guadalupe. Due to the Nahua and Spanish elements incorporated in the image said to have appeared on Juan Diego's tilma, earlier generations of Latine theologians reflected on Guadalupe's theological significance as *la Mestiza*, who "combines opposing forces so that in a creative way new life, not destruction, will emerge."[40] Guadalupe has been an emblem of mestizaje, at the heart of calls for cultural inclusion made in an aesthetic key.

This move, critics argue, has led US Latine theology to focus on issues of identity and cultural marginalization rather than honing in on the issues of economic and political injustice that orient Latin American liberation theology.[41] Jorge Aquino criticizes Goizueta in particular for his work's shift "from liberation theology's foundational concern with 'social-transformation' to an aesthetics of emphatic fusion," asserting a semiotics of representation at the expense of articulating a viable political theology that responds to structural injustices in the spirit of Latin American liberationists such as Gustavo Gutierrez and Leonardo Boff.[42] Guadalupe as la Mestiza leads to an evasion of questions about political and economic power that are fundamental to the project of liberation within the postcolonial and imperial context of the United States.

These critiques highlight the risks of allowing aesthetics to be sundered from ethics and caution against overemphasis on the former for fear it will lead to inadequate response to issues of economic and political injustice. Nevertheless, I contend that Goizueta's interpretation of the relationship between Guadalupe and Juan Diego is essential for articulating a political theology of Guadalupe in the context of the twenty-first century, especially given its concern with the ethical dimension of the relationship. Goizueta's exposition of the encounter between Guadalupe and Juan Diego as presented in the *Nican Mopahua* illustrates Juan Diego's realization of his own personhood in the context of a colonial society, where he is viewed and sees himself as "the people's dung."[43] In this manner Goizueta's ethical interpretation of the encounter between Guadalupe and Juan Diego is crucial to articulating a conception of solidarity that accounts for both human autonomy and relationality.

Margaret Farley's ethical account of the integration of individuality and relationality as obligating features of personhood offers a helpful framework for interpreting Goizueta's theology of the encounter between Guadalupe and Juan Diego. Farley anchors her description in the concrete reality of human persons that is both embodied and inspirited with concomitant needs for food, clothing, and shelter as well as the capacity for free choice, the ability to think, and the ability to feel.[44] Her conception of personhood resonates with the human capability approach, which emphasizes a range of sensory-based functions that are essential to individual human flourishing and the common good.[45] Yet Farley's conception differs from prevailing accounts of the capability approach by acknowledging the human capacity for transcendence as a foundation for comprehending a religious dimension of human experience.

From this description of human capabilities Farley outlines autonomy and relationality as two basic features of human personhood. She argues that these are obligating features of human personhood since they assert the necessity of treating human beings as *ends in ourselves* and thus prohibits using each other as *mere means*. In the case of autonomy, the human capacity for free choice means that we have the capacity to make decisions about our own lives, to set our own agendas. To treat a human as an end is to respect her autonomous capacity to set her own agenda rather than to treat her as a mere means to an end by absorbing her into one's own agenda. In addition to autonomy, Farley argues that the human capacity for relationship grounds the moral obligation to treat persons as ends in themselves. While human beings have the capacity for self-governance, we are also related to others in intrinsic ways. These relationships are essential to the formation of our identity, necessitating treatment of those with whom we are in relationship not merely as means for accomplishing our own goals but as ends in themselves and to whom we are responsible. As Farley writes, "Another way to say all of this is that as persons we are terminal centers, ends in ourselves, because in some way we both transcend ourselves and yet belong to ourselves."[46]

Farley's account of personhood illuminates the relational dynamics between Guadalupe and Juan Diego that Goizueta highlights in his exegesis of the *Nican Mopahua*, especially in Goizueta's emphasis on Juan Diego's realization of his dignity and agency within the context of a colonial society that has denied both features of his personhood. While Guadalupe sees Juan Diego as uniquely capable of conveying her message to Bishop Zumárraga, Juan Diego doubts his own capacity to be heard by those in power. When his first appeal to Zumárraga does not yield a positive outcome, Juan Diego asks Guadalupe to call upon someone with more power to advocate on her behalf: "I greatly implore you, my patron, noble Lady, my daughter, to entrust one of the high nobles, who are recognized, respected, and honored, to carry and take your message, so that he will be believed. For I am a poor ordinary man, I carry burdens with the tumpline and carrying frame, I am one of the common people, one who is governed."[47] Juan Diego's self-designation as "one who is governed" is a particularly striking statement when read within a human capability framework that is predicated on autonomy or, literally, self-governance. Guadalupe's request, he believes, is of such great importance that she should entrust it to a powerful person capable of exercising agency in relation to the ecclesial authorities. Juan Diego's request to send a powerful person to Zumárraga, along with his denial of his own agency, suggests that he does not regard himself as a political actor capable of confronting the colonial authorities.

As Goizueta notes, it is at this moment in the narrative that Guadalupe recognizes and affirms Juan Diego's dignity and agency: "In contrast to his own reluctance, la Morenita refuses to accept his deprecatory self-understanding and instead calls him 'the dearest of my children,' some-one capable of acting."[48] Whereas Juan Diego misunderstands himself as an object or tool "whose sole value comes from [its] usefulness," Guadalupe sees affirmation of his full personhood as a necessary aspect of her message. Beyond a mere utilitarian view of Juan Diego as a means for the end of having a basilica built on Tepeyac, Juan Diego's dignity and power are the very content of her message. She insists that it is necessary for Juan Diego himself to advocate to the bishop on her behalf: "Do listen, my youngest child. Be assured that my servants and messengers to whom I entrust it to carry my message and realize my wishes are not high ranking people. Rather it is highly necessary that you yourself be involved and take care of it. It is very much by your hand that my will and wish are to be carried out and accomplished."[49] Guadalupe chooses Juan Diego to be her advocate not in spite of his lowliness, but because of it. Guadalupe's message thus invokes the text of the Magnificat attributed to Mary of Nazareth: "He has brought down the powerful from their thrones, and lifted up the lowly" (Lk 1:52 NRSV). Lifted up by Guadalupe, Juan Diego becomes aware of his dignity through the acts of discerning goodness through beauty and in revealing truth to power.

Although Juan Diego is often lauded for his obedience to Guadalupe, Goizueta argues that Juan Diego's agency is even more evident in his decision to *disobey* Guadalupe.[50] When Zumárraga denies Juan Diego's request to build the basilica, Juan Diego appeals to Guadalupe to send a more powerful representative to appeal to the colonial ecclesial authorities on her behalf. But Guadalupe sends him back to the bishop, insisting that it must be Juan Diego to convince him of her request. Instead of returning to the bishop, however, Juan Diego decides to return to his home to tend to his uncle who is ill. Goizueta explains, "Ironically, Juan Diego's willingness to disobey Mary is a sign that he is, indeed, a person, with needs and desires that cannot simply be subsumed within someone else's—not even those of Mary herself."[51] Goizueta's argument for Juan Diego's agency resonates with liberal assertions of autonomy as the "capacity to run one's own life."[52] Instead of compelling or forcing him to obey her will, Guadalupe appeals to him as one possessing agency that ought to be respected. At the same time, Juan Diego's reasons for disobeying Guadalupe underscore Farley's account of human relationality as an obligating feature of personhood. Human beings are related to one another whether we acknowledge it or not. And our relationships are not self-evidently just. Juan Diego demonstrates the moral obligations asserted through our relationships with one another.

Goizueta further observes that Guadalupe treats Juan Diego as her equal in the context of their relationship. Guadalupe does not simply appear to a passive Juan Diego, speaking soothing words and giving him orders that she compels him to obey. She asks him questions. She heeds his responses. She argues with him. She gives him reasons. This dynamic alone would have been a remarkable relational experience for an Indigenous person in colonial Mexico.

This interaction between equal agents allows Goizueta to make an ethical distinction between an apparition or appearance and an encounter. In an appearance, Goizueta argues, an active subject appears to a passive object. Every encounter, however, is marked by a relationship between two active subjects. Juan Diego is not Guadalupe's simple, passive, or single-minded servant; he is a partner-in-relationship. Guadalupe and Juan Diego encounter each other in the context of an interpersonal relationship between two subjects, both with inherent dignity and capacity for moral agency. The narrative of the encounter is one of transformation: Juan Diego's self-perception as a passive object in colonial society changes to that of an active subject in relationship to Guadalupe and to colonial ecclesial authorities. As Goizueta explains, "The story of Guadalupe recounts a relationship which begins as the apparition of a subject (the Lady) to an object (Juan Diego) and ends as an encounter between two equal subjects, two full-fledged persons."[53]

Their encounter transforms Juan Diego's self-understanding, from passive object to active subject. Guadalupe reveals to Juan Diego (and to the colonial powers) his humanity, dignity, and agency. Juan Diego now recognizes himself not as an instrument of society, of the economy, or of the empire, but as an advocate on behalf of Guadalupe and the people whom she adopts as her own. In this way Juan Diego is fundamentally transformed by his encounter with Guadalupe.

Farley's description of the concrete reality of human persons and the obligating features of personhood helps to illustrate the ethical significance of Guadalupe's encounter with Juan Diego; Goizueta's interpretation of Juan Diego's empowering encounter with Guadalupe sheds light on the aesthetic dimensions of Farley's account of personhood. Guadalupe has a case to make

to Juan Diego, but she does not approach him in a strictly discursive or rational mode. She entices him *in xochi in cuicatl*, with flower and song:

> When he came close to the hill at the place called Tepeyacac, it was
> getting light. He heard singing on top of the hill, like the songs of vari-
> ous precious birds. Their voices were [unclear: swelling and fading?],
> and it was as if the hill kept on answering them. Their song was very
> agreeable and pleasing indeed, entirely surpassing how the bell bird,
> the trogon, and the other precious birds sing.[54]

Appealing to him with dazzling sights, sounds, and scents, Guadalupe acknowledges the human capacity for aesthetic experience in general and ability to
perceive *divine* beauty in particular. Read within Farley's framework, we see
Guadalupe affirming multiple dimensions of Juan Diego's personhood, including his capacity for sensory experience and self-transcendence. She treats him
as an end in himself, within a social, economic, and political context where he
has been instrumentalized and dehumanized.

In his comparative study of the meaning of the good life for pre-Colombian
Nahuas and for Aristotle, L. Sebastian Purcell argues that the Nahuas held a
view similar to Aristotle's *eudaimonia* (happiness or flourishing) but distinct
in significant ways. Purcell defends this claim with a comparative analysis of
eudaimonia and *neltiliztli*, translating the latter as "rootedness."[55] Whereas
eudaimonia is based on a teleological understanding of human flourishing,
neltiliztli is concerned with how one might live life on a "slippery earth" or
amid circumstances that are transitory and can be difficult, if not impossible,
to control. Rootedness seeks stability in a life characterized by manifest instability. This grounding is found not in the pursuit of human perfection, which
is seen as impossible in light of the transitory and "slippery" character of life.
Rather, rootedness is found in encounters with *xochitl in cuicatl*, which can
best be understood as poetry or beauty. It is in flower and song that one can
find permanence.[56]

An ethics of rootedness, with the assertion of flower and song as a way of
pursuing goodness amid conditions of instability, enriches the analysis of the
relationship between Guadalupe and Juan Diego. Juan Diego, enticed to go to
the peak of Tepeyac through flower and song, is invited to an encounter with
Guadalupe that generates deep delight and joy. It is through his encounter
with Guadalupe's beauty that he learns of his own dignity. As translated in
the *Nican Mopahua*, Guadalupe testifies that Juan Diego is "dignified" and her
beloved child. This affirmation, expressed through the aesthetic experience of
flower and song, convicts Juan Diego of his own worth and capacity. Through

his relationship with Guadalupe, Juan Diego comes to see himself worthy of speaking to Zumárraga and thus worthy of a place in a society in which his status is profoundly unstable. In other words, Guadalupe helps Juan Diego find his roots.

A political theology of Guadalupe and Juan Diego helps us to identify the significance of their relationship for the twenty-first century. This is not a story strictly about personal conversation, either of Juan Diego or Bishop Zumárraga. It is a story of political empowerment of the oppressed within the context of colonization. The encounter made evident Juan Diego's capacity for self-governance, an autonomy that is essential for liberty, as well as his fundamental dignity, which is the foundation to claims of human equality. This empowerment was central to cultivating his agency to confront the colonial ecclesial powers. In this way the story is relevant in a US democratic context, where the oppressed and marginalized resist the legacies of colonization, slavery, and segregation that still fester in our common life.

The ethical dimensions of their relationship are essential for understanding the event's political significance. Though Guadalupe's symbol can be (and has been) manipulated to support unjust ends, foregrounding the relational encounter between Guadalupe and Juan Diego highlights the symbol's potential to assert a vision of personhood that is amenable to the project of democracy. Guadalupe and Juan Diego are particular theological and religious symbols, but they express a vision of personhood and conceptions of justice and solidarity in support of common life in a twenty-first-century democratic context.

A Political Theology of Guadalupe and Juan Diego

In *The Miracle at Tepeyac* Teresa is a Salvadoran migrant fleeing violent political retribution promised to her family, which lives in the economic and political shadows of the United States. She resides in the part of the parish closed off for renovation and pays for silence from Juanito, the parish janitor, by completing chores for him. Teresa implores Juanito to continue to keep her secret and allow her to remain with her family in the shadows of the church. She asks Juanito, "Where are we supposed to go? This is the house of God and aren't we a part of God, too? Isn't that what the church is for?" Juanito responds by denying Teresa's theological claim: "That's a different kind of church. This is a United States church, the Señora and Padre Tomas don't worship that kind of God." Juanito's response unveils a terrible truth about his parish and about many churches in the United States: they are typically not places where the most vulnerable will find refuge. This insight in part explains Juanito's crass response to Teresa's plea for continued refuge, which will spare her life from certain death if deported to El Salvador: "That's not my problem, and it's not my church."[57]

Juanito and Teresa reside in the same church, but Juanito does not acknowledge the integral relationship that he has with Teresa. Declaring that the church is not his, he denies his responsibility for the lives of the people seeking sanctuary in its shadow. But Teresa's question about the church's responsibility to her as "part of God," or one created in God's image, asserts a fundamental theological truth: Teresa and Juanito are inextricably bound to one another. Their mutual creation in the image of a Triune God is the foundation not only of individual dignity but of fundamental relationship and attendant responsibilities to one another.[58]

The play's narrative follows Juanito's realization of his own dignity and worth as well as his responsibilities to the other members of his church and community. Interlacing Juanito's story with the story of Guadalupe and Juan Diego shows Juanito's conversion and empowerment through his encounter with Guadalupe's children: those who live on the margins of society and whom she empowers to recognize their own dignity, autonomy, relationality, capacities for aesthetic experience and self-transcendence, and political power.

The aesthetic method of interlacing, explains Cecilia González-Andrieu, plaits distinctive elements to incorporate them into a single strand.[59] This incorporation of threads does not reduce their distinctiveness; rather, interlacing allows for the disparate elements to be joined together while remaining distinct from one another, permitting each strand to be appreciated in a new way as it is brought into relationship with the other strands. Interlacing the account of the sixteenth-century encounter between Guadalupe and Juan Diego with the narratives of twentieth-century Latine people struggling for survival in the shadows of US political society and the Catholic Church allows the audience to see unexpected connections between the two stories.

The narrative interlacing in *The Miracle at Tepeyac* also reveals the connection between the political situations of Juan Diego, Juanito, and Teresa. Each character has been disempowered in the economic, social, and political realms of their society. Interpreting their stories together allows the audience to gain a better understanding of the conditions that undermine their individual and collective flourishing. Yet the play's narrative also allows the audience to interlace their own experiences of oppression into the braid. It allows them to relate the colonial ecclesial and political structures that Juan Diego endures with those of the characters and with the ones they encounter in their own lives.

Using the aesthetic method of interlacing, Su Teatro expresses a political theology of Guadalupe that can respond to the neocolonial dynamics of gentrification that are eviscerating Latine communities in Denver. The community interprets their own lives, experiences, and circumstances via the encounter between Guadalupe and Juan Diego. The relationship between Guadalupe and Juan Diego becomes an interpretive framework for the community's current struggles, exposing the invisible injustices they face on a daily basis. At the same time it allows the audience to imagine new possibilities for responding to their situation. Seeing themselves in relationship with Guadalupe invites identification with Juan Diego and allows the community to recognize Juan Diego's story in their own experiences of social upheaval caused by the neocolonial dynamics of gentrification at work in their communities.

This identification with Juan Diego, I argue, is essential to the liberative political appropriation of Guadalupe's symbol in the life of democracy. This identification is implicit in the use of Guadalupe's symbol in various social justice movements, including the UFW movement. According to Luís D. León, UFW leader César Chávez's life follows the classic pattern of a "hero's return," and identification of Chávez as a prophet in the movement.[60] This pattern allows Chávez to be interpreted as a Christ-like figure within the UFW. Interlacing the story of Guadalupe and Juan Diego with the UFW's story, however, causes Chávez to be interpreted as mirroring the narrative pattern of Juan Diego rather than the narrative pattern of Christ. Appearing under Guadalupe's banner positions Chávez, along with the rest of the movement's leaders and workers, as a contemporary Juan Diego, so to speak: exercising political agency, asserting fundamental equality, and demanding to be seen and heard by those in power. Guadalupe's banner becomes their symbol of justice, their chant that their fundamental human dignity—characterized by autonomy, relationality, and capacity for transcendence—be respected.

A political theology of Guadalupe and Juan Diego posits Guadalupe as a symbol of justice with a conception of fundamental equality that is essential to cultivating a thriving democracy in the twenty-first century. Interpreted within the US political context, Guadalupe is a symbol of solidarity, one that invites the formation of a democratic community committed to a vision of justice that requires the flourishing of every member of society.

OUR LADY OF THE NORTHSIDE

Performed against the backdrop of conflict and distrust between Our Lady of Guadalupe Parish and the Chicano movement, the presentation of *The Miracle on Tepeyac* in the parish basement articulates a case for the political significance of Guadalupe as one of the central religious narratives of Chicano Catholics. As political theology, the play allows for the reimagination of relationships between the parish and the movement, cultivating a renewed solidarity that undermines attempts to relegate Guadalupe to the supposedly private sphere of the Church or to evacuate her multivalent religious and cultural significance in public life.

On one hand, hosting Su Teatro's performance of *The Miracle at Tepeyac* allows the parish to structure its involvement in the Chicano movement with a Guadalupan grammar. This grammar inflects the parish's expression of Guadalupan devotion within its theology and practices while not forgoing the story's political implications. On the other hand, the performance in the context of the church allows the play to reflect more fully Guadalupe's multivalent significance for Denver's Chicanos. She is a political symbol, emblazoned on banners pleading for farmworker rights and immigrant justice. But she also signifies the ancestors' faith in God's love for the Juan Diegos of history: "He has brought down the powerful from their thrones, and lifted up the lowly; he has filled the hungry with good things, and sent the rich away empty" (Lk 1:52–53 NRSV).

The new relationship between the movements and the parish is captured in a mural of Our Lady of Guadalupe and Juan Diego painted behind the Eucharistic altar of the church. In 1976 Father Lara invited a parishioner to paint a mural of the Virgin of Guadalupe as a "beautiful Chicana from north Denver."[61] The mural featured an image of Guadalupe's encounter with Juan Diego on Tepeyac. For decades the mural was the backdrop for the parish's Eucharistic celebrations as well as its enactment of its robust social justice mission: "The church was a symbol of a fight for equality, and the mural was its emblem."[62]

In 2010 Our Lady of Guadalupe's new pastor ordered a white wall to be built in front of the mural, arguing that it detracts from the adoration of the Eucharist. The decision was upheld by the Archdiocese of Denver under the leadership of Archbishop Charles Chaput. Msgr. Jorge de los Santos, the vicar of Hispanic ministry of the archdiocese in 2010, defended the decision to cover the mural claiming, *contra* Esperanza's perspective, "the religion does not reside in the culture, but in the faith."[63] Many parishioners mourned the loss of the mural, citing its importance to Denver's Chicano Catholic community. "The mural stood for over 30 years as an inspiring source of devotion, pride and faith for thousands of parishioners, visitors from across the globe, and the Latinx community which has struggled for decades for true acceptance and respect by the institutional church."[64] In response, the archdiocese criticized the parish's efforts to draw public attention to the issue. The rejection of their petition following the public outcry has become a recurring theme in their response to pleas for mercy from Denver's Chicanx laity.[65]

A salient political theological point has been overlooked in this conflict. The decision to cover the mural with the white wall was both a theological and a political decision. It was an assertion of doctrinal orthodoxy but also an exercise of ecclesial power. Theologically the move suggested that the Eucharist is an act of communion with Christ but not with those with whom Christ is in relationship. It asserts a flattened Eucharistic anthropology that is unable to simultaneously assert Jesus' radical singularity while also acknowledging the centrality of both synchronic and diachronic relationship in the work of salvation. Politically the decision to cover the mural served as an affront to the parish's work in Denver's Chicano movement, in which it led the Chicano Northside in calls for social justice during turbulent times. Interlaced with the narrative of Guadalupe and Juan Diego, the Archdiocese of Denver reiterates the pattern of Bishop Zumárraga's distrust of Juan Diego's advocacy on behalf of Guadalupe. This pattern of distrust reorients the narrative of *The Miracle at Tepeyac*, which expresses a political theology of Guadalupe that "lifts up the lowly" and "brings the powerful down from their thrones," unmasking the assertion of ecclesial power and the erasure of Denver's Chicanx community.

Covering the mural (and thus hiding Juan Diego) asserts an implicit political theology of Our Lady of Guadalupe: it renders the symbol to be one of colonial triumph and reinforces a narrative of the conversion of Indigenous people to the Catholic Church without demanding a fundamental shift in either civic or ecclesial power dynamics in return. This Guadalupe is easily leveraged: baptizing the capitalist efforts of Banamex or showing support for a pro-life movement whose electoral advocate, Donald J. Trump, has guided his administration to separate migrant families and hold migrants and asylum seekers in detention centers with abhorrent conditions. This is the Guadalupe about which critics of US Latine theology's "aesthetic turn" express their wariness. Those who are concerned with the inscription of colonial power structures are right to be wary of this Guadalupe.

The Miracle at Tepeyac, performed in the context of Denver's Westside and Northside Chicano communities who are experiencing displacement from their neighborhoods via gentrification, shines a spotlight on the neocolonial dynamics of this social, economic, and political phenomenon. The play is an expression of lament, mourning, and anger but it is also one of love, consolation, and hope for the future. The play's use of interlacing allows the community to visualize a conception of justice that is essential for successfully articulating their grievances with a disempowered political, economic, and social position. Interlacing their experience with those of Juan Diego, Juanito, Teresa, and the other characters, the community comes to realize their own capacity to demand justice from ecclesial, political, and economic powers and to advocate for their own interests. The play equips the community with the political semiotics of Guadalupe and Juan Diego to assert its substantive justice claims.

The political theology of Guadalupe and Juan Diego illustrated in *The Miracle at Tepeyac* demands an invocation of Guadalupe in the realm of politics that accounts for the presence of the oppressed, especially the colonized. Juan Diego's presence undermines appropriation of the Guadalupe narrative as a means of asserting calls for diversity and reconciliation without an associated call for justice.

While a political theology of Guadalupe helps us to see the importance of Guadalupe in the calls for justice among Latine communities, it also gestures to Guadalupe's substantive justice meaning for the life of democracy in the twenty-first century. By highlighting Juan Diego's transformative moral and political experience on Tepeyac, the relationship between Guadalupe and Juan Diego acknowledges the narrative's essential connection to rectification of power imbalances in both ecclesial and political structures. It situates anyone who has encountered oppression in any dimension as Guadalupe's beloved child whom she empowers to recognize and embrace the autonomous and relational dimensions of their personhood within the work of justice.[66] From the walls of Denver's Northside to the streets of Charlottesville, a political theology of Guadalupe and Juan Diego places her on the side of those who have been subject to unjust legacies of conquest, colonization, slavery, segregation, racism, sexual violence, and deportation. It is a political theology of Magnificat, where Mary's soul is magnified as she bears witness to God's promise to "lift up the lowly."

A political theology of Guadalupe and Juan Diego informs a vision of just solidarity within the context of a pluralistic and democratic society. The relationship between Guadalupe and Juan Diego illustrates the centrality of solidarity for the life of democracy in the twenty-first century. This kind of solidarity is predicated on an account of personhood that features autonomy, relationship, aesthetics, and transcendence. More concretely, this view of solidarity bridges the narrative of Guadalupe's encounter with Juan Diego from the realm of poetry to the realm of politics and demands a conception of solidarity that grapples with the reality of social conflict.[67]

To be sure, Guadalupe's symbol has often been turned into an icon for a form of solidarity that celebrates difference without interrogating power differentials that hinder the pursuit of justice. But a political theology of Guadalupe and Juan Diego developed through the aesthetic method of interlacing resists assimilative appropriation by highlighting the conflictual aspects of the account. Interpreted in the midst of conflict, this story reminds us who has power, who has been denied power, and what is being done to rectify power imbalances. The account testifies to the necessity of "lifting up the lowly" and "bringing down the powerful from their thrones" in the context of twenty-first-century democracy in the pursuit of a pervasive social justice that seeks the good of all of society's members within a pluralistic society.

CONCLUSION

A political theology of the Virgin of Guadalupe, predicated on a relational anthropology in which the encounter between equals within the context of oppression is offered as the narrative's interpretive key, is essential for asserting the significance of the story within the context of US democracy in the twenty-first century. Guadalupe's symbol has been marshaled to defend myriad social causes, but its concrete engagement by Denver's Chicanos illuminates a lived theology that takes shape at the intersection of the religious and the cultural, the personal and the political. This political theology offers a framework for interpreting Guadalupe's function within the community without demanding the separation of its religious, cultural, and political content.

While this political theology reflects on the political concerns of the Chicanx Catholic community, it gestures toward similar intersections between religion, culture, and politics among groups that have encountered various dimensions of oppression. A political theology of Guadalupe and Juan Diego asserts the necessity of interpreting particular religious symbols within the common life of democracy and of identifying and rectifying the enduring inequalities that hinder the cultivation of a thriving democracy. Further, it suggests the need for articulating a conception of solidarity that is capable of accounting for the reality of social conflict even as it pursues deeper commitments to pursuing a common good.

In the next two chapters I evaluate the prevailing liberal political philosophies of John Rawls and Martha Nussbaum and unveil the implications of their respective theories for engaging religious and cultural particularity within the life of democracy. While other critiques of Rawls and Nussbaum have emphasized the limitations of their philosophies in relation to the use of religious rhetoric and discourse in the public square, my argument focuses on the aesthetics expressed in their work. This liberal aesthetic, I argue, undermines liberals' own project of generating equality within a pluralistic and democratic society. Despite the enduring credibility of liberalism's concern for forging a political consensus of justice in the context of pluralism, I argue that these forms of political liberalism provide an inadequate account for interpreting particular religious symbols (such as Guadalupe and Juan Diego) in public life. These philosophies consequently curtail the cultivation of the robustly participatory democracy toward which they strive. In response I offer an interpretive framework that allows for leveraging particularity toward a more participatory democracy that is predicated on a just solidarity.

NOTES

1. Garcia, "From Su Teatro Executive Artistic Director," 1.
2. Garcia, 1.
3. Gallegos, *Auraria Remembered*, 32; Garcia, "From Su Teatro Executive Artistic Director," 1.
4. Ashton, "Chicano Opposition to Crusade."
5. Dillard, "Police Search Denver Church," 3.
6. Johnson, "He Walks the Path of Christ," 10.
7. Sánchez, *From Patmos to the Barrio*, 97–98. Sánchez argues that the anticolonial usage of Guadalupe by Hidalgo y Costilla informed the use of Guadalupe as a symbol of economic justice by César Chávez and the UFW. Sánchez notes the parallel construction between the Grito de Dolores ("Death to the Spaniards! Long live the Virgin of Guadalupe!") and the rallying cry of the UFW ("Justice for the *compesinos* and long live the Virgin of Guadalupe!").
8. Flores, "Heart of the Neighborhood."
9. Tracy, *Analogical Imagination*, 102; Okey, *Theology of Conversation*, 79.
10. Laso de la Vega, *Story of Guadalupe*, 62–63; Purcell, "Eudaimonia and Neltiliztli," 13. Purcell explains the prevalence of *difrasismo*, or the expression of one idea in two words, in Nahuatl: "This sort of expression was extremely common in Nahuatl, and one must be careful to catch the metaphorical meaning at work. For if taken literally, the meaning of *difrasismo* is almost totally lost." Purcell highlights the example of *xochi in cuicatl*, which literally means "with flower and song" but metaphorically means something closer to "poetry."
11. Laso de la Vega, *Story of Guadalupe*, 84:2.
12. Rodriguez, *Our Lady of Guadalupe*, 17.
13. Poole, *Our Lady of Guadalupe*, 14.
14. Poole, 219.
15. Poole, 14.
16. Matovina, *Theologies of Guadalupe*, 29.
17. Matovina, "Theologies of Guadalupe," 64.
18. Gálvez, *Guadalupe in New York*, 79.
19. Gálvez, 78.
20. Pope Francis, "Holy Mass at the Basilica of Our Lady of Guadalupe," 1.
21. Marsh, Slade, and Azaransky, *Lived Theology*, 7.
22. Gadamer, *Truth and Method*, 267.
23. Gálvez, *Guadalupe in New York*, 76.
24. Lloyd and True, "What Political Theology Could Be," 505.

25. Laso de la Vega, *Story of Guadalupe*, 61.
26. Farley, *Just Love*, 211.
27. Cavanaugh, *Myth of Religious Violence*.
28. Hanisch, "Personal Is Political."
29. Schmidt, *Cachita's Streets*, 3.
30. Schmidt, 5.
31. Rodriguez, *Our Lady of Guadalupe*, 120.
32. Rodriguez, 121.
33. Castañeda-Liles, *Our Lady of Everyday Life*, 55–56.
34. Castañeda-Liles, 102.
35. Gálvez, *Guadalupe in New York*, 3.
36. Gálvez, 3.
37. Tirres, *Aesthetics and Ethics of Faith*, 58.
38. Elizondo, *Galilean Journey*, 5.
39. Goizueta, *Caminemos Con Jesús*; Goizueta, *Christ Our Companion*; García-Rivera, *Community of the Beautiful*.
40. Elizondo, *Galilean Journey*, 44.
41. Valentín, *Mapping Public Theology*; Aquino, "Prophetic Horizon of Latino Theology"; Medina, *Mestizaje*; Tirres, *Aesthetics and Ethics of Faith*.
42. Aquino, "Prophetic Horizon of Latino Theology."
43. Siller Acuña, *Para Comprender El Mensaje de María de Guadalupe*, 74.
44. Farley, *Just Love*, 210.
45. Nussbaum, *Creating Capabilities*.
46. Farley, *Just Love*, 210–13.
47. Laso de la Vega, *Story of Guadalupe*, 84:71.
48. Goizueta, *Caminemos Con Jesús*, 73.
49. Laso de la Vega, *Story of Guadalupe*, 84:71.
50. Goizueta, *Caminemos Con Jesús*, 73.
51. Goizueta, 74.
52. Appiah, "What's Wrong with Slavery?," 254.
53. Goizueta, *Caminemos Con Jesús*, 75.
54. Laso de la Vega, *Story of Guadalupe*, 84:63.
55. Purcell, "Eudaimonia and Neltiliztli," 10.
56. Purcell, 13.
57. Garcia, "Miracle at Tepeyac," 17.
58. LaCugna, *God for Us*; Hilkert, "Cry Beloved Image"; Hollenbach, *Common Good and Christian Ethics*; González, "Who We Are"; M. Clark, *Vision of Catholic Social Thought*; Flores, "Trinity and Justice."
59. González-Andrieu, *Bridge to Wonder*, 88.
60. León, "César Chávez," 56.
61. Griego, "Church Wall Hiding Our Lady of Guadalupe Mural."
62. Griego, "Church Wall Hiding Our Lady of Guadalupe Mural."
63. Griego, "Church Wall Hiding Our Lady of Guadalupe Mural."
64. Coday, "Denver Catholics Fight to Restore Guadalupe Mural."
65. Draper, "Faithful Again Demand Lady of Guadalupe Mural Be Uncovered."
66. Young, *Justice and the Politics of Difference*, 40.
67. Massingale, "Vox Victimarum Dei," 83.

2

John Rawls's
Liberal Imagination

"Imagine a Great City!" This was Federico Peña's slogan for his 1983 mayoral campaign.[1] Peña was mayor of Denver from 1983 until 1991. He was only the third Hispanic man elected as mayor of a major US city, joining Maurice Ferré of Miami (1973) and Henry Cisneros of San Antonio (1981). In 1992 Peña joined the Clinton administration, where he served first as secretary of transportation and then as secretary of energy. In 2008 he worked as a co-chair on another historic campaign: Obama for America.

Playing on the lyrics of John Lennon's 1971 hit song, Peña's 1983 campaign slogan invited Denverites to conceive of a more democratic city with greater participation among those who had often been left out of municipal government. Candidate Peña promised "continued efforts to provide equal access and opportunity to all Denver residents, particularly women, so that desire and ability will be the only limits on personal achievement and fulfillment."[2] Mayor Peña opened positions of public influence to those with ability and desire, making appointments to boards, commissions, and judicial seats that reflected the city's overall demographic profile.[3] In so doing he summoned forth a new generation of leaders who shared a commitment to implementing equal political access and economic development across the city.

Peña, a lifelong practicing Catholic, was a parishioner of Our Lady of Guadalupe Parish during his first mayoral campaign. A former altar boy who had spent the earliest years of his law career advocating for Chicano civil rights as a staff member with the Mexican American Legal Defense and Education Fund (MALDEF), Peña found a spiritual home at the parish that had become the heart of Chicano Catholicism in Denver. Elected to the Colorado House of Representative in 1979 before his fellow House Democrats elected him minority leader, Peña rose quickly to the forefront of Colorado politics. Even so, he spent Sunday mornings receiving the Eucharist in front of Carlotta Espinoza's mural of Guadalupe and Juan Diego commissioned by Jose Lara.

Formed at the feet of Guadalupe, Peña's campaign and administration reflected a Catholic faith inflected with a keen sense of social justice. He used his public platform to make room in Denver politics for those who had been underrepresented in city politics before his administration, including Chicano, Black, and Vietnamese constituents. Along the way he garnered the support of Chicano activist Rodolfo "Corky" Gonzalez and "Daddy" Bruce Randolph, the latter a pillar of the Black community celebrated for his charitable service to Denverites lacking stable housing.[4] This multiracial liberal coalition prepared the way for the election of Denver's first and second Black mayors: Wellington E. Webb in 1991 (and who also ran in the 1983 mayoral primary) and Michael Hancock in 2011. And in 2019, more than three-and-a-half decades after Peña's election, Latine representation on the Denver City Council finally reached a level proportionate to the city's Latine population when five Latinas were elected to the assembly, comprising 38 percent of the council.[5]

Peña's victory was catalyzed by Denver's Northside *Chicanismo* and *Guadalupismo*; on the night he was elected young people cruised the streets of north Denver chanting "Chicano Power!"[6] But it was also an experiment in lived liberalism. Graduating from the University of Texas in 1972, Peña was studying law just as it was beginning to metabolize John Rawls's liberal philosophies. Originally published in 1971, Rawls's *A Theory of Justice* identifies two principles of justice, lexically ordered: (1) defending each person's equal right to the most extensive basic liberties compatible with others while (2) defending social and economic inequalities so long as they ultimately lead to greater social equality.[7] Peña's mayoral record reflects Rawls's first principle through his commitment to increasing equal participation among those who were often left out of city politics. But it is the Peña administration's reflection of the second principle, the difference principle, that defines his mayoral legacy in Denver.

Taking over leadership in Denver's economically troubled early eighties, Peña prioritized infrastructure, business, and cultural development projects that aimed to raise Denver's national profile: a new international airport, a new professional baseball team, a new central public library. Peña's hallmark projects maintained his commitment to increasing diversity among the city's power brokers by diversifying the recipients of city building contracts, including hiring Latina-owned Alvarado Construction, which completed major work on the Colorado Convention Center and Denver International Airport. With these projects Peña doubled down on fortifying existing political and economic institutions, albeit in diversified versions of these positions and structures.

In this way Peña's public life was shaped by a Rawlsian liberal aesthetic that expressed a commitment to increasing equality while maintaining confidence that US political, legal, and economic institutions could deliver justice across the city's diverse population. This liberal aesthetic also influenced how Peña articulated his identity in public life. As one of the first prominent Latino politicians in Colorado or in the United States—with a lifelong commitment to the practice of his Catholic faith—Peña's approach to his ethnicity and religion in public life also reflected a Rawlsian commitment to relegating particular conceptions of the good to society's background culture in matters to pertaining to basic structures. In practical terms this meant that Peña learned to acknowledge the particularities of his identity without making them central planks of his political platform. Part political strategy and part survival mechanism, this pattern of relationship between race and ethnicity was manifest again in Barack Obama's 2008 campaign for president, for which Peña served as a national co-chair, especially in Obama's speech on race and religion in response to accusations of racist and anti-American sermons from his long-time pastor, Rev. Jeremiah Wright.[8]

From Peña's rise to Denver's City Hall to Obama's ascent to the White House, it is clear that Rawls's veiled aesthetics have shaped lived liberalism. Despite declarations of liberalism's demise from both the left and the right, Rawls's thinking continues to influence the shape of public life in incalculable ways. From court rooms to emergency rooms, from economic policy to foreign policy, Rawls's principles shape not only how we *think* about our common life but how we *see*, *hear*, and otherwise *experience* our common life. Said differently, Rawls's liberalism shapes the aesthetics of how we experience democracy in the United States and beyond.

How does Rawls's political philosophy, which is quite uninterested in aesthetics, come to have such a profound influence on the aesthetics of US democracy? Perhaps counterintuitively, it does so through Rawls's (in)famous method of abstraction, which invites readers into an imaginative thought experiment. The ahistorical original position requires that the reader conceive of the social contract not from the vantage point of a particular society or form of government but from "behind the veil of ignorance" where we "even assume that the parties do not know their conceptions of the good or psychological propensities."[9] Without knowing one's own position in society, Rawls argues, the free and rational person would choose principles of justice that are based on the possibility that they could be the least well-off member of society. Accordingly, this thought experiment generates principles that invite greater equality and participation among all members of society, with the difference principle stipulating that all social and economic inequalities are attached to "positions and offices open to all."[10] Rawls calls upon his audience to imagine the conditions of the original position necessary to identify fair principles of justice: "Thus we are to imagine that those who engage in social cooperation choose together, in one joint act, the principles which are to assign basic rights and duties and to determine the division of benefits."[11]

Peña's use of imagination during his campaign and as expressed in his governing strategies helps us visualize how Rawls's imaginative aesthetic shapes practical liberal commitments. Rawls's aesthetic pursues political stability—Rawls's term meaning institutions remain just even as they change rather than the impermissibility of any systemic change—that allows for people from different religious backgrounds to coexist within a democratic society.[12] In this sense Rawls's aesthetic allows for democratic society to visualize a Big Story, to employ García-Rivera's framework, about American identity that emphasizes the possibility that people from different religious, racial, and ethnic background can inhabit the same society under conditions of political equality. Nonetheless, Rawls's aesthetic requires a veiling of particular comprehensive doctrines, or particular conceptions of the good, in a manner that obscures from critical examination the unique identities, experiences, and commitments inherent in common life. This veiling prevents Rawls's liberalism from fulfilling its own original position commitment of seeing the world as it really is. The imaginative practice of veiling leads to concrete political practices that amount to ignoring inequalities and meaningful differences that are essential to understanding what justice requires. Obscuring injustices behind the veil, Rawls's liberalism fails to provide constructive resources for responding to them within society's basic structures.

Rawls's aesthetic limitation is particularly evident in his interpretation of religion. His conception of religion is molded by a narrow and shallow account of White mainline Protestantism in the mid-twentieth century. This leaves him with a compressed conception of religion that is too general to comprehend the public dimensions of nonwhite and non-Protestant religious beliefs and practices (such as Peña's Mexican American Catholicism). Relegating minoritized religion and culture to the background of deliberation about society's basic structures, Rawls's aesthetic cannot *visualize* the particular historical oppression endured by out-groups, especially injustices that are comprehended and expressed via religious symbols, religious language, or religious practices of minoritized groups. This inability to contend with actual histories of oppression undermines Rawls's own project of identifying justice principles that foster equality, participation, and fair distribution of power.

This chapter interlaces the thread of imagination from Peña's historic campaign and administration through Rawls's writings in *A Theory of Justice* and *Political Liberalism* to unveil the contributions and limitations of Rawls's liberal aesthetic to the life of US democracy.[13] I begin with an examination of imagination in Rawls's thought, with particular attention to the place of imagination in his aesthetics of the original position, the sense of justice, and public reason that Rawls sees as vital to maintaining just political institutions in the context of pluralism. I then interrogate Rawls's articulation of religion, an account that is based on a narrow account of White mainline Protestantism. Shaped by an individualized conception of soteriology, Rawls is fundamentally suspicious of religion as a force for the common good even as some of his assumptions about religion shape his highly individualistic political philosophy. He allows little possibility that religious practices can be generative social or public forces. I then turn to the works of Iris Marion Young, Ada María Isasi-Díaz, and Emilie Townes to illustrate the deleterious consequences of this aesthetic of abstraction in the everyday lives of people and communities rendered invisible within Rawls's liberal aesthetic scheme. I conclude the chapter by revisiting Alejandro García-Rivera's conception of the Big Story and little stories. Although Rawls's aesthetic allows us to visualize a Big Story of political stability in a pluralistic society, it obscures the little stories—including popular religious devotion to Our Lady of Guadalupe—that are essential for imagining conditions that allow for survival and flourishing of the oppressed. The life of democracy in the twenty-first century requires a political philosophy capable of seeing the little stories, without which the Big Story of pluralism is not possible.

RAWLS'S IMAGINATIVE AESTHETICS

"[Peña] seems to have more imagination."[14] The morning after the 1983 election, reporters scrambled to understand why Denver voters had decided to elect Peña, a thirty-six-year-old Mexican American lawyer, as their mayor. Peña came out ahead of incumbent Bill McNichols, who was eliminated during the primary, and Dale Tooley, a former district attorney and a three-time mayoral candidate. The *Rocky Mountain News*'s quotation of an anonymous voter from southwest Denver—across town and well away from Peña's northwest Denver Chicano stronghold—seemed to explain the situation well: Peña's vision for a more inclusive, more prosperous city resonated with voters from across the city's many racial, ethnic, religious, and economic groups.

Victory hadn't come easy. In addition to criticism about his relative youth and inexperience, Peña encountered both implicit and explicit attacks about his Mexican American identity. A poll question from Tooley operative Dick

Morris asked voters if they were comfortable voting for a Mexican candidate; nearly thirty years later Morris used the same racist tactics to undermine Obama's reelection candidacy.[15] The poll stunned many voters by unveiling blatantly racist sentiment that existed just below the surface of the city's mayoral contest. While some voters found the question to be distasteful or outright offensive, the intimation achieved its desired result of legitimizing doubts about Peña's ethnicity among some White voters. Phil Nash, a reporter for Denver's *Westword*, wrote of Peña, "There are still some people who say Denver isn't quite ready for Mayor Pena [*sic*]. And who really mean that Denver isn't ready for a mayor so young—and so Hispanic."[16]

Peña was openly irritated by Nash's suggestion that Denver might not be ready for his leadership. What did his ethnicity have to do with his ability to be mayor? Peña responded by emphasizing that ethnicity—both his own and that of his opponent—was irrelevant to the ability to lead Denver:

> The question I am asking is if Denver is ready for a person who has ideas, who has a track record, who is able, who has integrity, who is going to work hard, who is creative, who is thinking about the future, who is going to provide leadership for Denver in the 80s, who happens to be Hispanic. Is this city ready to discard a 73-year-old gentleman who is not ready for the 80s, who is tired, who has problems with management, problems with credibility because of his cabinet, who also happens to be Irish?[17]

In accord with his campaign slogan, Peña asked Denverites to imagine a city where race, ethnicity, age, class, prestige, and social status did not matter for decisions about leadership. He asked Denver to make a decision based solely on ability and willingness to lead. He asked voters to put on Rawls's veil of ignorance as they made their decision about the future of the city's democracy. In so doing Peña deployed Rawls's anonymous aesthetic, an aesthetic predicated on imagination.

Alan Wolfe argues that liberalism, in general, is averse to aesthetics. In his provocatively titled chapter "Why Good Poetry Makes Bad Politics," he indicts the aesthetics of Romanticism in particular for inflaming militaristic, nationalist, and ideological impulses.[18] While not opposed to the private virtues of poetry per se, Wolfe is chary of its public effects. "Romanticism," he writes, "touches on the deepest emotions, expands the human imagination, and produces world-class music and art."[19] Nonetheless, poetry tends to be a destabilizing force that interferes with the responsibilities of realism inherent in both domestic and international politics. Expressing affinity with Rawls's emphasis on political stability, Wolfe advocates for liberalism's turn to reason rather than passion as a stabilizing force in US public life. "When liberalism works—either at home or abroad—fewer people are killed in the name of a cause, fewer lives are disrupted to serve as characters in someone else's drama." Published in 2009, Wolfe's comment now reads as a prophecy of the state of democracy of the past two decades, a time when disorienting political upheaval has cast humanity into a reality television show–like experience with a particularly cruel premise. The global rise of ethnonationalist movements predicated on passionate allegiances as a basis for authority and authenticity and often bolstered by affective attachments to particular symbols (e.g., red trucker hats stitched with "Make America Great Again") has led to renewed calls for reason, fact, expertise, and even truth as the basis for government decision-making. "Let the passions reign in the museums and concert halls," Wolfe writes. "In the halls of government, reason, however cold, is better than emotions, however heartfelt."

Amanda Anderson, conversely, argues that liberalism *does* have a robust aesthetics that is manifest in certain forms of literature. This aesthetic is especially evident in novels that help illustrate liberalism as a lived commitment in a complex or "bleak" way and help the reader grapple with liberalism's tensions and ironies: works by Charles Dickens, Anthony Trollope, George Eliot, Elizabeth Gaskell, E. M. Forster, Ralph Ellison, and Doris Lessing. She places the theories of "bleak liberals" such as Theodor Adorno and Lionel Trilling in conversation with these authors, but excludes Rawls among contributors to this aesthetic.[20] Rawls is "famously inattentive to aesthetics," she writes.[21] While his work manifests a certain attitude of "serenity," she dismisses its contribution to a liberal aesthetics that can "press toward an account of the deeper discontents and aspirations that lie behind a pattern of attitudinal forms discernable across the tradition" that is characteristic of bleak liberalism.[22] Anderson argues for a liberal aesthetic capable of grappling with complex dimensions of social experience, a project that challenges systematic liberals and temperamental liberals alike. This latter group includes Martha Nussbaum, whose focus on the centrality of individual character to the liberal ethos, Anderson argues, prevents confrontation with the difficulties and limitations of lived liberalism.[23]

Indeed, there is a meditative quality to Rawls's work, as it asks for an *ascetic* detachment from the particularities that shape our own identities and a denial of information about who we are and where we stand in society. This detachment, Rawls claims, is not for its own sake. "We need a conception that enables us to envision our objective from afar: the intuitive notion of the original position is to do this for us."[24] To envision the objective from afar requires that we view *ourselves* from afar, or at least the particularities of our identities. He employs an economic example to illustrate this position:

> For example, if a man knew that he was wealthy, he might find it ratio-
> nal to advance the principle that various taxes for welfare measures be
> counted unjust; if he knew that he was poor, he would most likely pro-
> pose the contrary principle. To represent the desired restrictions one
> imagines a situation in which everyone is deprived of this sort of infor-
> mation. One excludes the knowledge of those contingencies which
> sets men at odds and allows them to be guided by their prejudices.[25]

Without prior knowledge of our position we must acknowledge the possibility that we could be the least-well-off member of society. In light of this
possibility we would not select principles that would harm our own interests.
It is only when we view our own position in society from behind the veil of
ignorance that we are able to identify principles of justice that will be truly
fair to all.

The meditative sensibility of Rawls's original position resonates with
Sarah Coakley's *théologie totale* and its emphasis on the necessity of ascetic
practices of attention that are at the foundation of aesthetic practices.[26] Coakley, of course, writes from an explicitly theological position, whereas Rawls
explicitly seeks to avoid any metaphysical commitments, especially theological ones. But Coakley's admonition for cultivating practices of attention
resonates with Rawls's description of the original position as an imaginative
space, where members of society attend to the premises on which conceptions of justice are founded.

Coakley's emphasis on the relationship between the ascetic and aesthetic
allows us to conceptualize the sensory dimensions of Rawls's theory. The theories part ways, however, on their respective proposed objects of attention.
Coakley argues for "the ascetical practice of contemplation as a preparation
for radical attention to the 'other'" (even if such practice must be counterbal-
anced by attention to oneself so as to check propensities and desires for such
attentions to become objectifying and/or imperialistic).[27] Although Rawls
asks that we forgo attention to our own particularities, he would not want us
to attend to the particularities of others either. Instead, the original position
calls for attention to one's own interests—without regard for the position or
interests of others—as the basis for decisions about the principles of justice.
Without knowledge of particular identities or social status—either of ourselves or of others—he argues that we would choose fair principles of justice
that would not disadvantage us if we were the least well off in society.

The original position is enticing to some. Imagine no knowledge of religion, race, or economic status. Certainly, we would select fair principles of justice in that world. Such an approach, however, neglects the challenges presented to the work of justice by concrete histories of oppression. Veiled to their identities and the identities of others, how would those in the original position be able to see and respond to the problems of police violence against Black and Brown people? How would they comprehend the complexities and particularities of lives taken by the hands of the agents of the basic structures intended to protect them?

Rawls would respond that the participants in the original position would have basic knowledge about the world. This knowledge would include, for example, statistics about the disproportionate rates of death by police violence against Black and Brown people. But without knowledge of particularities, how would such knowledge of the world account for the ongoing agony of Black deaths at the hands of police? How would it simulate the psychological and emotional effects of years of living in fear of leaving one's house and never coming home? While the original position allows for the basic assertion that policing is fair, it cannot comprehend the particular history of policing as it relates to slavery, Reconstruction, Jim Crow, school-to-prison pipelines, and other patterns of discrimination that undermine the stable basic structure that Rawls seeks. In this way Rawls's veiled aesthetic renders invisible countless aspects of human identity, experience, and relationship that are, in fact, crucial to pursuing stable principles of justice.

Although Rawls remains resolute in his claim that his principles of justice do not require any theological or metaphysical support for their stabilization, he concedes that there is a need for citizens to be attracted to the principles: "However attractive a conception of justice might be on other grounds, it is seriously defective if the principles of moral psychology are such that it fails to engender in human beings the requisite desire to act upon it."[28] The sense of justice fosters this desire. He uses this mechanism to identify the role of moral formation in his project of political stabilization.

In an Aristotelian turn, Rawls emphasizes the necessity of formation of particular abilities and goods among citizens. A sense of justice engenders a commitment to the project of justice. Concretely this means that the education of members of society matters for the cultivation of a stable conception of justice, particularly public education. "I assume that the sense of justice is acquired gradually by the younger members of society as they grow up. The succession of generations and the necessity to teach moral attitudes (however simple) to children is one of the conditions of human life."[29] The kind and quality of publicly available education thus becomes a matter of public interest.

In October 2019 the faculty of the University of Virginia (UVA) voted to adopt a newly constructed curriculum.[30] The foundation of the new curriculum is a set of courses called "engagements," or four half-semester courses that acquaint first-year undergraduate students with habits of mind that they will encounter during their studies in the university. Each student is required to take one course dedicated to each of four engagements: empirical and scientific engagement, engaging differences, ethical engagement, and engaging aesthetics. Aesthetic engagement courses ask, How does aesthetic perception create value and meaning in our lives? This question augments the aesthetic dimensions of Rawls's sense of justice. His commentary on the primary good of self-respect illustrates his thinking here. He distinguishes between things that are primarily good for oneself, such as exclusive goods like commodities and private property, and things that are good for society as a whole. For example,

> imagination and wit, beauty and grace, and other natural assets and abilities of the person are goods for others, too: they are enjoyed by our associates as well as ourselves when properly displayed and rightly exercised. They form the human means for complementary activities in which persons join together and take pleasure in their own and one another's realization of their nature.... Thus the excellences are a condition of human flourishing; they are goods from everyone's point of view.[31]

In identifying imagination and beauty as common goods Rawls argues for their necessity in a well-ordered society. These qualities, formed through education, promote political stability. For his conception of stability this means more than simply accepting institutions as they have been received. The sense of justice requires interrogating existing structures and making necessary changes to them when they do not foster justice. Habits of mind formed through aesthetic education—along with empirical, ethical, and difference education—are accordingly essential education that cultivates a just society.

It is significant that this aesthetic curriculum has been adopted at the university founded by Thomas Jefferson. Author of the Virginia Statute for Religious Freedom—an accomplishment that receives pride of place on his gravestone at Monticello—Jefferson founded the university with the explicit intent to keep theology at the margins of academic discourse. He gave architectural representation to this commitment by replacing the chapel typically located at the center of a university with a library housed inside of a luminous rotunda. Religious studies, of course, is now a vibrant department at UVA. Several of its faculty members contributed to developing, piloting, and passing the university's new curriculum. The provision for an aesthetic engagement allows for students to study aspects of religious traditions that are perceptual or simply not strictly discursive. This change has the capacity to challenge the very notion of religion developed and engaged in twenty-first-century democratic discourse. Nevertheless, Mr. Jefferson's university still embodies some of the tensions between religion and public life that are manifest in Rawls's work. The study of religion—whether normative or descriptive—is often framed as ancillary to public education and, subsequently, to the life of democracy. But religion must always make a case for being in the room. And that case must be translated into what Rawls refers to as "public reason."

Public reason, like the other dimensions of Rawlsian liberalism, is grounded in the aforementioned necessity for political stability in plural society. Rawls stipulates that citizens must justify their political decisions to each other using publicly available language, values, and standards. Whereas the original position aims to exclude knowledge about one's own position within society from deliberations about basic structure, Rawls uses public reason as a mechanism for allowing reasons to emanate from particular comprehensive doctrines toward stabilization of the conception of justice. Like the original position and the sense of justice, public reason contributes to Rawls's liberal aesthetics that influence democratic practices.

The standard of public reason applies to deliberations on matters of basic justice—essential constitutional provisions, for example—but not to matters of general justice that we discuss in the background culture. Rawls explains: "[Public reason's] limits do not apply to our personal deliberations and reflections about political questions, or to the reasoning about them by members of associations, such as churches and universities, all of which is a vital part of the background culture."[32] While operating in the background culture, citizens may use language, concepts, and ideas that correspond to their particular worldviews. Translation is necessary, however, in matters pertaining to basic structures. This demand extends to every aspect of public life that comes into contact with deliberations about institutional justice, including voting: "Otherwise, public discourse runs the risk of being hypocritical: citizens talk before one another one way and vote another."[33]

Religious ethicists have criticized Rawls's demand for public reason as too narrowly restricting discourse, and thus participation, in democracy. While the requirement for public reason is compatible with Christian aims to communicate religious truths with broader publics using accessible language, Eric Gregory argues that Rawls's strict demand for public reason in matters pertaining to public justice is impractical, historically naïve, strategically self-defeating, and antidemocratic.[34] Echoing Rawls's concerns for the potentially destabilizing aspects of religion, Gregory concedes that "a more freewheeling ethic of citizenship can be dangerous." Nevertheless, he asserts that these challenges are congruent with the life of a thriving democracy: "Democratic deliberation means that we should let a thousand flowers bloom in the garden of political discourse."[35] There is no need to reject the concept of public reason wholesale, but it needs to be capacious enough to accommodate religious interventions into public life even if such interventions cause a degree of volatility in the life of democracy.

Echoing Gregory's concerns, Cathleen Kaveny argues that limits on religious speech prevent the cultivation of a participatory democracy predicated on trust. She is concerned that the requirement for translation renders public discourse inauthentic. She explains:

> If we enter into an ostensibly frank discussion on a given controversial issue, such as abortion or gay adoption, we expect that if we refute the arguments put forward by our interlocutors, it is at least possible they will change their minds. But this may not be the case if our interlocutors are not offering us the *reasons they actually hold*, but rather are mustering an ad hoc argument drawn from the language of public reason to support their position. If we urge our interlocutors to put forth the arguments that are not really theirs, our interlocutors will not change their minds if we defeat them but instead search for a more resilient replacement approach to make their case in the public square.[36]

While Rawls cautions against hypocrisy if we allow religious reason to guide our public actions, Kaveny worries that a strict demand for public reason will actually lead to a hypocritical discourse, where we believe one thing and say another. Discourse of this kind, she argues, is inadequate for forging a democratic culture predicated on participation and trust.

Jeffrey Stout's analysis resonates with these critiques, emphasizing the possibility that Rawls's conception of common reason falters by suggesting that it is the only configuration for public reasoning: "Rawls is quick to move from imagining the basis on which citizens 'can reason in common' to concluding that only by conducting our most important political reasoning on this basis can we redeem the promise of treating our fellow citizens fairly in matters pertaining to the use of coercive power. And this conclusion leads, in turn, to a restrictive view of the role religious reasons can play in the public forum."[37] Stout draws our attention to a crucial point: the claim that our most important reasoning—that which pertains to society's basic structure—must be pursued free from religious reasoning, denies the possibility that citizens can treat each other fairly while maintaining religious particularity in public life.

Rawls's struggle to interpret concrete examples of substantive arguments about basic justice that are made using religious language reinforces these critiques. In a discussion of the religious rhetoric employed by abolitionists and Martin Luther King Jr., Rawls argues that neither violate public reason despite the religious content of their messages: "Both the Abolitionists' and King's doctrines were held to belong to public reason because they were invoked in an unjust political society, and their conclusions of justice were in accord with the constitutional values of a liberal regime. I also said that there should be reason to believe that appealing to the basis of these reasons in citizens' comprehensive doctrines would help to make society more just."[38] Despite his affirmation that their speech met his *proviso* concerning public reason, Rawls remains uncertain about the relationship between these movements and public reason: "I do not know whether the Abolitionists or King ever fulfilled the *proviso*. But whether they did or not, they could have. And, had they known the idea of public reason and shared its ideal, they would have."[39]

This test case asks whether Rawls's requirement is tenable in a political context influenced by participants holding myriad conceptions of the good, including religious ones. Stout answers in the negative. On one hand he sees Rawls's introduction of the proviso as an improvement on more restrictive manifestations in previous works. But even with the proviso, religious reasons are insufficient as public reasons: "Religious reasons are to contractarian reasons as IOUs are to legal tender," writes Stout. "You have not fulfilled your justificatory obligations until you have handed over real cash."[40] Even so, Stout is disturbed that cases such as the abolitionists and King "barely squeak by" on these criteria. For this reason, Stout asserts, "it is hard to credit any theory that treats their arguments as placeholders for reasons to be named later."[41]

The critiques of Gregory, Kavaney, and Stout gesture to a problem deeper than language in Rawls's thinking about public reason. Rawls's demand for reason shapes public discourse, but it also shapes public aesthetics. It delineates what is in the foreground and what is in the background of public life. If religious speech challenges Rawls's proviso, then religious symbols such as Our Lady of Guadalupe confound it. When emblazoned on a banner in support of the United Farm Workers, Guadalupe's symbol is leveraged to make a substantive justice claim about society's economic system, a foundational system in society's basic structure. A torch carried from Guadalupe's basilica in Mexico City to Saint Patrick's Cathedral in New York City as a protest for immigration justice asserts a substantive claim about society's basic structure as it concerns its definition of citizenship. Claims made about society's basic structure via religious language, narratives, or symbols cannot simply be evacuated of their religious meaning. Rawls's assertion that they can and should be evacuated displays a tension between his mechanisms for stabilizing religious participation in public life and the necessity of fostering robust popular participation within the context of a twenty-first-century democracy. Delving more deeply into Rawls's conception of religion illustrates the implication of his aesthetics for the life of democracy.

RELIGION AND LIBERAL IMAGINATION

Rawls does not treat religion as a distinctive category, but rather includes it under the more general heading of comprehensive doctrine or conception of the good.[42] Nevertheless, concerns about religious pluralism and conflict set an important context for the development of his liberal political theory. Rawls is ambivalent about religion's potential to contribute positively to public life. On one hand he views religion as a particular type of conception of the good that can contribute to the formation of an overlapping consensus necessary for political stability. On the other he cites religion as a destabilizing force that is particularly susceptible to promoting violence and injustice. This ambivalence about religion is evident in his political theory, when he seeks to simultaneously enlist particular comprehensive doctrines (including reasonable religious doctrines) as potential allies in the project of identifying a stable and freestanding conception of justice and protect society's basic structures from the potentially volatile aspects of these particular views of the good. The conception of religion reflected in Rawls's political philosophy is a White, mainline Christian theology of the mid-twentieth century.

The study of theology was central to Rawls's education as an undergraduate at Princeton University. As a senior he wrote a thesis on sin and faith.[43] He briefly considered pursuing ordination in the Episcopal Church, but decided instead to join the US Army during wartime.[44] Rawls abandoned personal and academic interest in theology after his military service, citing the profound evil and incomprehensible injustice of the Holocaust.[45] He came to understand the God of Christianity as fundamentally unjust: "To interpret history as expressing God's will, God's will must accord with the most basic ideas about justice as we know them. For what else can the most basic justice be? Thus, I soon came to reject the idea of the supremacy of the divine will as also hideous and evil."[46]

In addition to his suspicion that divine providence is an affront to justice, Rawls also characterizes Christianity as an essentially "solitary religion" by which "each is saved or damned individually."[47] He associates the quality of religion through the individual practitioner in isolation from wider communities of believers. He suspects that "a person's religion is often no better or worse than they are as persons."[48] This individualized account of religion resonates with his understanding of the individual as the primary subject of salvation. He argues that the pursuit of individual salvation becomes a distraction from issues pertaining to broader society: "While it is impossible not to be concerned with ourselves, at least to some degree—and we should—our own individual soul and its salvation are hardly important for the larger picture of civilized life."[49] The Confessing Church notwithstanding, Rawls criticizes German Christians for being more concerned with their personal salvation than with resisting the evil of Hitler's regime.

Rawls's operative conception of Christian religion is thus a fundamentally privatized relationship between the self-interested individual and God. This privatized account of Christianity is reflected in his treatment of religion in general and in his political philosophy in particular. His conception of religion adheres to a particular understanding of a White mainline expression of Christianity. While he generally acknowledges differences among religious traditions, his designation of religion as a particular subset of comprehensive doctrines does not allow him to adequately describe the diverse structures between particular religious traditions or even the internal diversity within particular religious traditions themselves.[50] This compressed conception of religion is amenable to Rawls's focus on individuals as autonomous agents capable of reasoning about the basic principles of justice without having any specific information about either themselves or their fellow citizens, even as he insists that participants in his thought experiment would know basic facts about the world. In this view religion expresses yet another manifestation of self-interest that influences decisions about the principles of justice from behind the veil of ignorance. Given its private and individual nature, Rawls understands religion as that which can be easily sloughed from the individual's exercise of reason within the context of public life. This account of religion permits Rawls to conflate it with other comprehensive doctrines that he would have individuals relegate to the margins of decisions about society's basic structure.

Along with his critique of Christianity's potentially coercive effect on personal character, Rawls expresses concern for religion's capacity to foster violence. Political liberalism took shape against a backdrop of proliferating religious pluralism and dangerous political instability in the sixteenth and seventeenth centuries. This specific religious conflict spanned the period from 1517, when Martin Luther purportedly nailed ninety-five theses to the door of All Saints Church in Wittenberg, until the signing of the 1648 Treaty of Westphalia that ended the Wars of Religion.[51] During this time, Rawls claims, Europe witnessed the astronomical human costs of religious violence. In light of the political turmoil spawned by religious intolerance, Rawls attempts to articulate a coherent theory of political stability, one whose social institutions remain just even as they are inevitably altered due to changes in social circumstances. Accordingly, he asserts the fact of reasonable pluralism, including both religious and nonreligious comprehensive doctrines, as essential to a liberal theory of justice. He asks, "How is society even possible between those of different faiths? What can conceivably be the basis of religious toleration?"[52] In the context of religious conflict, acquiescence to the political rule by those from a different faith is tantamount to heresy. Accordingly, Rawls articulates a theoretical framework that resists the instability that results from clashes of comprehensive doctrines, including those concerning religious belief.

It is essential to note that Rawls does not dismiss the potential contributions of particular comprehensive doctrines, including religious ones, to society's common life. Reasons emanating from one's own comprehensive doctrine can contribute to matters concerning society's basic structures as long as they are translated into public reasons that are accessible to all members of society. Further, he emphasizes the permissibility and desirability of religious discourse in the background culture or in the realm of public conversation that is distinct from the basic structure of society.[53] Ideas emerging from particular comprehensive doctrines as a part of the background culture are essential to civic life, especially regarding deliberations pertaining to public issues.[54] Indeed, a vibrant background culture is important in a society characterized by reasonable pluralism, where not all persons subscribe to the same comprehensive doctrine.[55]

Thus, Rawls's concern for the destructive dimensions of religious conflict does not engender a necessary association between pluralism and cataclysmic conflict: "This pluralism is not seen as a disaster but rather as the natural outcome of the activities of human reason under enduring free institutions."[56] In Rawls's view, a dynamic pluralism can foster equality and justice, which are essential to the life of democracy. But this pluralism must be regulated in order to promote stability that protects diversity rather than instability that inflames conflict.

Rawls's theory is based on a historical interpretation of the Protestant Reformation that indicts religion as a uniquely influential catalyst of violence. This historical narrative undergirding Rawls's theory has been subject to interrogation. William Cavanaugh, for example, claims that the modern interpretation of religion as the primary catalyst of seventeenth-century European violence is a "creation myth" that endeavors to strictly delineate religion and politics.[57] This interpretation casts religion as a violent and destabilizing force that must be pursued completely separate from the public sphere. On the contrary, Cavanaugh argues, religion and politics were not neatly separated until the dawn of modernity. The narrative of religion's potential for political instability and generation of violence offers only an incomplete picture of the dynamic between church and state in the context of violence.

Cavanaugh's political theological account of the use of torture by Augusto Pinochet's regime in Chile helps elucidate his argument for the state's own potential for using violence to achieve unjust ends. He argues that it is necessary to examine the social dimensions of state-sponsored torture in which the social body is the primary target of the state's actions.[58] While religion in modernity has been uniquely accused of perpetuating violence, Cavanaugh argues that religious practice can play a crucial role in resisting state-sponsored violence.[59] He uses the Catholic Eucharist as an example of the capacity of religious practice to resist the violence of the state's program of torture and disappearance through believers' practice of communion with one another: "Torture creates victims; Eucharist creates witnesses, martyrs. Isolation is overcome in the Eucharist by the building of a communal body which resists the state's attempts to disappear it."[60] Cavanaugh thus suggests the possibility of framing particular religious beliefs and practices as resistance to the abuses of both individual bodies and of the social body by unjust political regimes.

Cavanaugh's historical and theological analysis of the relationship between church and state raises questions about the adequacy of the account of this relationship that undergirds Rawls's political philosophy and thus his aesthetics. Rawls gives the modern nation-state more credit for protecting pluralism than it is due. Furthermore, this interpretation continues to shape perceptions of religious engagement in public life, including interventions by religious actors and institutions into situations of injustice and violence as being a violation of this sacrosanct philosophical convention.

The uncritical juxtaposition between religion and public life has manifold consequences for the life of twenty-first-century democracy, especially for communities whose intersecting ethnic, racial, and religious liminality has relegated them to the edges of the public institutions that comprise society's basic structure. At the same time, neither the state's capacity for violence nor religion's capacity for resisting violence invalidates Rawls's concern for religion's potential volatility. In his political theology of martyrdom, Rubén Rosario Rodríguez argues that surging political violence among twenty-first-century religious extremist groups that employ corrupted theologies of martyrdom continues to contribute to a destabilized global political order.[61] While much attention has been given to the manipulation of theologies of jihad to justify political Islam, Rodríguez also points to the use of sacred scriptures by Christian fundamentalists in the United States to justify involvement in the War on Terror and the use of military force by Zionists in Israel to assert contemporary national boundaries in terms of ancient Israel's borders as examples of the use of religious reasons to promote and to justify violence.[62] In each of these cases religious extremist groups seek to commandeer the state's apparatus for violence in order to institute their particular agendas. The surge of religiously motivated political violence underscores Rawls's concern for stabilizing a freestanding conception of justice that does not use the state's monopoly on violence to enforce any particular religious or ideological agenda.

Nevertheless, Rodríguez cautions against associating the political violence perpetrated by religious extremist groups with entire religious traditions or with religion itself. He notes that three prominent examples of the use of violence by religious groups represent discourses largely marginalized within their respective traditions and appropriate traditional theological narratives for the sake of enacting their religious goals at the national and global levels.[63] This use of scripture and theology to justify violence thus demonstrates the necessity of pursuing basic structures that resist the destabilizing violence carried out by extremist religious groups in their pursuit of political goals under the banner of religious belief. It also shows the need for subtle examination and engagement of the religious traditions themselves within the life of democracy. Rodríguez explains:

> Normative doctrinal statements ought only to be made in dialogue with the diachronic and synchronic diversity within a tradition— demanding methodological humility that insists that no single representative or isolated community within the greater tradition can speak authoritatively and with finality for the whole tradition. Consequently, radical fringe groups cannot determine doctrinal orthodoxy nor establish correct practice for an entire religion, and conversely, a dominant majority cannot impose its doctrinal formulations onto minority dissenting groups within that religion.[64]

Rodríguez exhorts a pluralistic view of religious traditions themselves. This applies to doctrines related to justice, violence, human identity, and pluralism. Echoing Cavanaugh, Rodríguez also asserts the potential of religious groups to contribute positively and substantively to the resistance of state-sponsored violence, as is evident in the witness of Óscar Romero. Religious groups can enact and perpetuate violence but likewise they can also resist violence through discursive, practical, and aesthetic means.

Rawls's conception and categorization of religion does not permit the acknowledgment of such complexities among or within religious traditions. His articulation of the problem of religious violence does not adequately assess the interchange between religion and violence nor the potential role of religious traditions in undermining violence. This limitation in thought consequently influences his thinking about religion as a source of political empowerment and participation, especially among minoritized communities.

RACE, RELIGION, AND DEMOCRACY

The exclusion of religious particularity from deliberation about the basic structure prevents Rawls's theory from effectively engaging the inherent religious influences not only of prominent public religious figures such as Martin Luther King Jr. but also of individuals and communities whose public engagement in democracy from particular religious, racial, and cultural perspectives directly affects society's basic structures. Delving into this problem, this section evaluates Rawls's aesthetic as it pertains to engaging these particularities in the life of democracy.

Feminist philosophy has critiqued Rawls's prioritization of objectivity, arguing that the false universalization of thought and rationality exalts the subjectivity of those with power while relegating less-powerful people and groups to social, political, economic, and sexual margins. I will unpack the problems of Rawls's demand for impartiality as illustrated in the feminist political theory that has influenced the expression of mujerista and womanist theologies' critiques of objectivity claims. These critiques emphasize the limits of Enlightenment hierarchical reasoning in promoting an authentically participatory democratic life.

Iris Marion Young questions the very foundations of the modern ideal of impartiality. Young argues that "the ideal of impartiality in moral theory expresses a logic of identity that seeks to reduce difference to unity. The stances of detachment and dispassion that supposedly produce impartiality are attained only by abstracting from the particularities of situation, feeling, affiliation, and point of view."[65] This attempt at impartiality does not yield the desired result. Instead, impartiality generates a dichotomy between the universal and the other: general and particular, public and private, reason and passion, impartial and partial. The necessity of unity works to relegate difference to the margin, with all things located outside of the center being considered absolutely other. Difference is transformed from mere variation to a dichotomous us-versus-them structure that cannot comprehend plurality. Rather than recognizing the importance of difference, the supposedly impartial position ends up working against it, struggling to comprehend the nuances of concrete situations that can significantly influence the possibility of fostering and ensuring just social arrangements.

The contours of Young's argument reveal the issues of impartiality in particular articulations of political liberalism. She explains: "The ideal of impartial moral reason corresponds to the Enlightenment ideal of the public realm of politics as attaining the universality of a general will that leaves difference, particularity, and the body behind in the private realms of family and society."[66] This distinction between the public and private realms, Young argues, operates to exclude groups traditionally associated with the body and feelings—women, Black people, American Indians, Jews, and other socially marginalized groups—from public discussions on societal justice; their contributions are perceived as irrational, partial, and of limited or no use to the project of impartiality pursued in society.

This structure reinforces philosophies fertilized by Enlightenment philosophy's pseudo-scientific view of Whiteness as the highest manifestation of reason. While philosophers differed on the specifics of their structures of racial hierarchy, these distinctions quickly reduced to a binary between Whiteness and Blackness. As J. Kameron Carter argues, Whiteness is the telos of Enlightenment philosophy:

> Thus whiteness is both "now and not yet." It is a present reality, and yet it is also still moving toward and awaiting its perfection. The teleological end, which is the consummation of all things within the economic, political, and aesthetic—in short, within the structural—reality called "whiteness," is on the one hand made present and available now in white people and in white "culture." And on the other hand, it is through these white people and culture that the full reality of whiteness will globally expand to "eschatologically" encompass all things and so bring the world to perfection.[67]

A conception of supposed impartial rationality excludes individuals and groups that deviate from the White standard from public forums of deliberation and collective decision-making, which are essential to democratic governance. As Young explains, "Difference thus becomes a hierarchical opposition between what lies inside and what lies outside the category, valuing more what lies inside than what lies outside."[68] It is this center-periphery dynamic that constricts public life for minoritized people and communities in the United States.

Young argues that Rawls's project reproduces the monological reasoning that she identifies in the work of his Enlightenment forebears. Although Rawls builds his theory on the presupposition of a plurality of selves, his original position renders impossible any meaningful interaction between parties. As Young explains,

> The constraints on reasoning that Rawls builds into this original position in order to make it a representation of impartiality . . . rule out not only any difference among participants in the original position, but also any discussion among them. The veil of ignorance removes any differentiating characteristics among individuals, and thus ensures that all will reason from identical assumptions and the same universal point of view. The requirement that participants in the original position be mutually disinterested precludes any of the participants from listening to others' expression of their desires and interests and being influenced by them.[69]

Young's position resonates with the fundamental concern of this investigation: How is it possible to create any genuine interaction among plural selves and moral communities in a context that prizes the position that human beings—finite and capable of reason only in the context of our finitude—are able and expected to tap into universal reason?

Young's concerns about liberalism's faux objectivity help formulate an implicit critique of liberalism vis-à-vis liberationist theological ethics, including the works of Ada María Isasi-Díaz's mujerista ethics and Emilie M. Townes's womanist ethics. Rawls is not a major interlocutor for either Isasi-Díaz or Townes, but reading their works through Young's lens helps amplify their reasons for rejecting the false claims to objectivity that hinder the pursuit of justice in racially, culturally, and religiously pluralistic societies, where people on the underside of the Enlightenment's racist pseudoscience have been marked as unreasonable.

Isasi-Díaz develops a vision of justice emanating from mujerista theology, or a theological discourse that prioritizes the voices of grassroots Latinas working for justice. "*Mujeristas* privilege Latinas' lived experiences," she explains, "not because grassroots Latinas are morally better or holier than others but because we believe that since they do not profit from the present [social and economic] situation, they are capable of imagining a radically different future. They can do this better than those who benefit from current structures and who are, therefore, tempted to protect them."[70] The method of privileging the voices, perspectives, and experiences of marginalized communities in moral reasoning is in opposition to Rawls's method, which sets up the original position as a means of *avoiding* privileging a particular position in setting up the basic structure of society.

Although she does not directly engage Rawls's theories, Isasi-Díaz's footnotes reveal the influence of Young's critique of liberalism on her mujerista ethical framework.[71] Isasi-Díaz's work contains an implicit critique of Rawls's theory of justice that prioritizes impartiality for the sake of avoiding social bias in the process of establishing just social institutions. The subjectivity of some is subordinated to the supposed objectivity of others (those with power, whose subjectivity masquerades as reason and truth): "In *mujerista* theology we understand objectivity as the need to disclose our subjectivity, to make known our motives, our prejudices, the worldview that colors our way of acting. In *mujerista* theology we have insisted on partiality instead of impartiality and, together with other liberation theologies, we have privileged the poor and the oppressed, valuing their way of dealing with reality as important for all those who seek justice."[72] Particularity does not hinder justice; partiality toward the oppressed promotes the healing of social wounds as articulated in Matthew 25. For Isasi-Díaz, then, an adequate image of justice is not a blindfolded woman holding a scale but rather a gathering of people chatting over cups of *café con leche* while reflecting on their experiences of oppression, stories of survival, reasons for doubt, and sources of hope.[73]

This implicit critique of liberalism is essential to Isasi-Díaz's construction of a mujerista ethics of difference. While she asserts that differences are an essential aspect of human identity, she is critical of the tendency to make moral evaluations about differences as seen in the modernist pseudoscientific construction of a racial hierarchy: "If we are to bring about a paradigm shift in how we understand differences, we need to emphasize the role of differences in relationships rather than relating them only to what separates."[74] Isasi-Díaz advances a conception of difference anchored in a relational account of personhood. In the context of relationship, difference can be used to either undermine or advance equality. Communities characterized by solidarity are thus essential for justice.

Similarly, Townes's womanist ethics unmasks the liberal pursuit of objectivity as a pernicious task. She argues that false notions of objectivity cause and perpetuate unjust harm. The pursuit of objectivity masks the causes of injustice that threaten the survival of Black women. She writes,

no i am not here for the killers
>   when it comes to solidarity
>   >   which i assume is another way to say justice
i am not interested in them
>   except for how to decrease their numbers
>   and their power
i have no wish to be objective about their behavior, methods, ideologies,
or strategies
when I do the work of justice
>   it is with and as an advocate for the victims
>   >   actual
>   >   possible
>   >   imagined
>   of evil
it is subjective, it is emotional, it is passionate, it is very interested
and if I cannot find others who are interested and committed to this
>   then there is no solidarity
>   and our differences not only separate us
>   >   they make us adversaries
>   >   >   or enemies[75]

Supposed objectivity harbors cooperation with evil, Townes argues. She asserts the necessity of partiality in the rejection of evil. Townes thus advocates for partiality as a necessary condition for siding with the poor and dispossessed, those who Jon Sobrino calls the victims of history.[76]

These ethical critiques of the limits of universal reason interrogate a notion of reason as being incapable of making sense of difference. The problem with the disembodied "view from nowhere" is that such a view does not exist. The affirmation of this idea creates a unified center against a periphery, where deviant approaches are coalesced around a conception of the other that represents embodiment, emotion, feeling, and so on (or aspects of personhood associated with female identity and nonwhite identity) as things that stand against reason. In this way moral philosophies that claim to privilege no particular position actually end up privileging a very specific position: the position of the powerful. These critiques unveil a fundamental concern with Rawls's political aesthetics: his reliance on abstraction renders his framework inadequate for rigorous engagement with justice claims that emanate from particular communities by advocating for intentional ignorance of the context from which these claims emerge.

For his part, Rawls is unapologetic about the role of abstraction in the development of his political philosophy. He argues that these conditions are necessary for framing an adequate device of representation that does not privilege a particular comprehensive doctrine. Abstraction is not an end in itself, but rather a necessary component of the project of constructing a free-standing political conception of justice. It offers crucial perspective in public conflicts that need it the most. The theoretical work of abstraction is thus fundamental within liberal democratic society.

The arguments of Young, Isasi-Diaz, and Townes reveal the problem with particularity in Rawls's thought. While his theory seeks to foster equality, the demand for impartiality risks preferencing the subjectivity of dominant communities. Indeed, the goal of Rawls's aesthetics is to obscure history, preference, and ideology in the hope of foregrounding just social institutions. Yet the intentional ignorance of the original position renders the framework unable to address histories of exploitation, domination, colonization, and marginalization that threaten the stability of just institutions. If our most challenging political problems demand abstraction, what is the basis, either theoretical or practical, for responding to historic injustices that hinder both participation and stability in political life? What features are necessary for a framework for religion in public life that fosters both political stability and democratic participation?

CONCLUSION

From the pulpits of Black churches in northeast Denver to the parish hall of the Northside's Our Lady of Guadalupe, Federico Peña saw that a high voter turnout among politically marginalized racial and ethnic minorities would be required to put him over the top.[77] Indeed, the voters in these churches formed the base of his electoral coalitions in 1983 and again in 1987. But his years in civil rights activism had taught him a more pertinent lesson: Peña appreciated the cultural, religious, and political significance of religious institutions in Black and Brown communities. Those institutions were a place where marginalized people, who often felt despised by the cultural, political, and economic forces of White supremacy, were able to realize their "somebodiness" in a democratic context.[78] This understanding of the significance of religious institutions in the life of democracy has shaped the latest chapter in his lifelong work for justice, equality, and representation.

Now in his early seventies, Peña is a political rock star in Colorado. Still active in public service and philanthropy, Peña engages his potent political legacy on behalf of issues crucial to Denver's Latine community: education, immigration, health care. The Federico F. Peña Southwest Family Health Center and Urgent Care provides free and low-cost health services in south-west Denver, home to many Latine and Asian-American communities. In 2020 Colorado governor Jared Polis appointed Peña chairmen of the advi-sory council guiding the state's economic recovery from COVID-19, which has disproportionately harmed Colorado's Latine population.[79] Polis, who also made political history as the state's first openly gay and first Jewish gover-nor, underscored Peña's unparalleled public reputation by turning to him for crucial leadership in a time of local, national, and global crisis.

Indeed, Peña has spent his public life participating in liberalism's Big Story on both the local and national levels. But in the eighth decade of his life he is increasingly aware of how the little stories of his Catholic faith have shaped his commitment to justice, equality, and solidarity and inspired his work in public life. Peña expresses a particular joy in participating in parish life over the course of his lifetime. Growing up in Brownsville, Texas, his childhood parish would call upon the five Peña brothers "whenever they needed a team of altar boys."[80] At Our Lady of Guadalupe Parish he helped purchase stained glass windows to honor the church that had nourished him during his early years in Colorado politics.[81] At Our Lady of Visitation—the parish he joined upon his return to Denver from Washington—he ran the pickle stand during the church festival with his wife, Cindy Peña. He has spent many hours of his life in the company of presidents, CEOs, and public officials. But the parish is where he goes, along with his Latine community, to feel like "somebody."

In November 2016 the Archdiocese of Denver stunned parishioners at Our Lady of Visitation by announcing its plans to close the parish.[82] Claiming that Our Lady was a struggling parish, the archdiocese eventually shuttered the small-but-active Hispanic church, built in 1954 from two box cars on land donated by parishioner Benito Garcia. Archbishop Samuel J. Aquila made the decision without consulting the parishioners. The decision shocked and devastated the church; many of the families had been members of the "little pink church" for generations. Like the Chicanos of Saint Cajetan's in Auraria before them, Our Lady of Visitation's members began to organize to save the church. Peña, whose father-in-law had been a deacon at the parish for thirty years, leveraged his legal acumen and political capital to seek justice from the archdiocese. Working with a canon lawyer, Peña and the other members of the Goat Hill Society (named after the hill where the church stands, "*el alto de la chiva*") took their case to the Vatican, where they gained a small victory by having the church's status changed from a mission church to a parish, even as procedural opacity and disciplinary issues within the Curia threatened to derail their case. The Goat Hill Society also forged solidarity with other Latine Catholics fighting to save their churches from closure by dioceses across the country. Nonetheless, the "little pink church" remains shuttered indefinitely. Parishioners organized a vigil for the parish in April 2017. One of the parishioners held a banner with a picture of Our Lady of Guadalupe surrounded by the name of the church: "Our Lady of Visitation." Standing next to the banner, Peña gave a rousing speech addressed to Aquila: "Though this church is small and the people here are humble, we're very proud—as you can tell from the people who are here today. We only want to worship at this church, this very simple, humble church, that has been our place of worship for almost seventy years."[83] In accord with a political theology of Guadalupe and Juan Diego, Peña now finds himself bearing Guadalupe's banner, advocating for justice in the face of an intransigent archbishop. Peña has promised to fight to save the parish as long as he lives.

In a tantalizing plot twist, Peña's life has become not a model of Rawlsian reason enacted in public life. Peña has found a new public voice in the gaps between liberalism's promises of equality and inclusion, in the US Catholic Church's struggle to act justly in relation to its ever-growing Latine population, and in the ongoing search for "rootedness on the slippery earth" among Denver's Chicanx communities. Peña's story raises a crucial question for liberal aesthetics: Can they be adapted to more adequately engage religious and cultural particularity in the life of democracy? The next chapter investigates Martha Nussbaum's contributions to liberal aesthetics to respond to this question.

NOTES

1. Peña, "Fundraiser Invitation."
2. Krieger, "Tooley, Pena's Goals for City Similar," 1.
3. Peña, "Mile-High Achievements."
4. Peña, "Campaign poster."
5. Gutierrez, "Denver's Latino Population."
6. "A Mile High," 22.
7. Rawls, *Theory of Justice*, 60.
8. "Barack Obama's Speech on Race."
9. Rawls, *Theory of Justice*, 12.
10. Rawls, 60.
11. Rawls, 11.
12. Rawls, 457–58.
13. Rawls, *Theory of Justice*; Rawls, *Political Liberalism*.
14. "Poll: Many Say Tooley Tactics Backfired," 10.

15. Levin, "Dick Morris Says Obama Won't Win."
16. Nash, "Pena For Your Thoughts," 15.
17. Nash, 15.
18. Wolfe, *Future of Liberalism*, 123.
19. Wolfe, 125.
20. Anderson, *Bleak Liberalism*, 17.
21. Anderson, 100.
22. Anderson, 2.
23. Anderson, 14.
24. Rawls, *Theory of Justice*, 22.
25. Rawls, 18.
26. Coakley, *God, Sexuality, and the Self*, 91.
27. Coakley, 83.
28. Rawls, *Theory of Justice*, 455.
29. Rawls, 462.
30. UVA Arts and Sciences website, "General Education."
31. Rawls, *Theory of Justice*, 443.
32. Rawls, *Political Liberalism*, 215.
33. Rawls, 215.
34. Gregory, *Politics and the Order of Love*, 61–62.
35. Gregory, 63.
36. Kaveny, *Prophecy without Contempt*, 55–56 (emphasis in the original).
37. Stout, *Democracy and Tradition*, 68.
38. Rawls, *Political Liberalism*, l.
39. Rawls, ln27.
40. Stout, *Democracy and Tradition*, 69.
41. Stout, 70.
42. Laborde, *Liberalism's Religion*, 4.
43. Galston, "Driven Up the Rawls."
44. Nagel, *Brief Inquiry into the Meaning of Sin and Faith*.
45. Rawls, "On My Religion," 265.
46. Rawls, 263.
47. Rawls, 265.
48. Rawls, 267.
49. Rawls, 265.
50. Kaveny, *Prophecy without Contempt*, 27.
51. Pettegree, *Brand Luther*, 71.
52. Rawls, *Political Liberalism*, xxiv.
53. Rawls, 14.
54. Rawls, 215.
55. Rawls, 36.
56. Rawls, xxiv.
57. Cavanaugh, *Myth of Religious Violence*, 2.
58. Cavanaugh, *Torture and Eucharist*, 3.
59. Cavanaugh, 234.
60. Cavanaugh, 206.
61. Rodríguez, *Christian Martyrdom and Political Violence*, 126.

62. Rodríguez, 173.

63. Rodríguez, 173.

64. Rodríguez, 242.

65. Young, *Justice and the Politics of Difference*, 97.

66. Young, 97.

67. Carter, *Race*, 89.

68. Young, *Justice and the Politics of Difference*, 102.

69. Young, 101.

70. Isasi-Díaz, "Mujerista Narratives," 230.

71. Isasi-Díaz, *La Lucha Continues*, 218.

72. Isasi-Díaz, 212.

73. Isasi-Díaz, 211.

74. Isasi-Díaz, 222.

75. Townes, *Womanist Ethics and the Cultural Production of Evil*, 154–55.

76. Sobrino, *Christ the Liberator*.

77. Federico Peña, in conversation with author, February 2019.

78. Harris, *Something Within*, 74.

79. Hill and Kenney, "Polis Announces Emergency Economic Advisory Council."

80. Federico Peña, in conversation with author, February 2019.

81. Federico Peña, in conversation with author, February 2019.

82. Campbell, "Catholic Church Shutters Beloved Hispanic Parish."

83. Prince, "Goat Hill and Our Lady of Visitation Parish, Part Two."

3

Martha Nussbaum's
Liberal Aesthetics

"I am sure you were beautiful at one time. Now you are run down. You must have been majestic, for a small town to build such a small church. And look at us now. An entire wing is boarded up and in disrepair, so we crowd into what we jokingly call the 'New Church.'"[1] The *Miracle at Tepeyac* interlaces the story of a small-town Hispanic parish in decline with scenes from Guadalupe's encounter with Juan Diego. Set in a fictional parish in an unnamed Colorado tourist town, the play depicts a once-thriving church buckling under the weight of diocesan neglect, mistreatment, and abandonment. Membership has declined. Funding has disappeared. The crumbling church building exists in a constant state of unfinished renovation.

In this scene from the play, Padre Tomas laments the deterioration of his church. As he longs to desert the dilapidated, dying church for a desk job at the archdiocesan office, his faith in the parish is revivified by a cadre of some forgotten members: Señora Gabaldon, the underappreciated parish housekeeper, who runs the church in Padre Tomas's absence; Juanito, the undereducated parish janitor, who resents his lowly status in the church; Teresa, the undocumented refugee hiding with her family in the unfinished part of the church; and Kevin, the young man dying from an unnamed disease (likely AIDS).

While the characters spend the majority of the play in conflict with one another, eventually they come together as they accompany Kevin in the hours leading to his death in the midst of the church's sanctuary. Kevin asks Juanito, as the church's true caretaker, to give him his last rights; Padre Tomas consents. Kevin dies in Teresa's arms, creating a stunning Westside Pietà on the stage of the Angelica Martinez Performance Hall at Su Teatro. After Kevin dies Padre Tomas wonders about Kevin's family. Juanito replies that Kevin did not have a family but that the people living and working in the church were his family. Juanito also confesses to Padre Tomas that Teresa's family lives inside the part of the church undergoing renovation. Reporting Teresa and her family to the authorities would result in their deportation back to El Salvador. "Padre Tomas," says Juanito, "there is your church. What are you going to do with it?" Juanito's question challenges Padre Tomas to recognize his duty to defend the members of his little church, each vulnerable in their own way. He begins by offering sanctuary to Teresa: "Teresa, [you] and your family will stay. There are no immigration laws in the house of God."[2] With these words Padre Tomas turns the dying church into a sanctuary for the most vulnerable members of the community caught in the crosscurrent of draconian immigration laws and demoralizing church politics.

This culminating scene serves as the emotional climax of *The Miracle at Tepeyac*. Even as the community laments Kevin's death, they realize their deep love for each other and for their forgotten church. This love cultivates solidarity among a community that has often been at odds with one another; solidarity becomes the basis for their collective resistance against unjust immigration laws that would force Teresa and her family to face the death squads waiting for them in El Salvador.

While grief and joy intermingle in the scene, the audience is also offered a glimpse of the Auraria neighborhood's anger at their removal from their own "once beautiful church." Their anger is born of lament for the loss of Saint Cajetan's Parish, the thriving parish that was the spiritual home of Chicano Catholics in the Auraria neighborhood.[3] Now removed from their home, Su Teatro weeps "by the rivers of Babylon" (Ps 137 NRSV), playing the songs of their homeland while mourning the loss of a home to which they will likely not return.[4] Like the speaker of Psalm 137, their mourning turns to anger. *The Miracle at Tepeyac* expresses the community's continued sense of outrage and betrayal decades after their removal from Auraria and becomes a "hidden protest" against the civil and ecclesial forces that displaced the Auraria residents.[5] The story also illuminates the situation of other Denver neighborhoods, where through the forces of gentrification Black and Brown residents are being priced out of neighborhoods that they cultivated and sustained. These emotions—directed at their neighborhood, their community, their home—might be called *political emotions*.

Martha Nussbaum defines a political emotion as a cognitive appraisal of value directed at the nation, but it doesn't take much imagination to see how the term might encompass emotions directed at local political communities as well.[6] *The Miracle at Tepeyac* illustrates the potential of aesthetic experience to form political emotions that are necessary for the life of democracy in the twenty-first century. At the same time, Su Teatro's portrayal of the relationship between Guadalupe and Juan Diego demonstrates the inadequacy of

Nussbaum's liberal aesthetics to comprehend the substantive contributions of marginalized communities, including Black and Brown communities, to public discourse about justice.

Like religion, emotion is commonly construed as a destabilizing force, particularly within politics. Yet, as Joshua Hordern notes, political philosophers and religious ethicists have asserted that emotion is important to political relations, even as we continue to strive for a more adequate account of the nature and extent of their influence.[7] Building her analysis on a cognitivist account of emotion, Nussbaum contends that emotions are actually a stabilizing force within society, necessary for helping us maintain our focus on problems that need to be solved even if they do not necessarily tell us how to solve these problems. She argues that literature, along with other narrative-based art forms such as theater and film, are crucial to forming emotions that take the state as their object and contributing to political stability in democratic society (maintaining just social institutions even as these institutions are inevitably altered in response to changing social circumstances).[8]

In the previous chapter I demonstrated the inability of Rawls's liberal aesthetics to recognize particularity from behind the veil of ignorance by overlooking histories of oppression that undermine projects of equality that are central to liberalism's vision for common life. But Nussbaum cautions against dismissing Rawls's liberalism on the grounds that it does not sufficiently allow for an account of moral psychology. Situating herself as the inheritor of Rawls's argument, she offers an account of political emotions oriented toward cultivating a just society.[9] She argues that Rawls's theory contains insights for engaging emotion in public life, more so than one might suspect.[10] She uses Rawls's formulation of the sense of justice discussed in chapter 2 as a cornerstone of her own account of the politically stabilizing potential of emotions, senses, and imagination. Infusing Rawlsian political theory with her own theory of political emotions, Nussbaum unveils a liberal aesthetics in which the generation of emotions through encounters with literature and other narrative-based art forms is fundamental to sustaining the life of democracy in a pluralistic society.

In this chapter I argue that Nussbaum's liberal aesthetics improve on Rawls's mechanisms for engaging religious particularity in society and offer a corrective to his prohibitive demands for strict impartiality and public reason. Nussbaum constructs a liberal political aesthetic that aims to protect religious and cultural diversity while promoting greater participation in the life of democracy among multifarious constituencies. Still, Nussbaum's liberal aesthetic does not offer sufficient ground for constructive engagement of these particularities in a pluralistic society, including substantive claims about the content of justice that orient the political advocacy of minoritized communities in the twenty-first-century United States. Her framework for engaging both the emotional and religious aspects of art are governed by the same conception of public reason articulated by Rawls. Her demand that these particularities be treated as "civic poetry," transposed to a key discernible to political liberals, hinder efforts to cultivate democratic solidarity that respects persons in both their individual and relational integrity. Nussbaum's liberal aesthetics demonstrate liberalism's lingering inadequacy for constructive engagement of particularity in the life of democracy.

This chapter is organized into three parts. The first part exposes Nussbaum's articulation of the human capability approach, with particular attention to what I shall call the aesthetic capabilities: (1) senses, imagination, and thought, (2) emotions, and (3) play. Nussbaum identifies these capabilities as essential to what humans are to do and to become, thus situating aesthetic capabilities as foundational to identifying fundamental human rights that are essential to justice. The second part examines Nussbaum's theory of emotions. Arguing that emotions are cognitive appraisals of value, Nussbaum asserts a dynamic interaction between human thought and human emotion. Building on Rawls's articulation of the sense of justice, Nussbaum argues that political emotions are necessary for fostering and stabilizing a pluralistic and democratic society. The third part interrogates Nussbaum's theory as it pertains to specific expressions of particularity in public life, including the religious, cultural, and social contexts of racially and ethnically minoritized communities in the United States. While Nussbaum argues that religious aesthetics can legitimately be interpreted as "civic poetry," and acknowledges the capacity of religious traditions to foster justice in a pluralistic and democratic society while continuing the Rawlsian prohibition against comprehensive doctrines that influence society's basic structures, I argue that her theory does not allow an adequate framework for engaging substantive contributions to the common good from minoritized perspectives.

AESTHETICS, CAPABILITIES, AND HUMAN RIGHTS

Nussbaum's liberal aesthetics reflect her understanding of emotion, imagination, and the senses as integral human capabilities. The capability approach is a conceptual framework designed to offer a comparative quality-of-life assessment that identifies the basic conditions needed for social justice.[11] This approach asserts that the minimal level of justice requires that ten core

capabilities be available to every person. She does not prioritize any one capability over another: "All ten of these plural and diverse ends are minimum
requirements of justice, at least up to [a] threshold level."[12] The key question
for the capabilities approach is, "What is each person able to do and to be?"[13]

Nussbaum's list of capabilities has evolved over time, coalescing into a
list of ten things human beings ought to do and/or become regardless of
particular life circumstances: (1) life, (2) bodily health, (3) bodily integrity,
(4) senses, imagination, and thought, (5) emotions, (6) practical reason,
(7) affiliation, (8) relationships with other species, (9) play, and (10) control
over one's environment (both material and political).[14] The list emphasizes
capabilities that are centrally concerned with embodied aspects of human
life and experience. These capabilities attempt to articulate a holistic view of
human identity that considers a broad range of human capacities as being
central to our flourishing.

While Nussbaum strives to articulate a comprehensive framework for
human capability, it is evident that senses, imagination, thought, and emotions are central to her list. In fact, some of the other capabilities Nussbaum
identifies appear to hinge on these four. Although her earlier work on the relationship between literature and emotion emphasizes the necessity of literary
formation for judges, Nussbaum's more recent works argue that these capabilities are crucial for adequate public reasoning among all citizens in liberal
democracies.[15] Emotions allow citizens to form relationships and appreciate
their associations.

Although Nussbaum does not articulate a formal theory of justice in the
style of Rawls, her capability approach forms the basis for her understanding
of justice. Capabilities identify what is due to each person if they are to live
a life "worthy of human dignity," as Nussbaum says.[16] If the aesthetic capabilities are essential human capabilities, then human rights projects should
aim to foster the necessary conditions, structures, and laws that make their
development possible. Nussbaum emphasizes that the list of capabilities is
quite general and should be specified within particular national contexts.[17]

Of course, the project of acknowledging universal rights is a highly contro-
versial one, especially as it concerns the pursuit of justice in a global context
characterized by unimaginable religious and cultural pluralism that is simultaneously rife with vast social, economic, and political inequalities. As many
critics have argued, the concept of universal human rights is far from being
unanimously accepted as some cross-cultural invariant. Grace Y. Kao's incisive work on human rights in plural social contexts illustrates the contours of
the debate concerning the role of metaphysics in human rights philosophy.
While human rights discourse has enduring international significance, worries

persist about the purported universality of rights claims. Kao cites the American Anthropological Association's critique of the universality of rights discourse, expressed prior to the promulgation of the United Nations' Universal Declaration of Human Rights, that such a declaration would actually consist of a "statement of rights conceived only in terms and values prevalent in the countries of Western Europe and America."[18] Such a declaration would not be universal, but rather a *universalizing* imposition of particular rights (Western ones) onto other values and contexts (non-Western ones). What to one culture might be a defense of an individual's rights might, to another culture, be the evisceration of the community. What might be an individual virtue in one culture might be a communal vice in another.

Nussbaum offers two ripostes to such critiques. First, her argument for contextual engagement guards against claims that her work succumbs to the Western myopia often attributed to human rights discourse. Nussbaum employs an inductive, dialogical, and intercultural method for identifying the capabilities.[19] Focusing on the development of capabilities in particular contexts, Nussbaum argues that "this approach can provide a situationally sensitive, contextual mode of making ethical judgments and interventions."[20] Second, although Nussbaum regards her method as attending to contextual particularity, she does not withdraw her support for an overarching project of articulating human rights across the particular positions she engages. While acknowledging the Western origins of human rights, Nussbaum suggests that this root does not necessarily invalidate its universal claim. Yet despite her effort to construct a framework that engages with particular contexts, Hilary Charlesworth argues, Nussbaum's ethic is better described as "transversal" rather than properly "universal."[21]

Despite Nussbaum's attempt to develop a capability framework that is responsive to the nuances of particular contexts, S. Charusheela argues that Nussbaum's theory expresses an ethnocentric and universalizing character. Charusheela contends that Nussbaum shifts the ethnocentrism of universalism from her ethical framework into her social analysis.[22] She illustrates this sleight of hand through Nkiru Nzegwu's social analysis of the human capability of literacy, a skill that Nussbaum identifies in her specification of the aesthetic capability of senses, imagination, and thought.[23] Examining the political consciousness and acumen of Igbo women in Nigeria—including evidence of lower levels of political consciousness and participation among literate women in this community who have internalized Western hierarchical notions—Nzegwu questions whether literacy is correctly included as an intrinsic value for enhancing women's political consciousness. At the same time, Nzegwu illustrates how the Western expectation of literacy as a minimum requirement for political participation has placed constraints on unlettered Igbo women. Nzegwu anticipates objections that her argument will sound nativist, like "a radical recreation of a pre-colonial reality that is of little relevance to Africa's post-colonial condition."[24] Nonetheless, a social analysis of the political and social function of literacy in Nigerian society lays bare the Western assumptions latent in Nussbaum's universal claims concerning human flourishing:

> [Each] particular application of the universal approach requires— usually assumes—a social analysis. And, for each instance of application that makes a claim about what is necessary for promoting universal flourishing, we can ask—indeed, need to ask if we come from a critical perspective committed to ending oppression— whether ideological claims that uphold power are embedded in the analysis being used, and whether alternate social analyses may lead us to different conclusions.[25]

Despite Nussbaum's attempts to guard against ethnocentrism, Nzegwu's social analysis of the political significance of literacy in the Nigerian context unveils the enduring ethnocentrism latent in Nussbaum's articulation of the capability approach.

Concerns about putative universal validity raise a central question for advocates of any universalizing discourse: Are human rights truly universal? Or, as Kao asks, "Are human rights concepts actually western ones masquerading under a cloak of ethical universalism or otherwise concealing a disreputable claim to power?"[26] If the universalist language conveyed from Aristotle and Aquinas is simply a cover for White, Western values, then any list of inherent rights risks an assertion that Western values are universal ones. Yet an outright dismissal of assertion of universal rights (or transversal rights, as the case may be) risks eroding the best justification for defending human beings from the most exploitative dynamics of a global political economy predicated on inequality and the exploitation of human and other natural resources. While a universal assertion of human rights risks reasserting Western values, rejecting universal rights in the context of rampant transnational patterns of exploitation risks forgoing binding moral claims as a basis for a globally responsive ethic. What, then, is the basis for the affirmation of universal dignity that is the foundation for identifying, articulating, instituting, and defending human rights?

Charusheela is confident that a social analysis will expose the problems of universalist reasoning and serve as an adequate basis for rights discourse. Reading Charusheela's admonition within the context of theological discourse, however, unveils an often unstated, unacknowledged, and perhaps even unrecognized tension between the project of postcolonial social theory and that of liberative, theoethical responses to the many-faceted reality of oppression. Both criticize liberalism for its unacknowledged universalizing tendencies. But Christian theological ethics in a liberationist key remains accountable to the theological claim of fundamental dignity by virtue of humanity's creation in the image of the Triune God: *imago Dei, imago Trinitatis.* It thus cannot dismiss the possibility of the existence of "true universals," which are distinct from "false universals" that perpetuate oppression.[27] Liberative ethics reasserts the urgent task of defending the universality of fundamental human dignity as an essential foundation for the work of resisting oppression. This explains in part why engagement with Nussbaum's work remains prominent in Catholic social ethics: she asserts that human beings are ends in themselves and are thus bearers of certain fundamental rights. And while those who employ discourses without accountability to universal theological claims of human dignity are free to dispense with universals, it is difficult to conceive how abandoning claims of universal human dignity or pursuing an authentic common good concerned with cultivating conditions that make possible the thriving of all people could possibly be a desirable strategy in the fight against multifaceted manifestations of oppression.[28]

Kao addresses the potential problem with the ethnocentric objection to human rights. Even if we assume that human rights emerged from the West, this fact would not necessarily invalidate their universal applicability. To think so, she argues, "would be to succumb to the genetic fallacy."[29] Postcolonial critics are justified in their suspicion of intellectual colonization and the risks associated with Western-originating ideas that shape institutions and practices. Still, the outright rejection of universal human rights on such a basis sets a dangerous precedent for engagement with ideas pertaining to global justice and equality. The validity of a concept is not necessarily reducible to the provenance of its origin. That would overlook the potential value of any concept discovered by another group: "We would be wise to think twice about dismissing an idea simply because it is not indigenous—or even endorsing it simply because it is."[30] Kao reminds us of the philosophical weakness—and political risk—of accepting or rejecting ideas simply based on their origins. Acknowledging assertions of Western ideological hegemony in human rights discourse, she nonetheless remains confident in the possibility of articulating a truly universal human rights framework. It is necessary to distinguish between the universal and the merely local. Similarly, human rights advocates must determine what is a legitimate implementation of a right versus a deviation from a globally valid standard.

Defending the need to assert moral universals in the project of defending human rights, Kao highlights Nussbaum's account of the capability approach as straddling the divide between minimalist and maximalist frameworks for human rights.[31] The capability approach succeeds not simply in identifying a list of central capabilities. Rather, Kao argues, it "helps to clarify what it actually means to secure a human right to someone, correctly acknowledges the unavoidability of presupposing a conception of the good for human beings in the process, and properly situates human rights claims alongside the moral entitlements that nonhuman animals might be said to have."[32]

What is required to guide rights projects that are truly global while staving off the enduring risk of ethnocentrism in rights discourse? Discussing the role of religion in the global project of human rights, Linda Hogan demonstrates the work of aesthetic engagement (which she designates primarily as engagement with the arts) as expanding the subject, scope, and application of human rights without forgoing the claim of universal human dignity that is essential to Christian theological ethics. Hogan asserts that the history of human rights is characterized by a gradual expansion of recognition of rights from belonging only to a "particular group of property-owning white males" to an ever-expanding and truly universal group.[33] Hogan attributes encounters with poetry for the ever-expanding understanding of the subject of human rights. This encounter with the arts offers a "glimpsed alternative" that expands our understanding of who is entitled to these rights. Such a sensory engagement with the "glimpsed alternative" is crucial for expanding our moral concern. She argues, "The arts—perhaps more than any other artifact—are the primary means through which this glimpsed alternative is articulated."[34] The engagement of the senses through the arts is thus essential to the expansive trajectory of human rights; they allow us to imagine a subject of human rights that is truly universal.

A comprehensive focus on what humans are able to be and do enables Nussbaum to situate emotion and aesthetic perception as central tenets of basic human functioning. Specifically, Nussbaum identifies a set of aesthetic capabilities that enable persons to live fully human lives. If human capability is concerned with what humans are able to do and to be, then aesthetic capabilities are vital to human identity and flourishing. Beyond a generalized expression of the centrality of these capabilities, Nussbaum uses them as a basis for a schedule of human rights that at once asserts a universal and common humanity while also accounting for human particularity and experience in a politically concrete manner. If human capabilities are vital to human identity, then they ought to be central to political considerations. The next section explores this relationship.

NUSSBAUM ON EMOTION

Nussbaum's aesthetic capabilities also shed light on the place of aesthetics in the life of US democracy. Nussbaum pursues the connection between aesthetics and public life via emotions. Specifically she argues for a cognitivist account of emotions in which they are integrated with reason. This account is the basis for Nussbaum's definition of political emotions—which differ only from other emotions in that they take the nation as their object—as essential for achieving Rawls's conception of political stability.[35] These political emotions are the foundation of Nussbaum's account of liberal political aesthetics in which she asserts the place for aesthetic engagement, especially literature and other narrative forms of art, in the life of democracy. After explaining Nussbaum's cognitivist account of emotions and political emotion, I will examine Nussbaum's liberal aesthetics, showing the strengths and limitations of these aesthetics toward engaging particularity in the life of democracy.

Cognitivist Account of Emotion

Nussbaum defines emotions as intelligent responses to the perception of value: "Intellect without emotions is, we might say, value-blind: it lacks the sense of meaning and worth of a person's death that the judgments internal to emotions would have supplied."[36] While emotions are often derided as irrational and unreliable, Nussbaum argues that they are an indispensable aspect of moral formation and direct the moral agent toward what is good.

She uses Charles Dickens's novel *Hard Times* to illustrate this relationship between intellect and emotion.[37] Thomas Gradgrind, a utilitarian economist and family patriarch, teaches his children and pupils to rely on reason alone, resisting the interference of emotion and imagination into their intellectual formation. His suspicion of emotion extends to engagement with literature, which he sees as subversive.[38] Literature is a destabilizing force capable of generating emotions that threaten to upend the cool calculations of human reason. In this view literature is a threat to ethics. Gradgrind advocates for a utilitarian view of ethical decision-making, one in which determinations of the greatest good are calculated without accounting for the personal or particular consequences of decisions. Dickens depicts the devastating consequences of Gradgrind's utilitarian teachings for his students' education and for his children's ethical formation. His children, in particular, do not learn to make the valuable connection between emotional response and intellect that Nussbaum asserts is critical for their individual flourishing.

Even so, Gradgrind's children still express an astonishing emotional aware-ness, given their deficient emotional and imaginative formation. For example, Louisa Gradgrind states that her lack of emotional education has made her "unjust." Despite her sense of being malformed in her ability to perceive the suffering of others, Louisa's recognition suggests that she senses the importance of this capability to her flourishing and senses that something is amiss without it. Sissy Jupe, the daughter of an aging circus clown and one of Gradgrind's students, on the other hand, demonstrates an emotional resilience that belies her utilitarian education. Nussbaum summarizes:

> Sissy is told by her utilitarian teacher that in "an immense town" of a million inhabitants, only twenty-five are starved to death on the streets. The teacher, M'Choakumchild, asks her what she thinks about this—plainly expecting an answer expressing satisfaction that the numbers are so low. Sissy's response, however, is that "it must be hard upon those who were starved, whether the others were a million, or a million million."[39]

Sissy's response reveals what Nussbaum calls imagination or fancy, or the "ability to see one thing as another, to see one thing in another."[40] Sissy looks beyond the aggregate figure and sees the circumstances of particular per-sons. Sissy's response bears sympathy with Nussbaum's capability approach, implicitly recognizing that twenty-five starving people, ends in themselves, are hardly being given the chance to do and become all the things they would be able to if they were not starving to death. Sissy also acknowledges the inherent dignity of the suffering minority, refusing to subordinate the inter-ests of the individual to those of the community. The flourishing of the com-munity as a whole does not negate the suffering of the few individuals who experience the immense suffering of starvation.

Emotions are thus instructive because they help us to maintain focus on the human elements of complex issues; they sear into our conscience the gravity of the social problems that we face as a society. As Nussbaum notes, "The emotions do not tell us how to solve these problems; they do keep our attention focused on them as problems we ought to solve."[41] With this in mind, Nussbaum offers emotion not as a panacea for social ills but as a neces-sary orienting function that colors our rational approach to an issue.

Nussbaum argues that emotions and thought are connected in an integral manner.[42] She rejects assertions that emotions are separate from—and sub-ordinate to—reason: "Emotions are not just the fuel that powers the psycho-logical mechanism of a reasoning creature," she writes. "They are parts, highly complex and messy parts, of this creature's reasoning itself."[43] Given this integral relationship, she articulates a cognitivist account in which emotions are directed at a particular object.

Taking on specific objects, emotions then do not resemble the uncontrollable "forces of nature" that are often the basis of their derision. They are judgments of value and they see their objects as containing importance. The value of an emotion's object, Nussbaum argues, is connected to a perception of value in relation to a person's own flourishing. In general, humans do not spend their days paralyzed by fear of every calamity that might occur in our world, even if they know such disasters have profound implications for other people's lives. What causes us fear has to do with what is most important to us, or what Nussbaum refers to as our "own cherished relationships and projects." Nussbaum illustrates this dynamic with a description of her emotions related to the hospitalization and eventual death of her own mother:

> What inspires grief is the death of someone beloved, someone who has been an important part of one's own life. This does not mean that emotions view these objects simply as tools or instruments of the agent's own satisfaction: they may be invested with intrinsic worth or value, as indeed my mother surely was. They may be loved for their own sake, and their good sought for their own sake. But what makes the emotion center around this particular mother, among all the many wonderful people and mothers in the world, is that she is my mother, a part of my life. . . . Even when they are concerned with events that took place at a distance, or events in the past, that is, I think, because the person has managed to invest those events with a certain importance in her own scheme of ends and goals.[44]

Emotions—as opposed to moods or feelings—are connected to objects that one perceives as important to her own ends, goals, and flourishing. They are connected deeply to one's thoughts about particular objects. Nussbaum thus interlaces emotion with reason, plaiting them together as two strands in a cord. While they remain distinct from one another, neither can perform its proper function without reference to the other. Certainly, Nussbaum cautions her readers about the excesses of emotion, conceding that "there may even be special reasons for regarding them with suspicion, given their specific content and the nature of their history."[45] Her interpretation of *Hard Times* suggests, however, that there are similarly weighty reasons to regard with suspicion any claims of reason unanchored in emotion.

As a cognitive appraisal of value, then, emotion is essential to the moral formation of humans fundamentally constituted by both autonomy and relationality. While emotion is crucial to personal moral formation, it is also essential to the public pursuit of justice. Nussbaum argues that when directed at the nation as their object, emotions such as compassion and love are essential for political stability in liberal democratic society. Still, she cautions that emotions like anger and shame can destabilize society. The next section elaborates the specific features of political emotions as articulated by Nussbaum, including the benefits and risks of particular kinds of emotions to the pursuit of justice.

Political Emotions

If emotions are cognitive appraisals of value, as Nussbaum claims, then a feminist reading would also suggest their significance in both personal and political facets of social experience.[46] Employing her basic definition of cognitive emotion, Nussbaum elaborates the relationship between the emotional and the political:

> All societies are full of emotions. Liberal democracies are no exception. The story of any day or week in the life of even a relatively stable democracy would include a host of emotions—anger, fear, sympathy, disgust, envy, guilt, grief, many forms of love. Some of those episodes of emotion have little to do with political principles or the public culture, but others are different: they take as their object the nation, the nation's goals, its institutions and leaders, its geography, and one's fellow citizens seen as inhabitants of a common public space.[47]

Taking the nation as their object, political emotions are uniquely situated to reflect the key commitments of a liberal democratic society: equality, justice, and freedom, for example. While political emotions—whether love, hate, compassion, anger, hope, or shame—have a catalytic effect in public life, Nussbaum contends that they are essential for cultivating political stability or the cultivation of just institutions within society's basic structure.[48] "Political emotions are a source of stability for good political principles, and of motivation to make them effective," she writes. "So it will naturally focus on making people experience certain emotions in certain contexts with particular objects (the nation itself, its goals, its specific tasks and problems, its people)."[49] Democratic nations thus rely on political emotions that can stabilize democratic goals: justice, equality, and participation, for example.

Political emotions are critical to political stability in two ways. First, they advance societal values by modeling and encouraging emotional attitudes that solidify just political norms. Take the US presidency as an example. The office has developed over generations to position the president as a "First Citizen" of the United States.[50] One aspect of this role has been to serve as "mourner in chief" during times of national devastation and tragedy. Abraham Lincoln exemplified this role through his Gettysburg Address, which captured the devastation of the battle while instilling hope for a nation made whole.[51] The fact that Lincoln neglected to address slavery in that address foreshadows national silences and elisions on racial injustice and White supremacy that continue to haunt the United States while demonstrating the power of the First Citizen to shape the moral imagination of a nation in both implicit and explicit ways. More recently, Barack Obama embodied the role of mourner in chief during his eulogy for the Hon. Rev. Clementa Pinckney, who was murdered, along with eight members of his congregation, by White supremacist Dylan Roof during a Bible study session at Mother Emanuel African American Methodist Episcopal Church in Charleston, South Carolina. Inhabiting the diction of a Baptist preacher, Obama offered a stirring address. Concluding his remarks, he paused for a moment before singing "Amazing Grace! How sweet the sound, that saved a wretch like me!"[52] The congregation and the nation joined their president's hymn, channeling their sorrows and hopes into song. Obama deftly employed aesthetics of Black Christian liturgy to form political emotions of both lament and sympathy in the wake of a terrorizing hate crime.

At their best, political emotions generate the sympathy for other citizens necessary for establishing and enforcing just laws and institutions. Sympathy is a central aspect of a political culture that seeks the personal and collective flourishing of its members. "When you feel sympathy for the poor," writes Nussbaum, "it is fine to view that as an occasion for philanthropy, but it is better to use that energy to create a decent tax system and a set of welfare programs." Emotions, she argues, are crucial to creating and sustaining just laws and institutions. Indeed, institutions are at their best when they embody the insight of these political emotions.[53]

This dual operation of political emotion is integral to Nussbaum's theory. Emotions are both stabilizing and in need of stabilization. While strong emotions oriented toward just immigration reform, as evoked in the final scene of *The Miracle at Tepeyac*, for example, might motivate advocates to formalize their concerns into a just law, the law itself is necessary for times when other emotions might threaten justice for this group. In this way Nussbaum situates political emotion at the center of political stability and the pursuit of just laws and institutions in society's basic structure.

For example, political emotion emanating from the religious particularity of African American movement leaders in the early 1960s was a key factor in passing landmark US civil rights legislation, including the Civil Rights Act of 1964 and the Voting Rights Act of 1965. Recently the substantial political gains made during this era have suffered from unraveling public and legal support, especially the undoing of key enforcement mechanisms of the Voting Rights Act that were intended to prevent disenfranchisement in districts with historical precedent for such actions. This uncertain legal and political landscape threatens to destabilize political society by allowing discrimination, segregation, and other inequalities to seep further into the basic political structure of the United States. The paucity of public sympathy for racially marginalized persons is one culprit of this destabilization. As Nussbaum claims, sympathy for fellow citizens is a foundational emotion for a liberal and plural democracy. Political emotions, then, are a vital force in resisting political inequality. Moreover, since political emotions can be intense, they ought to be tutored by reason; a society devoid of that formative tutoring will lack the emotional intelligence necessary to stabilize democracy and make institutional gains supportive of the common good.

Emotions such as sympathy, argues Nussbaum, sustain efforts to institutionalize equality. Unfortunately, people in the United States often struggle to muster sympathy for people outside of their own social groups, especially White people for nonwhite people. The 2013 acquittal of George Zimmerman in the shooting death of Trayvon Martin served as a reminder of the lack of sympathy of White people for Black people, including Black children. Specifically, many White citizens have demonstrated a lack of sympathy for the epidemic of shooting deaths of unarmed Black people at the hands of law enforcement officers. The discourse associated with the shooting death of Tamir Rice—a twelve-year-old Black boy who was shot to death by a Cleveland police officer while playing in the park with a toy gun—is indicative of this lack of sympathy. In the aftermath of his death, public officials sought to demonstrate his fault in the matter.

An approach informed by sympathy must begin with lament, with weeping at the loss of a human life.[54] In the absence of sympathy for Black people who fear for their lives at the hands of institutions of the basic structure that alleges to pursue justice for all from behind the veil of ignorance, the public will struggle to establish and sustain basic civil rights protections against personally dehumanizing and politically destabilizing discrimination. Yet the ongoing problem of racial injustice in the United States demonstrates a continued need to prioritize these issues in public discourse and to graft just laws and institutions onto society's basic structure.

The Movement for Black Lives presents a significant challenge to Nussbaum's account of political emotions. Specifically, her account does not allow a place for public expression of emotions associated with experiences of racial injustice, including anger. In *Anger and Forgiveness* she rejects the possibility of anger having a justifiable normative basis.[55] She argues that anger essentially involves a desire for payback. She chides individuals and groups who have used anger to express public grievance, arguing that anger is not only unnecessary for the pursuit of justice but also a hindrance, "a large impediment to the generosity and empathy that help construct a future for justice."[56] Interpreted within the context of racial justice, Nussbaum asserts the necessity of forgoing Black anger as part of a strategy of securing White generosity and empathy. By her account, appeasing one's oppressor and avoiding engendering feelings of discomfort seem integral to any practical strategy of securing rights and justice.

Perhaps discerning the limitations of her own normative prohibition against anger, Nussbaum suggests a normative justification of a subspecies of the emotion that she calls transitional anger. She views this form of anger as ethically permissible, given its future-oriented emphasis on reconciliation, as opposed to payback as in the dominant species of anger. She employs Martin Luther King Jr.'s "I Have a Dream" speech as a paradigm case for transitional anger, exegeting his metaphor of "insufficient funds" to illustrate anger that she deems acceptable: "For instead of demonizing White Americans, or portraying their behavior in terms apt to elicit murderous rage, he calmly compares them to people who have defaulted on a financial obligation."[57] Nussbaum assumes that the expression of Black anger in the face of violent, enduring oppression would automatically result in murderous rage against White people. Here she exploits a pernicious stereotype of Black people as perpetuators of anger-fueled riots, engaging in what Emilie Townes has called the "fantastic hegemonic imagination," which "'plays' with history and memory to spawn caricatures and stereotypes."[58] Nussbaum marshals the stereotype of the angry Black person to elevate and extol King's "almost saintly" public persona as a paradigm of a Black person who translates his anger into a forward-looking, hopeful moral vision.[59] Evaluating her normative criticism of anger in the context of nationwide and worldwide protests in outrage over the death of George Floyd at the hands of agents of the basic structures that alleged to protect him, Nussbaum's response reads as a demand for expressions of Black frustration that forgo anger and thus avoid making White people feel uncomfortable.

Nussbaum's rejection of a normative basis for anger disallows engagement of substantive arguments about justice from communities of color who have experienced the various faces of oppression within society's basic structures.

American Pietà, a painting by Michael Owens, depicts a Black mother cradling her son who has been shot to death. The two figures appear against the backdrop of a tattered US flag. The mother's eyes are cast down, gazing on the lifeless little boy lying in her arms. She covers his limp hand with hers, still offering him tender care as she has done through his entire existence. This image foregrounds the outrageous evil and injustice of the loss of innocent lives within institutions that are allegedly designed to protect them. Viewed within the context of a twenty-first-century US social and political context, the image indicts an anti-Black, White supremacist culture that views the lives of Black people as both criminal and disposable. It exposes society's basic structures as failing to deliver justice to Black parents and their children. The image does not destabilize the basic structure; it discloses the inherent instability of a conception of justice that cannot deliver justice equally to all people.

Positive emotions such as compassion and love are not mutually exclusive with anger and lament. Nonetheless, Nussbaum's disqualification of negative emotions from public life due to their potentially destabilizing influence reproduces the similar anti-emotion dynamics that she identifies in *Hard Times*. Disqualifying certain emotions from engagement in public life, in fact, undermines the kind of political stability that pursues justice and can respond to the political realities of the United States, a society where the basic structures have failed to deliver equality time and time again.

As the inheritor of Rawls's argument, Nussbaum reasserts public reason as the standard for engagement in the public square. And while she does permit emotions to be expressed within the realm of reason, her own account does not allow for the expression of all emotions with substantive implications for justice in society's basic structures. Her account of emotion stands in stunned silence in the face of a Black mother weeping at her son's grave. Nussbaum might respond, if only this mother's anger would transition to forgiveness, society's structures would certainly serve justice to her. But this account fails to recognize the role of potentially destabilizing forces such as emotion and religion in the project of political stability as Rawls defines it—offering an account of justice that is responsive to changes in society. This limitation rooted in Nussbaum's adherence to an Enlightenment conception of reason is also evident in the liberal aesthetics that emanate from her thought. Art can be engaged only as long as it is evacuated of the radicality of its particularity.

Nussbaum's cognitivist account of emotions is the foundation for her account of political emotions. While political emotions identify the potential of love, compassion, and sympathy to contribute to political stability, Nussbaum does not adequately account for the public role of anger in response to the failure of institutional structures to deliver justice to Black and Brown people. This narrow account of political emotions shapes Nussbaum's liberal aesthetics, especially its ability to comprehend the intersecting particularities of race and religion in the life of democracy.

Literature and Aesthetics

While Nussbaum does not refer to her own project in specifically aesthetic terms, it is clear that her cognitivist theory of emotion forms the basis for a liberal political aesthetics. This aesthetic makes the case for the engagement of art, especially literature, in public life. It asserts the significance of art for forming political emotions like love and compassion toward the identification of a stable conception of justice. Nevertheless, Nussbaum inherits liberalism's suspicion of the destabilizing influence of religion, race, and culture in public life. Similar to Rawls, her liberal aesthetic places excessive limits on the engagement of the just claims expressed through literature, theater, images, and music emanating from groups unjustly relegated to the margins of political life in a democratic context.

Literature and the literary imagination can be subversive, argues Nussbaum; narratives fuel imagination and desires in ways that can undermine political, economic, and social power.[60] Literature has been treated as optional or ornamental in an educational marketplace that views the humanities with suspicion. Nonetheless, Nussbaum argues for literature's essential role in legal education, especially in forming literary imagination that shapes normative moral reflection.

Literary imagination, Nussbaum contends, is essential for cultivating public emotions that are critical for forging and sustaining justice in a politically liberal society. Emotion is a vital, if unappreciated, force in liberal societies. The most influential political leaders (she identifies Martin Luther King Jr. and Mahatma Gandhi as paradigms of liberal leadership) understand "the need to touch citizens' hearts and to inspire, deliberately, strong emotions directed at the common work before them."[61] Effective liberal leaders are able to generate sentiments of sympathy and love that both promote social unity and respect diversity and pluralism.[62] In addition to sympathy and love, societies must wrestle with complex emotions that profoundly influence the pursuit of public justice: anger, fear, disgust, envy, guilt, and grief, just to name a few.[63] She stresses the need to manage or curtail these emotions, especially in law and policy making, so that they do not generate division and hierarchy. Generating and managing emotions is a challenge for liberal societies. But without these emotions political society would lack an important resource for cultivating robust commitment to the common good.

In Nussbaum's work, imagination formed through reason and emotion is indispensable in the pursuit of justice in a politically liberal society. In *Poetic Justice* Nussbaum argues that literary education and formation is a critical factor for the development of public officials who have custody of public institutions that shape social justice in society: judges, lawyers, legislators, and the like. In later works Nussbaum broadens the scope of her argument to assert the necessity of literary formation for all citizens of liberal democratic societies. "Literature is in league with emotions," argues Nussbaum.[64] Literature, imagination, and emotions are integrally connected. Nussbaum explains: "[Emotions] have a complicated cognitive structure that is part narrative in form, involving a story of our relation to cherished objects that extends over time. . . . This, in turn, suggests that in order to talk well about them we will need to turn to texts that contain a narrative dimension, thus deepening and refining our grasp of ourselves as beings with a complicated temporal history."[65] Aesthetic engagement is critical to emotion; aesthetic capabilities are crucial for emotional formation that is supportive of political liberalism.

Nussbaum resists romanticizing the role of literature in public life. Literature can struggle to break free from the unjust biases and moral vices of its particular context. This failure of moral imagination is apparent in the way that social groups devise narratives and symbols that protect their power, shield themselves from outsiders, and reify their particular ideologies without engaging realities beyond their own contexts. In view of what Nussbaum calls "fancy," however, good literature—or that which either implicitly or explicitly fosters liberal values—can transcend social boundaries and develop a much larger view of reality by deeply engaging particular contexts and forming the imaginative capabilities of readers. In its concern for the ordinary—or what US Latine theologians call *lo cotidiano*—literature provides a concrete and context-specific description of moral circumstances that elicit ethical reflection. Nussbaum emphasizes the importance of engaging concrete circumstances that shape human emotions and desires. This kind of engagement is native to literature and necessary for forming emotions such that they can engage with public discourse.

Although she suggests that the novel presents "universalizable" prescriptions, she also emphasizes the plural realities of literary audiences. The reader of a novel is always situated in a particular context. Each reader will approach a story from within that context. For this reason novel reading is essentially comparative, requiring readers to enter into conversation with one another in order to interpret the work well.[66] In this way novel reading has the potential to be a truly democratic form of aesthetic engagement, adding grist to the mill of public deliberation across difference in which every perspective is as valuable as every other.

The importance of context in Nussbaum's liberal aesthetics arises from its centrality in her theory of emotion. She asserts that an adequate account of public emotions is highly contextual and is able to account for the history, tradition, and problems of a particular context. Toward this end, people must be engaged as they are, even if one ultimately hopes to reshape their loves and concerns toward fostering the common good.[67] Attending to a particular circumstance provides the flexibility necessary to keep pace with the vicissitudes that accompany the task of conceptualizing emotion in a way that has applicability across contexts. This is especially important in the pluralistic environment of liberal democracies. Nussbaum's theory of political emotion thus strives to attend to the contextual particularities that influence the development of political emotion and civic culture necessary to sustain reflexive equilibrium in a liberal democracy.

This contextual approach to emotion attempts to form a theoretical framework for responding to particularity. As Nussbaum emphasizes, the theory acknowledges that different persons, groups, and communities will respond to narratives, symbols, and artwork in different ways. "Political love is and should be polymorphous," she writes. "The love of parents for children, the love of comrades, and romantic love all are capable of inspiring a public culture in different ways, and we should not be surprised or disappointed if different groups of citizens react to the same public speech or artwork in different emotional ways."[68]

Nussbaum updated her work to address the necessity of emotional and imaginative formation for citizens more broadly, though her original emphasis on public officials still foregrounds the public significance of these qualities. Literature, she argues, has the capacity to reinforce the value of human life that is integral to legislative and judicial practice. US Supreme Court justice Steven Breyer, commenting on his experience of engaging with literature, emphasized the significance of emotional and aesthetic formation among judges serving in the public interest, stressing that every person and every family is different: "Each one of those persons in each one of those houses and each one of those families is different, and they each have a story to tell. Each of those stories involves something about human passion."[69] Breyer's insight is not ancillary to his public work; it is an indispensable component of his judicial reasoning. Nussbaum explains: "The ability to think of people's lives in the novelist's way is, Breyer argues, an important part of the equipment of a judge."[70] Given her focus on the role of aesthetics in judicial formation, Nussbaum's decision to limit her argument to Anglo-American realist literature is not arbitrary or artificial. This genus of literature, she argues, is particularly well suited for illustrating moral particularity in a way that gestures to broader public implications. Film and poetry often share the same narrative properties and emotional expressiveness as novels, and thus Nussbaum considers them potentially legitimate sources for public moral reflection.

And yet Nussbaum's use of judicial formation as a lens for viewing the role of aesthetics in moral formation contains important limitations. The novel, she claims, is the central morally serious but popularly engaging fictional form in our culture. This narrow focus on the novel comes at the expense of accounting for potential ethical significance of nonliterary media—images, music, symbols, icons—in aesthetic formation necessary for sustaining a stable, participatory public life. Concerning other media, she argues that it is often "dreamlike and indeterminate in a way that limits its role in public deliberation."[71] Thus, media that might be considered too mystical or religious fails to meet Nussbaum's criteria for moral seriousness. In *Political Emotions* Nussbaum broadens the kind of media that can be fruitfully engaged in the cultivation of emotions helpful for sustaining a stable conception of justice in society's basic structures, using the opera *The Marriage of Figaro* as an illustration of the public potential of emotions. In accord with her framework's concern for context, she allows that not all art forms are suitable for generating political emotions for all societies: "I am not, then, proposing that modern democracies use the opera as a device to kindle public emotion of the right sort. Although it may surely do so in people who love it, it is insufficiently inclusive today to implement its own values on a wide scale."[72] Her broadened criteria would allow for works such as *The Miracle at Tepeyac* to be counted among works that can generate desirable political emotions such as compassion and love, at least the portions of the work directly concerned with properly "civic" matters: immigration, poverty, literacy, gender, sexuality, and health care. Without the narrative grounding of particular events that mimic concrete reality, however, certain art forms do not have the capacity to shape public reasoning and morality.

In its strict delineation to particular kinds of narratives, this aesthetic theory excludes many kinds of media—including works foreign to modernist standards of reason and rationality—from the list of legitimate sources for public engagement. For example, Nussbaum's definition could exclude much of the literature emanating from the magical realist stream of Latin American and US Latine writers such as Julia Alvarez and Gabriel García Marquez, Isabel Allende and Rodolfo Anaya. This literary tradition often mixes the marvelous and the mundane, the material and the spiritual.[73] The force of *The Miracle at Tepeyac*'s social critique and justice claims, derived from the interlacing of a political theological account of the relationship between Guadalupe and Juan Diego, would be rendered inadmissible for aiding the formation of political emotions. Whereas Rawls's theory casts doubt as to whether Martin Luther King Jr. or Harriet Tubman could meet the proviso for public translation, Nussbaum's theory casts doubt on whether art, literature, and music that is illegible to Western intellectual standards can be legitimately engaged in the formation of political emotions. In this way Nussbaum advances an *aesthetic* public reason.

If there is an integral relationship between intellect and emotion, then Nussbaum's criteria for works suitable for the formation of public emotions proves too narrow. The human heart is not moved by reasonable explanation or concrete illustrations alone; it requires the mystical, transcendental, dreamlike, and indeterminate elements of music, abstract painting, ballet, and religious narrative and imagery. In accord with Nussbaum's own definition of fancy, human emotions are shaped not only by the way the world is but also by hope of what *could be,* as expressed through our artistic endeavors. Nussbaum misses an opportunity to further elaborate the relationship between intellect, emotion, and aesthetics in a way that bolsters robust particularity in the manner required for the life of a thriving democracy.

Artistic expression in the broadest sense conveys public ideas that can enhance common discourse. It is necessary to expand what is considered art in order to promote justice and advance human flourishing and the common good. It is also necessary to expand the parameters of what counts as legitimate public art, including narratives and symbols, for the sake of enriching public engagement. Expanding this definition can promote greater incorporation of religious narratives and symbols into liberal philosophical and political structures and strengthen justice in liberal society. The next section will delve into the implications of this limitation in Nussbaum's aesthetics, especially as it pertains to the engagement of Latine religious narratives and symbols in public life.

RELIGION AND LIBERAL AESTHETICS

Nussbaum's liberal aesthetics help us to consider the way that aesthetics might support the life of democracy. Like her interlocutor Rawls, Nussbaum acknowledges the potentially legitimate role of religion in liberal democracy.[74] Yet she reiterates Rawls's demand that religion must be appropriately situated within public discourse. Her own interpretation of King's "I Have a Dream" speech elucidates this argument. Whereas Rawls's struggles to make sense of *whether* King's work violates the division between the background culture and any deliberations about the basic structure (see the analysis in chapter 1),

Nussbaum is confident that King's rhetoric *is appropriate* for public deliberation. But Nussbaum achieves this confidence by designating King's sermon as
a form of "civic poetry":

> Symbols that are resonant sometimes come out of a religious tra-
> dition, but they can be appropriated into the general language of a
> society without being exclusionary, if they are advanced in connection
> with a robust pluralism. Thus King draws a lot of his imagery from the
> prophets (though also from Shakespeare and popular music); he uses
> those references, however, as a kind of civic poetry, and he makes it
> very clear that he looks to a future that include everyone on a basis of
> equality. . . . So political liberalism reminds us to remain vigilant about
> the problem of pluralism and the dangers of hierarchy and establish-
> ment, but it does not doom the public culture to banality or silence.[75]

Nussbaum's framework depicts King's sermon as a symbol of public significance free from the destabilizing anger of the Hebrew prophets that animate
his words. It is as if King really intended those prophetic images to be helpful
illustrations of a liberal concept.

But King was a Baptist preacher. Amos and Shakespeare are not of equivalent authority or significance to his substantive claim about injustice regarding
the basic structure of the United States. The prophets were not another color
on King's palette; they were the content and substance of his proclamation
of justice directed at the nation. By reducing the significance of King's sermon to a masterpiece of civic poetry, Nussbaum's liberal aesthetic reinforces
Enlightenment intellectual hegemony and demands that King forgo his religious, cultural, and racial particularity to defend his fundamental humanity
and equality in US public life.

King's vision, steeped in a prophetic tradition with a full-throated theological voice, loses its particular power and resonance when viewed simply
through the aesthetic lens of "civic poetry." It loses the bite of its prophetic
proclamation of justice when read as an admonition simply for "civic
empathy."[76] Ultimately Rawls's and Nussbaum's respective frameworks succumb to the same problem: they both claim that religious, cultural, and racial
particularity are potentially beneficial for cultivating the common good in the
context of a pluralistic public life but ultimately fail to offer a structure for
engagement of them in the life of liberalism.

Nussbaum is perhaps more permissive of religion and cultural particularity in public life than Rawls. But her aesthetics are ultimately too prohibitive;
religious symbols lose their particularity in their transition to public symbols,

forgoing their resonance and deeper implications for the pursuit of justice and equality in the life of a participatory democracy. Cecilia González-Andrieu amplifies this issue in her analysis of the aesthetics of Christian martyrdom, a tradition into which she situates King alongside Dietrich Bonhoeffer and Óscar Romero:

> We cannot attribute their unflinching steadfastness in Christ to the secular understanding suggested by a "notion." Thus, we note even if speaking of Christianity as a "notion" puts at ease a secularized public suspicion of religion, it also labels the entire content of the exhibition "notional," which means speculative or theoretical—the word also used in other reports. To say that Romero, King, and Bonhoeffer died for a notion must be denounced as a lie, and this helps to understand the truth claims of Christian art.[77]

Perhaps martyrdom, especially highly visible and publicly significant instances of martyrdom, can be read as a civic event that testifies to the truth—or falsehood—of a particular claim or idea. González-Andrieu's point, however, is that an interpretation of these events as merely public vitiates both the particularity and richness of their meaning. King's martyrdom, for instance, testifies to his unyielding desire for racial justice in the United States; it is irreducibly public and religious in nature. Its interpretation requires an adequate framework for engaging those realities. To be clear, the demand for public translation of particular narratives, symbols, and art forms is not unreasonable. The problem arises when the symbols are stripped of their religious and cultural particularity in a way that blunts their meaning.

What is the alternative to Nussbaum's liberal aesthetics of civic poetry? I suggest that Kristin Heyer's conception of civic kinship yields a more promising framework for interlacing racial, ethnic, and religious solidarity. Civic kinship is predicated on a relational anthropology emphasizing that humans are constituted fundamentally by both autonomy and relationality.[78] While relationships can be sites of abuse, Heyer suggests that a model of solidarity that envisions society in terms of familial belonging is better able to account for both human distinctiveness and commonality. She writes, "The mutual dynamics of solidarity . . . remind participants that integration is an endeavor in which all parties have something to offer."[79] The language of integration is often taken to imply that marginalized people and cultures must forgo that which makes them distinctive in order to assimilate to a dominate culture. Yet Heyer stresses that authentic solidarity requires recognition of full equality and rights of those on the margins as a fundamental condition of "intercultural transformation of a culture and its members" that "diverges from static versions of culture that risk 'collective narcissism' on the part of those who manipulate tradition at the service of social control rather than cultural development."[80] While the metaphor of civic kinship does imply the development of a common space to which members of different groups come to belong, this development requires distribution of social and cultural power in a way that resists the undermining of any particular person or group within society. Danielle Allen invites us to consider a metaphor of wholeness as one capable of knitting together the distinctive parts of a diverse body politic, one with a history of White supremacy and anti-Blackness that troubles any project of simple unity. Civic kinship, when anchored in an adequate account of justice, resonates with Allen's metaphor.

Whether as civic kinship or whole garment, the common good requires a conception of solidarity that does not capitulate to Enlightenment hierarchical bifurcation to produce a permanently minoritized group. Rather, it requires a conception predicated on a rectification of persistent power imbalances that thwart the attainment of a just solidarity.

CONCLUSION

If Rawls and Nussbaum falter in their attempts to offer frameworks for encountering particularity in public life, what might an adequate framework look like? Similar to Nussbaum, Alejandro García-Rivera avers that aesthetics is essential to uniting individuals and communities around a common cause across religious and cultural difference. García-Rivera, employing both Latine theology and American pragmatist (or, more properly, pragmaticist) philosophy, argues that aesthetics can unite parties across difference without undermining the richness of their particularity; aesthetics serve as a common interpretive term and a canvas for expression and interpretation of difference. The challenge for García-Rivera is whether this framework is grounded in a conception of justice sufficient to foster public participation and political stability directed toward the societal common good.

NOTES

1. Garcia, "Miracle at Tepeyac," 5.
2. Garcia, 28.
3. Flores, "Heart of the Neighborhood," 26.

4. Flores, "Psalmist's Lament," 24.

5. Alvarez, *In the Time of the Butterflies*, 26.

6. Nussbaum, *Political Emotions*, 2.

7. Hordern, *Political Affections*, 24–25.

8. Rawls, *Theory of Justice*, 457–58.

9. Nussbaum, *Political Emotions*, 9.

10. Nussbaum, 8–9.

11. Nussbaum, *Creating Capabilities*, 18.

12. Nussbaum, *Frontiers of Justice*, 175.

13. Nussbaum, *Creating Capabilities*, 18.

14. Nussbaum, 33–34; Nussbaum, *Frontiers of Justice*, 76–78.

15. Nussbaum, *Poetic Justice*, xv.

16. Nussbaum, *Creating Capabilities*, 31.

17. Nussbaum, 40.

18. Kao, *Grounding Human Rights in a Pluralist World*, 2.

19. Cahill, "Justice for Women," 87.

20. Charusheela, "Social Analysis and the Capabilities Approach," 1137.

21. Charlesworth, "Martha Nussbaum's Feminist Internationalism," 76–77.

22. Charusheela, "Social Analysis and the Capabilities Approach," 1136.

23. Charusheela, 1140.

24. Nzegwu, "Recovering Igbo Traditions," 444.

25. Charusheela, "Social Analysis and the Capabilities Approach," 1143.

26. Kao, *Grounding Human Rights in a Pluralist World*, 2.

27. García-Rivera, *Community of the Beautiful*, 92.

28. Young, *Justice and the Politics of Difference*, 48–63.

29. Kao, *Grounding Human Rights in a Pluralist World*, 26.

30. Kao, 26–27.

31. Kao, 4–5. Maximalists permit (and in some cases require) "thick" religious or philosophical conceptions of the good as the basis for articulating fundamental human rights. Reacting to the Westernization of rights discourse, minimalists aim for a "thin" account of rights that does not rely on religious or philosophical premises.

32. Kao, 8.

33. Hogan, *Keeping Faith with Human Rights*, 179.

34. Hogan, 180.

35. Rawls, *Theory of Justice*, 454.

36. Nussbaum, *Poetic Justice*, 68.

37. Dickens, *Hard Times*.

38. Nussbaum, *Poetic Justice*, 1–2.

39. Nussbaum, 68.

40. Nussbaum, 36.

41. Nussbaum, 69.

42. Nussbaum, *Upheavals of Thought*, 40.

43. Nussbaum, 3.

44. Nussbaum, 30–31.

45. Nussbaum, 2.

46. Hanisch, "Personal Is Political."

47. Nussbaum, *Political Emotions*, 2.

48. Rawls, *Theory of Justice*, 457–58.
49. Nussbaum, *Political Emotions*, 134–35.
50. Flores and Mathewes, "First Citizen."
51. Lepore, *These Truths*, 295.
52. Obama, "Remarks in Eulogy for Clementa Pinckney."
53. Nussbaum, *Political Emotions*, 135.
54. Massingale, "Systematic Erasure of the Black/Dark-Skinned Body," 121.
55. Nussbaum, *Anger and Forgiveness*, 5.
56. Nussbaum, 8.
57. Nussbaum, 31.
58. Townes, *Womanist Ethics and the Cultural Production of Evil*, 7.
59. Nussbaum, *Anger and Forgiveness*, 33.
60. Nussbaum, *Poetic Justice*, 2.
61. Nussbaum, *Political Emotions*, 3.
62. Nussbaum, 3.
63. Nussbaum, 2.
64. Nussbaum, 53.
65. Nussbaum, *Upheavals of Thought*, 3.
66. Nussbaum, *Poetic Justice*, 8–9.
67. Nussbaum, *Political Emotions*, 200–201.
68. Nussbaum, 382.
69. Nussbaum, *Poetic Justice*, 79.
70. Nussbaum, 99.
71. Nussbaum, 6.
72. Nussbaum, *Political Emotions*, 19.
73. Arellano, *Magical Realism and the History of Emotions*.
74. Nussbaum, *Political Emotions*, 388.
75. Nussbaum, 388.
76. Miller, *Friends and Other Strangers*. Employing a metaphor similar to Nussbaum's, Miller suggests the cultivation of "civic empathy" as an appropriate framework for acknowledging religious particularity in public life without having to actually engage religion in public life.
77. González-Andrieu, *Bridge to Wonder*, 66.
78. Farley, *Just Love*, 211.
79. Heyer, *Kinship across Borders*, 153.
80. Heyer, 153.

4

Lifting Up the Lowly

"Calling out around the world, are you ready for a brand new beat?"[1] Bathed in a spotlight, a singer belts out the lyrics of the Martha and the Vandellas song "Dancing in the Street." A chorus of four singers harmonizes with her melody. The performers wave their hands, beckoning the audience to join in with their a cappella rendition of the song. Though tentative at first, the audience begins to clap and sway. After finishing her litany of cities, the lead singer modifies the lyrics a little bit, singing, "At Su Teatro, we're dancing in the street!"[2]

The performers are members of The SOURCE, Denver's African American community theater company. They perform "Dancing in the Street" as part of the musical revue *The Five Points/Wrapped Around My Soul*. Written and directed by playwright Jimmy Walker, the show is a theatrical exploration of life in Five Points, one of Denver's oldest African American neighborhoods and the heart of the city's Black community. The show explores the challenges and triumphs of life in Five Points during the mid-twentieth century. Redacting soulful performances of dozens of R&B hits from the 1950s, '60s, and '70s with short spoken interludes about life in the neighborhood, the performance testifies to the power of soul music as a form of both spiritual consolation and political empowerment. The SOURCE's performance transports the audience to the streets of Five Points to reflect on its past, present, and future.

The SOURCE performs *The Five Points/Wrapped Around My Soul* in the Frank Trujillo Salon del Arte, a black box theater at Su Teatro that has a banner of Our Lady of Guadalupe taken from a promotional poster for *The Miracle at Tepeyac* draped above the door. Su Teatro owns the theater complex on Santa Fe Drive adjacent to the former Auraria neighborhood. Su Teatro currently houses The SOURCE and cooperates with their sister company to ensure access to the theater space, even collaborating on some of their shows. The companies have shared a theater space before, with The SOURCE housing Su Teatro in its early years.[3]

The Chicanx audience at Su Teatro might not realize the accidental radicality of "Dancing in the Street." Often asked if the song had intended to provoke riots, the Vandellas' lead singer, Martha Reeves, exclaimed, "My Lord, it was a *party* song!"[4] But by "calling out around the world" for young people—young Black people—to take to the streets, the Vandellas sang the anthem for the social, political, and cultural upheaval of the 1960s. "In June 1964 the social, political, and cultural upheaval that would be known as 'the sixties' was about to explode" and Martha and the Vandellas "had just sung its anthem."[5] Young Chicanos were dancing in the streets in the 1960s too. Just blocks away from Su Teatro, at Denver West High School, Chicano students took to the streets during the 1969 Blowouts to protest the school's discriminatory treatment of minority students. The walkouts are remembered by another Su Teatro play, *Chicano Power 1969: Fire in the Streets/War of the Flowers.*[6] "Dancing in the Street" plaits together two protest traditions from two communities that have often been at a distance from one another despite their common struggles and resonant traditions.

The relationship between Black Americans and Mexican Americans in the United States at times has been marked by conflict. People of both groups have been subject to segregation, discrimination, and violence. But geographical, cultural, and even religious differences left few occasions for fostering deep interpersonal or communal commitments between the two communities prior to the mid-twentieth century. Racial differences also hindered the creation of coalitions, especially the decision by middle-class Mexican Americans to self-identify as White. Mexican-American organizations such as the League of Latin American Citizens (LULAC) and the American GI Forum strategically employed their government classification as White to pursue assimilation into White institutions, economic structures, and cultures that they believed would generate greater opportunities for advancement in the United States.[7] This strategic use of Whiteness backfired, both legally and socially, and led to losses in the courtroom and in the culture.[8] Further, as discussed in chapter 1, conceptions of mestizaje that elevate Whiteness obscured the existence of both Black and Indigenous identity that lie at the very heart of Latine identity.

Nonetheless, the social movements of the 1960s and 1970s shifted relational dynamics among the Black and Chicano movements, unearthing deep connections and common ground among the communities. Scholarship about the social movements of those decades often study them as discrete entities. "On the contrary," argues Lauren Araiza, "the social movements of the 1960s–1970s were marked by a pattern of continuous interaction and dynamic exchange."[9] Interactions among these distinct-yet-related movements influenced racial discourse among Chicanos and recast an understanding of Chicano racial identity from White to Brown: "The ineffectiveness of the Whiteness strategy, coupled with the domestic and international movements of the 1960s, led some Mexican Americans to develop a Chicano identity that rejected Whiteness in favor of "Brown" identity. *Chicanismo* included racial pride, cultural expression, active resistance to discrimination, and unity with people of color around the world, including African Americans."[10] This shift in racial discourse among Chicanos helped construct a frame for engaging the common experiences of oppression among Black and Brown people. While tensions remain, a shared consciousness of racial oppression allowed for cultivating solidarity among like-minded Black and Brown organizations in the movement.

Against the backdrop of these tensions and synergies, The SOURCE's performance of *The Five Points/Wrapped Around My Soul* at Su Teatro highlights the social ligaments between Denver's Black and Chicanx communities. Both communities have experienced racial discrimination and White supremacist violence throughout their histories in the city. Both communities contend with the degrading effects of racist political, economic, and social structures that spur poverty and violence in their neighborhoods. Both communities employ the arts—especially community theater, murals, music, poetry, and other public art—as part of their resistance against social devastation. As a result, both have cultivated vibrant cultural hubs in their neighborhoods, coalescing grassroots artists, activists, and intellectuals in the shared work of fostering trust, cooperation, and beauty. Now both communities confront the erasure of their neighborhoods as rapid gentrification consumes their artwork, their organizations, and their institutions.

Gentrification in Five Points has eliminated local Black businesses, affordable housing options, and community cultural institutions that have sustained the neighborhood for generations. Black businesses, social clubs, and homes have been replaced with White-owned microbreweries, boutique coffee houses, and cycle studios. These new businesses cater primarily to a White and wealthy clientele, a de facto exclusion of participation by most of the neighborhood's long-time residents. In November 2017 a coffee shop in Five Points posted a sandwich board sign on the sidewalk that read, "Happily Gentrifying the Neighborhood Since 2014." The opposite side said, "Nothing says gentrification better than a fresh brewed cortado."[11] Intended as humor by the White shop owners, the signs brought at least two hundred protesters from across the city to Five Points. The protest's organizer, Tay Anderson, responded, "I don't see it as being a joke. I see it as being offensive to African-Americans and Latinos who were pushed out of this community."[12] Two months later, at a gentrification summit convened in response to the protests, Anderson included Native Americans in her talking points: "Kicking Blacks, Latinos, and Native Americans out of their homes is not a joke."[13]

Performed against the backdrop of the social upheaval that gentrification causes for longtime communities, *The Five Points/Wrapped Around My Soul* calls on the power of "music, sweet music" to resist the erasure of Black and Brown communities from Denver's cityscape. Artistic collaboration between The SOURCE and Su Teatro demonstrates the place of aesthetic experience in cultivating a just solidarity in a pluralistic society. Whereas Rawls's and Nussbaum's liberal aesthetics restrict engagement of social, religious, and cultural particularities, The SOURCE and Su Teatro model a capacious method for interpreting particularity via aesthetic experience. Sharing stories about their neighborhoods, these theater companies and their audiences cultivate solidarity that is not predicated on the false objectivity of Whiteness as unveiled in chapters 2 and 3. Interpreting each other's stories across differences of race, religion, and culture, The SOURCE and Su Teatro cultivate a community of the beautiful that is committed to holistic flourishing of Black and Chicanx people and neighborhoods. This solidarity, which "lifts up the lowly," is essential to cultivating an authentic common good that is predicated not on the metaphor of oneness, as Danielle Allen explains, but on the metaphor of wholeness, where distinct parts of the body politic are knit together into a democracy that can bring about "trustful coherence without erasing or suppressing difference."[14]

How does the community of the beautiful cultivate solidarity that seeks wholeness? Reflecting on Mary's Magnificat and Our Lady of Guadalupe, Alejandro García-Rivera emphasizes the necessity of "lifting up" members of a community who have been relegated to the background using the aesthetic principle of foregrounding. García-Rivera employs Josiah Royce's semiotic illustration of the obverse collection (or the O-collection) to illustrate this aesthetic norm. Like the cluster of interconnected points that forms the O-collection, lifting up one point allows it to be foregrounded without breaking the relationship between all of the points. This configuration allows for the foregrounding of one or more points at a time and reconfigures the relationship in order to lift up other points from the background. Building on García-Rivera's aesthetic insight, I argue that lifting up the lowly is a crucial principle for an aesthetics of the common good, a common good that supplants a project of "oneness" with "wholeness" and allows distinct identities to be stitched together to cultivate solidarity. I turn to Latine theology to articulate an aesthetics of the common good that invites wholeness.

This chapter is organized into three sections. First I elaborate the relational context of Latine theology that gives rise to García-Rivera's theological aesthetics, especially its account of the pluralism within the context of community. Then I examine García-Rivera's theological aesthetics of lifting up the lowly to illustrate its capacity to navigate the tensive dynamic between pluralism and community that is manifest in Latine theology. Finally I return to *The Five Points/Wrapped Around My Soul* to illustrate the significance of García-Rivera's theological aesthetics for forging a just solidarity (that is, one that promotes the necessary social conditions for the flourishing of each member of society) that is the foundation of the societal common good.

THE RELATIONAL CONTEXT
OF LATINE THEOLOGY

In *Community of the Beautiful: A Theological Aesthetics* García-Rivera argues that the act of interpretation, or coming to know the mind of another, necessarily takes place in the context of difference and relationship. García-Rivera's theology must be read within the broader context of Latine theology, which emphasizes the inherently relational character of human beings by virtue of our creation in the image of a Trinitarian God (*imago Trinitatis*) over and against theologies that have rendered excessively individualistic accounts of anthropology (doctrine of the human) and soteriology (doctrine of salvation). Latine theological anthropology is therefore characterized by the thick notion of familial belonging that is prominently featured in Latine cultures.

The emphasis on human relationality expressed in Catholic theological ethics in general resonates with the Latine community's experience of thick relational contexts. This account of relationality is crucial to Goizueta's theological interpretation of the relationship between Guadalupe and Juan Diego: she empowers him to recognize his dignity and political power within colonial ecclesial and civic structures that have treated him as "the people's dung."[15] In this way Goizueta's framework gestures to the liberative potential of the thick account of relationship in Latine Catholic theological anthropologies, especially when interlaced with adequate concepts of dignity and autonomy.

But while Latine theology has done well to illustrate the theological and ethical necessities of a theological anthropology inflected by special relationships, it has often struggled to convey the individual dignity of particular members of the community, especially within the context of families. Several Latine theologians have criticized the subordination of vulnerable individuals (women, children, LGBTQ folx, persons with disabilities) within

Latine families. These theologians offer a more comprehensive conception of the dynamic between relationship and difference that strengthens the basis for a justice framework and is supportive of the concerns of communities engaged in social struggles, such as the kind seen in Denver's Black and Chicanx communities.

A Familial Worldview

Latine cultures are profoundly communal, anchoring individual existence within the context of community and specifically within the context of family. This emphasis is reflected in the structure of the Spanish language: for example, *Nosotros* (translated as "we") really means "we-others" (nos-otros).[16] This recognition of fundamental human relationality orients Latine approaches to broader theological questions about individuality in community. If human beings are fundamentally relational, it means that we are ethically obligated to attend to the dynamics of our relationships to ensure that they promote the flourishing of particular human beings as well as society at large.

Latine theology expresses a particular thick conception of relationship as a constitutive aspect of human identity. The individual does not—indeed cannot—exist outside of the communities and families with whom she has relationships.[17] Relationships are a vital dimension of personal identity. This fundamentally relational condition gives rise to the responsibility to view the good of others as central to one's own flourishing.

This specific expression of relational anthropology is crucial to Latine theological contributions to Christian family ethics. Latine theological anthropology promotes greater social orientation among families, as is evident in the structure of Latine families.[18] Latine families grow not only through marriage and birth but also through the Sacraments (Baptism, Marriage, and Ordination, for example) as well as through the extension of the family through neighborhood relationships and other forms of social belonging. These kinds of familial relationships are celebrated in *The Miracle at Tepeyac*, where the church members become one family who join together in each other's struggles. But it is also modeled in *The Five Points/Wrapped Around My Soul*, where the musicians reveal the Five Points neighborhood as a family struggling to stay together in the face of existential threats—poverty, violence, exclusion, and the dismantling of the neighborhood by wealthy newcomers.

Nevertheless, patterns of abuse can fester *within* families.[19] While family is a central cultural, theological, and ethical category for Latines, we must avoid romanticizing the family and grapple with concrete instances of exploitation, marginalization, powerlessness, and violence within family structures.

For example, while there are similar rates of domestic abuse reported among Latina and non-Latina White women, a lower rate of Latinas report abuse to authorities.[20] A constellation of factors contribute to underreporting: Latinas underutilize public resources and protections in these situations due to language and cultural barriers as well as distrust of law enforcement. This distrust is exacerbated among Latinas lacking recognized citizenship documentation. Furthermore, while underreporting of domestic abuse is engendered by the prevailing legal and political structures, another significant contributing factor that discourages Latinas from seeking assistance is excessive protection of family interests.[21] Thus, while Latinas may not be at significantly higher risk for domestic abuse than other women, cultural and social factors can converge to prevent protection and justice for Latinas who suffer abuse and violence at the hands of their families.

The absence of an adequate conception of autonomy has led some Latine theologians to expresses skepticism about the liberating potential of Latine relational anthropology. Orlando Espín asks, "Has Latino/a theology been romanticizing Latino/a family life and Latino/a culture and history, thereby contributing to the perpetuation of sins and idols; and if so, how do we defend our *Latinidad* while we also seriously critique our own dehumanizing behaviors and attitudes?"[22] Michelle A. González adds, "A community that is constructed at the expense of certain individuals is not one that can be celebrated within a Christian vision of the human."[23] They both argue for the necessity of interrogating Latine family dynamics even as Latine theology attempts to draw positive theological insights from the lived experiences of Latine communities.

In the absence of a robust account of autonomy, it is unclear how Latine theology can articulate an adequate framework for right relationships within the context of relationality that supports both communal and personal flourishing. It is necessary, then, for the *familia* of Latine theologians to address the potential abuse of vulnerable and marginalized family and community members by articulating a vision of just relationships that affirms the significance of personal autonomy but doesn't forgo the social orientation of families and communities.

Toward a Just Relationality

Latine theology continues to seek ways to articulate the connection between difference and relationship in a manner that preserves its anthropological insight but also rejects injustices perpetuated against members of a community, especially the most vulnerable. Nancy Pineda-Madrid has written about the role of women and women-identified people resisting feminicide in Ciudad Juárez and the systematic killing of women on the US-Mexico border simply because they are women.[24] Her analysis demonstrates the role of unjust relationships in the structures that have led to the slaughter of women throughout the region. Specifically, her soteriological analysis of the feminicide demonstrates how women's interests have been subordinated to the interests of the drug cartels, which perpetuate the slaughter and mutilation of women's bodies to mark turf and consolidate their economic power. Her analysis also indicts the local Catholic Church and the Mexican government, both of which have failed to defend the women of the region in the face of this brutality. Resonating with Delores Williams's classic theological conception of Black women's surrogate suffering, Pineda-Madrid demonstrates how women have been sacrificed as a defense of the interests of particular ecclesial and political communities.[25] The destruction of women in order to consolidate and preserve power evokes Ivone Gebara's critique of the idolatrous construction of gender in Latin America, which sees women as primarily oriented toward the service of the interests of the men in their lives rather than the service of God.[26]

An awareness of these idolatrous relational dynamics figures prominently in the resistance against feminicide in Ciudad Juárez. Women who have been murdered are memorialized through the pink crosses that are scattered throughout the region, especially in places where bodies have been found. Each pink cross is inscribed with the name of a woman who has been victimized by feminicide, reclaiming her life for Jesus Christ from the systems that enabled her murder with impunity. The pink crosses symbolize a rejection of the orientation of women of Juárez as servants of systems of violence and political power. The pink crosses thus undermine the idolatry of conceptions of gender that view women's bodies as objects of sacrifice for the sake of protecting patriarchal order in the church, the government, or the global economy.

Significantly, Pineda-Madrid notes that the protesting women have not selected Our Lady of Guadalupe as the symbol of their resistance.[27] The women see the use of Guadalupe as a symbol of shame against women, especially in the realm of sexuality. In this instance the women working together on the grassroots level have determined that the tendency of Guadalupe to be leveraged as a symbol critiquing women's sexuality does not serve their cause. Of course, the cross itself has also been used as a symbol of violence and oppression, including violence against women. For this reason the decision of the women of Juárez to paint the cross pink is theologically significant. It asserts their interpretation of the Crucified Christ as being on the side of those who experience violence. Inscribing the name of each murdered woman on the cross reasserts her identification with Jesus Christ as the source of her humanity. It identifies the women who have been victimized— whether murdered themselves or not—as people made in God's image and redeemed with Him.

Similarly, Néstor Medina argues that the construction of relationship in Latine theology can be harmful to communities that fall outside of Latine imagined racial norms. He takes on giants of Latine theology, illustrating the limitations, inadequacies, and even the harms of mestizaje theologies that have dominated the tradition. Specifically, Medina emphasizes the role of mestizaje in rendering Black and Indigenous people invisible in Latine theology. Writing in 2009, Medina's work was on the forefront of demonstrating the anti-Black and anti-Indigenous tendencies within Latine theology, even in theologies explicitly committed to liberation.

Examining the works of Virgilio Elizondo and Gloria Anzaldúa, Medina employs Guadalupe to illustrate the racial dynamics of mestizaje. While acknowledging that Guadalupe is a multivalent symbol, Medina argues that Elizondo frames Guadalupe as a "providential reconciliation" of two disparate peoples.[28] This reconciliation forms a new people: not simply Spanish or simply Indigenous, but Mexican. But it is the erasure of the Indigenous— biologically, culturally, and religiously—that Medina takes issue with in Elizondo's interpretation. Even the appellation "Juan Diego" erases the man's original Indigenous name, "Quauhtlatoatzin" (He Who Speaks with the Snakes), appropriating him and obliterating his Indigenous self for the cause of Christian mission. Medina explains:

> In my view, Juan Diego is made *mestizo* by removing his indigenous background at the time of the encounter, and by some is made to represent the culturally *mestizo/a* population. The implication is that Guadalupe does not mean only liberation and the irruption of a "new" people. For some indigenous peoples, Guadalupe has also functioned as a symbol imposed upon their communities in order to have them abandon ancient religious symbols and practices. Their religious traditions have been replaced with mestizo/a Christianity, and Guadalupe is the perennial reminder of the conquest and eradication of the indigenous religious traditions.[29]

Medina's analysis raises a major question for Latine theology: Can Guadalupe say anything about the oppression and resistance of Indigenous people while simultaneously erasing Indigenous biology, culture, and religion?

Anzaldúa, conversely, emphasizes the fluidity of Guadalupe's identity. This view of Guadalupe allows Anzaldúa to claim the symbol as an embrace of multidimensional identity, including one's Indigenous identity. "To embrace Guadalupe," Medina explains, "is to (re)claim her indigenous ancestry. . . . In other words, mestizaje is the medium through which the authentic indigenous roots are reclaimed."[30] Accordingly, Anzaldúa "leaves the door open for taking the Indigenous religious elements in Guadalupe much more seriously than previous interpretations on mestizaje have."[31]

Nonetheless, Medina criticizes both Elizondo's and Anzaldúa's treatment of Indigenous identity in their respective interpretations of Guadalupe. Indeed, whether she is regarded as a symbol of "providential reconciliation" in an encounter that brings forth a new people or as a symbol of the survival of Indigenous religious elements despite violent attempts to destroy them through the mechanisms of colonization, Guadalupe as la mestiza does not allow for the survival of Indigenous religion. Medina asserts the need for an interpretation of Guadalupe as "the concrete symbol of the obstinate resistance and struggle of the indigenous peoples to survive, to the extent of transforming key Christian symbols by bringing them close to their own ancestral religious traditions and practices."[32] He gestures to syncretic religious practices—including attendance at Catholic Mass—that function to allow Indigenous people to preserve their particular customs, symbols, and rituals in the context of colonization.

Medina's analysis opens a crucial horizon in Latine theological reflection on religious and cultural pluralism. He demonstrates the racial and cultural limitations of Latine theologies that extol Guadalupe as simply a liberative symbol. Just as Pineda-Madrid compels a reckoning over the use of Guadalupe to undermine the dignity of women-identified Mexicans fighting against the terror of feminicide, Medina demands a nuanced theological representation of Guadalupe as a symbol that interrogates the role of mestizaje in the erasure of Black and Indigenous identity among Latines. Taken together, their critiques demand an ethical framework for engaging difference that rejects the subordination of gender and race in the pursuit of a false construction of oneness within Latine theology.

These critiques of the use of Guadalupe to enforce patterns of domination and subordination demand an ethical response. I argue that Latine theological ethics already contains resources for responding to the problem that Pineda-Madrid and Medina clarify. Specifically, Isasi-Díaz's mujerista ethics provide crucial guidance for situating relationships in the context of pluralism without requiring racial, gender, or sexual subordination to foster a flourishing common life.

Isasi-Díaz argues for the necessity of an ethical method capable of both recognizing and interpreting difference within community.[33] How we conceive of difference, she emphasizes, influences the possibilities for constructing a just social order. Isasi-Díaz cautions against the misinterpretation of difference. Misinterpretations are the basis for prejudice and hatred that undermine community. Prejudice and hate motivate chants to build walls, cage children, and jail political opponents, for example.

To avoid a xenophobic response to difference, some seek to avoid acknowledging or engaging difference altogether. This kind of interpretive malpractice leads to the argument that difference must be either eliminated through assimilation or completely disregarded in the decision-making that pertains to society. As was considered in chapter 2, Isasi-Díaz also rejects refusals to acknowledge difference. Difference is inherent between and among people, families, neighborhoods, and regions. Attempts to eliminate difference preserve social marginalization. An understanding of difference as "absolute otherness," she explains, "leads to a conceptualization of those who are different as outsiders, with those belonging to the dominant group having the power to decide what is normative (themselves) and what is deviant (others). As long as this continues to be the prevalent understanding, there is no possibility of having just personal relationships, or of creating just societal structures that will not benefit some groups at the expense of others."[34] The risk here is that difference results in privilege for dominant persons and groups falsely considered normative and continued marginalization for persons and groups that do not conform to this norm.

Difference can be misinterpreted to the detriment of communal flourishing, argues Isasi-Díaz. But a robust commitment to community need not eclipse the good of individual persons. Maintaining the dynamic between the good of individuals and the good of the community is essential to a thriving society. A community that promotes individual flourishing, she says, "does not subsume the person but rather emphasizes that the person is constituted by this entity and that the individual person and the community have a dialogic relationship through which the person reflects the *familia/comunidad*."[35] The dialogical relationship between the person and the community is key to promoting equality and participation within Latine communities and beyond. Accentuating the dynamic between difference and relationship, Isasi-Díaz's argument resonates with the conception of solidarity characterized by mutuality, equality, and participation expressed in Catholic social thought.

García-Rivera, in a vein similar to Isasi-Díaz's, investigates the meaning of difference within relationships. Discerning the meaning of difference, he argues, is necessary to avoid despairing over it.[36] "Faced with the reality of difference," he writes, "we see only the difference itself and not the meaning of difference. If difference, and human difference in particular, has no meaning but is simply difference itself, then despair and cynicism fill in the void of our lack of understanding."[37] García-Rivera's study of the dynamic between difference and relationship is the foundation of his theological aesthetics.

THE COMMUNITY OF THE BEAUTIFUL

While the analysis of Latine theology and ethics discloses the tension between difference and relationship, García-Rivera's theological aesthetic offers a method for navigating the concepts. Building on the semiotics of Charles Sanders Peirce and Josiah Royce, García-Rivera offers the aesthetic norm of foregrounding as a cornerstone of fostering communities that allow for the respect of individuals.[38] This norm suggests the ethical centrality of what he calls "the community of the beautiful": a community that is formed through the common act of aesthetic interpretation and foregrounding, or "lifting up the lowly." García-Rivera thus offers a crucial response to the reductive treatment of difference that hinders prevailing secular discourses from promoting the full participation of marginalized groups in democratic society (including the liberal positions of Rawls and Nussbaum).

Similar to Isasi-Díaz, García-Rivera asserts that difference and relationship are fundamental conditions of creation. Emphasizing the simultaneous conditions of unity and distinction, he argues that the fundamental state of being (ontology) is simultaneously relational, individual, and aesthetic. Establishing relationship alongside individuality as the fundamental characteristics of being, García-Rivera argues that the act of interpretation can be facilitated through the aesthetic method of foregrounding, that is, engaging a particular aspect of a larger whole.

García-Rivera bases his argument highlighting the aesthetic character of the act of interpretation on the *analogia entis*, the analogy of being. All of creation is united in its basic state of existence. Still, creation is also defined by difference: both difference from the Creator and difference among all creation. "*That things are* makes the claim that all creatures have something in common," he writes. "They all participate in being what they are. *What things are*, on the other hand, makes a seeming antithetical claim that each creature possesses a unique particularity that makes it what it is."[39] García-Rivera employs this idea in order to buttress his understanding of unity and difference *both* vertically (between Creator and creatures) *and* horizontally (among creatures). While both are theologically significant, the relevant point here is the simultaneous basic condition of unity and difference among creatures. This condition is the starting point for García-Rivera's reflection on the character of being.

Having established the unity and particularity of the created order, García-Rivera turns to Charles Sanders Peirce's pragmatic philosophy to elaborate the claim that being is fundamentally relational. He draws on Peirce's logic of signs to establish this claim. Peirce's semiotics is concerned with the relational character of logic. While the most elementary logical relation consists in the comparing or contrasting of two objects or in the relationship between signified and the signifier, Peirce recognizes that this comparison requires a third term that interprets this comparison: the interpretant. The interpretant, together with the signified and the signifier, comprise a sign.[40] Peirce's semiotics underscore the relational character of logic.[41] The comparison of two individuals is an act of thought that forges a relationship between them. This comparison is impossible without a third element to unite them. Thus, from within the logic of signs the "third term" makes relationship between two discrete entities possible.

While Peirce's philosophy expresses the relational character of the act of interpretation, Josiah Royce reiterates the necessity of particularity in this semiotic scheme. Specifically, Royce highlights the necessity of individuality in the act of interpretation. While being is intrinsically relational, it is also fundamentally individual. The logic of signs, then, leads to the formation of a community of interpretation that transforms the isolated individual into a member of a community.[42]

From this acknowledgment of relationship and particularity Royce is able to construct a conception of interpretation, or what he calls the "community of interpretation," that emphasizes the formation of community in the context of difference and pluralism. Royce offers two philosophical concepts to illustrate the dynamic between individuality and relationship at work in the act of interpretation. The first of these concepts is boundary crossing.[43] Boundary crossing requires the disruption of one's perspective through encounter with the other. Boundary crossing underscores the transgressive quality of aesthetic engagement. The second concept Royce calls loyalty, which is the will to interpret a mind other than one's own. The shared act of interpretation forges a community of interpretation.[44] At the heart of this community lies a *will* or *desire* on the part of the interpreters to enter into the shared act of interpretation. This will to interpret, to enter into community across difference, serves as a source of atonement and reconciliation and draws together a community in the context of difference: "Done in the context of the knowledge of good and evil, such interpretation amounts to a reconciliation of an individual to a community of interpretation. It is, in a sense, an 'at-one-ing,' i.e., drawing into and becoming 'one' with community, which heals the tragic consequences of evil." In this way the act of interpretation facilitates the tension between community and difference by drawing individuals together through a common act. Royce's description of the act of interpretation resonates with the illustration offered by the performance of *The Five Points/ Wrapped Around My Soul* on Denver's Chicanx Westside, where two particular groups transgress social, cultural, and even physical boundaries separating their communities in the hope of coming to knowing the mind of the other.

While the modern mind often conceives of relationships as existing only between two individuals (or groups, or communities, or nations), Royce avers that this logic of signs can be extended to accommodate relationships between multiple individuals or polyadic relationships.[45] He uses the concept of the O-collection to describe these multifaceted relationships. Invoking the O-collection, Royce argues (1) that there can be multiple relationships between individual elements and (2) that particular individuals can be understood only within the context of these relationships. To visualize the O-collection, imagine a cluster of interconnected points. In this cluster it is possible to lift up a particular point from the background and bring it to the foreground. It is possible to bring a point from the margin to the center. It is possible to configure the cluster so that multiple points are in the foreground or multiple points are in the center. It is even possible to reposition one's position in relation to the cluster itself so that the background becomes the foreground and the margin becomes the center. All of these configurations and reconfigurations, nevertheless, allow for the points to remain in relationship with one another. In this way the O-collection illustrates a fluid arrangement of polyadic relationships that García-Rivera will find desirable for describing the aesthetic character of relationships: "God's ordaining power," García-Rivera proclaims, "constitutes an interrelated world of unique individuals. Every intelligible creature may be said to be part of an O-collection!"[46]

Employing Royce's semiotics, García-Rivera argues that every creature is (1) fundamentally relational, (2) irreducibly individual, and (3) inextricably contextual. García-Rivera argues that this account of human relationship and difference is fundamentally aesthetic, meaning that its perceptible form—its "felt qualities"—are crucial to what is appreciable and meaningful.[47] Drawing on the polyadic character of the O-collection, García-Rivera offers the aesthetic method of foregrounding as a way of engaging particularity within the context of community. "Foregrounding," he explains, "is a special type of comparison which animates as it compares. Against a backdrop, foregrounding accentuates some elements of that background thus animating the whole."[48] Through foregrounding it is possible to lift up a particular individual, to examine and engage it, without extricating it from the larger constellation of relationships that grounds it in the order of creation. This method, which García-Rivera terms "lifting up the lowly," permits aesthetic engagement with genuine particularity in the context of community.

He illustrates this aesthetic practice through the example of Our Lady of Guadalupe. For suffering Christians of Latin America, "In [Guadalupe], cosmic order and redemption, origins and ends, are shown their profound unity. Such unity, however, could only be seen through the eyes of Juan Diego who was walking towards home and, surprisingly, subversively, and even beautifully was shown a home he never expected."[49] The aesthetic practice of foregrounding, or highlighting a particular piece of the background, lifts up Juan Diego's aesthetic encounter with Guadalupe as a common term for interpretation. In this act interpreters come into contact with the felt qualities of the story that shape imagination and affections. In lifting up Juan Diego's narrative, this particular story emerges from the background as a rich source of aesthetic engagement.

The relational character of García-Rivera's aesthetics gestures toward the significance of aesthetic experiences—which encompass both making and encountering art as well as our everyday experiences—in cultivating solidarity, justice, and the common good. I will return to the example of *The Five Points/Wrapped Around My Soul* to illustrate the social and ethical significance of García-Rivera's aesthetics.

THE COMMUNITY OF THE JUST

Similar to other Latine theologians, García-Rivera considers justice to be an orienting concern in his theology. He frames this affirmation of justice within an argument for the existence of universal truths. He writes, "Ideologies do not claim a reference to the true, but service to a dominant power. Because falsehoods exist that lie about their claim to universal reality does not mean that universals are not real. Indeed, how else can one respond to such falsehoods? If we cannot love justice, then what motivates us to expose the stereotype? If we cannot experience kindness, the how can we reject the lies of the cruel?"[50] Goizueta reasserts García-Rivera's emphasis on the relationship between beauty and justice: "There can be no beauty without justice; the gratuity of God's love can only be experienced in and through the struggle for justice—even if that justice receives its fullest meaning only in the form of gratuity, mercy, reconciliation, and worship."[51] Together García-Rivera and Goizueta argue that the "love of justice" is necessary to refute "false universals."

While García-Rivera and Goizueta emphasize the necessity of loving justice, neither offers a positive definition of justice that can systematically orient the corrosive marginalizing effects of oppression. The consequences of this lack of systematic account become evident in the practical application of aesthetic solidarity. All kinds of communities are united across their differences around aesthetic experiences, but what are the ethical mechanisms in place to evaluate whether these communities are in fact committed to justice? How ought we evaluate the moral quality of the community formed in the act of interpretation without a positive conception of justice to guide our discernment?

Reading García-Rivera's interpretation of Guadalupe through Medina's critical lens highlights this problem. Like Elizondo, García-Rivera stresses the centrality of the Guadalupe event in uniting the Spaniards and the Nahuas into a single people. "The 'difference' that divided two peoples," he explains, "becomes an act of union which was, at its heart, redemptive. This redemptive act, this union of 'difference,' takes the form of a symbol, or, rather, a set of symbols and signs, known as Our Lady of Guadalupe."[52] But, as Medina argues, it is this providential reconciliatory view that undermines the genuine racial, cultural, and religious differences inherent in Latine identity. Medina's critique of Guadalupe as La Mestiza calls to mind the view of the common good that Danielle Allen critiques in *Talking to Strangers*. Allen's differentiation between oneness and wholeness lays bare essentializing common good discourses, even well-intentioned ones, based on Guadalupe's special care for the poor. A vision for the common good based on a political theology of Guadalupe and Juan Diego calls for a shift from oneness to wholeness. It invites a stitching together of a community under the conditions of equality, mutuality, and reciprocity rather than violently dominating and extinguishing people, cultures, and religions en route to a new creation. It is this interlacing of communities that we see at work in the cooperation between The SOURCE and Su Teatro.

FIVE POINTS ON THE WESTSIDE

García-Rivera's emphasis on the transgressive power of aesthetic interpretation resonates with the illustration of *The Five Points/Wrapped Around My Soul* offered earlier. Performed on Denver's Westside for the Chicanx community, *The Five Points/Wrapped Around My Soul* promotes "unification of what was previously dispersed and fragmentary." This unity is achieved "precisely through the 'third' of comparison and interpretation."⁵³ In accord with this framework, Jimmy Walker's review invites the audience to reinterpret this common term to form and sustain community across difference. In this way García-Rivera's argument resonates with Martha Nussbaum's liberal aesthetics in its recognition of the power of poetry, music, and art to unite members of plural societies across their differences. Aesthetic experiences, Nussbaum argues, "take people out of themselves and forge a shared community."⁵⁴ Differences become smaller, she says, when people laugh, grieve, or sing together.

Yet García-Rivera's interpretive method interrogates political liberalism's skepticism about the potential of robust particularity, including religious particularity, to be instructive when fostering just institutions that promote the societal common good. To employ the language of liberalism, the relevant insights of *The Five Points/Wrapped Around My Soul* come from the center of comprehensive doctrine(s) that are native among Denver's Black community rather than from a version of the message that is evacuated of its religious and cultural particularities. By refusing to reduce cultural and religious particularity to "civic poetry," *The Five Points/Wrapped Around My Soul* becomes a site for communal interpretation across difference—a relational, particular, and aesthetic act that cultivates solidarity between The SOURCE and Su Teatro in pursuit of shared social values: equality, participation, and justice.⁵⁵

Su Teatro and The SOURCE thus form a community of solidarity through which they bear witness to each other's stories of struggle, resistance, consolation, and empowerment. Their collaboration began on a practical level, with the sharing of theater space. In the 1970s the Black community theater companies that were the forebearers to The SOURCE offered Su Teatro space to perform its work. Su Teatro eventually bought its own theater (formerly the Denver Civic Theater) and now it houses The SOURCE.⁵⁶ While the companies have remained distinctive entities, they have come to participate in each other's stories. For example, Dee Burleson, who starred in *The Five Points/ Wrapped Around My Soul*, also starred as Juanito in Su Teatro's December 2017 production of *The Miracle on Tepeyac*. Burleson's presence in *The Miracle on Tepeyac* gave visual representation to an Afro-Latine identity that is often rendered invisible in public and artistic representations of Latine cultures. To cast Burleson as Juanito, the modern-day Juan Diego, was to subvert the mestizo paradigm that Medina critiques in his analysis of Elizondo.

The relationship between Su Teatro and The SOURCE gestures to a framework for solidarity that accounts for the role of the arts in forming communities committed to equality, mutuality, and participation. Their relationship adds flesh to concepts of solidarity that have emerged within Christian ethics and Catholic social thought. On one hand the two companies illustrate characteristics of solidarity that are prevalent in this discourse. On the other their relationship reveals the ways that treatments of solidarity that traditionally remained in the conceptual register have not been able to enact an embodied solidarity that puts these principles into practice.

The Five Points/Wrapped Around My Soul demonstrates how the aesthetic incarnates solidarity.[57] Eschewing the public reason model of political liberalism, The SOURCE makes no effort to merely translate the northeast Denver African American experience of life in the Five Points neighborhood to the Westside Chicanx community on Santa Fe Drive. It offers no verbal or written explanation of any aspect of the performance, either in the play bulletin or in front of the audience. Yet this particular narrative resonates deeply among Chicanx audience members, conjuring laughter, tears, sighs, and moans throughout the course of the evening. It isn't our neighborhood, but we can relate. After the show the cast shuffles out from backstage to mingle with the audience. Here people from different parts of the city inaugurate political conversations about the struggles of gentrification facing their neighborhoods. They begin to imagine practical solutions to their shared struggles. Under the banner of Guadalupe hung above the entrance to the Salon del Arte they discover affective bonds with people from the other side of the city. Aesthetic encounter forges a community across difference committed to a common social purpose. Performing their stories for and with each other, The SOURCE and Su Teatro inaugurate a community of the beautiful. They work together to "lift up the lowly" as part of a dynamic, polyadic relationship capable of loving difference in the pursuit of justice.

CONCLUSION

"All we need is music, sweet music."[58] When it comes to justice, society needs more than "sweet music" in order to establish a minimal level of solidarity that fosters human flourishing and the common good. It demands basic structures that defend political stability and sustain democratic participation. Reading García-Rivera's aesthetics, however, we see that the arts are also crucial to an aesthetic formation that fosters solidarity and justice in pluralistic and democratic societies. Aesthetic engagement can shape the imaginative and affective capacities necessary for cultivating a just society.

This analysis opens a window into García-Rivera's theological aesthetics, revealing the capacity of aesthetics to form communities across difference through the act of interpretation. Aesthetic engagement offers new sites for interpretation. It helps us to transcend the artificial racial, ethnic, geographic, and religious boundaries that thwart the pursuit of justice and the common good. This aesthetic encounter ignites the will to interpret a mind other than one's own, generating the energy needed to attend to particularity across difference. It foregrounds a particular narrative that gestures toward that which is held in common without reducing particularity to "civic poetry." In this way aesthetic engagement empowers us to encounter particularity in the context of the whole.

NOTES

1. Martha and the Vandellas, "Dancing in the Street," *Dance Party* album, Motown, 1964.
2. Walker, review of *The Five Points/Wrapped Around My Soul*.
3. Kennedy, "Denver Production 'Gospel at Colonus.'"
4. S. Smith, *Dancing in the Street*, 2 (emphasis in the original).
5. Kurlansky, *Ready for a Brand New Beat*, xxi.
6. Singer, "Su Teatro's New Play."
7. Araiza, *To March for Others*, 6.
8. Araiza, 6.
9. Araiza, 2.
10. Araiza, 6.
11. Hoffman, "Demonstrators Protest Ink! Coffee."
12. Hoffman, "Demonstrators Protest Ink! Coffee."
13. Phillips, "Anti-Gentrification Activists."
14. Allen, *Talking to Strangers*, 20.
15. Siller Acuña, *Para Comprender El Mensaje de María de Guadalupe*, 74.
16. González, "Who We Are," 73.
17. Goizueta, *Caminemos Con Jesús*, 50.
18. Flores, "Latina/o Families."
19. Rubio, *Family Ethics*.
20. Tjaden and Thoennes, "Extent, Nature, and Consequences."
21. Lipsky et al., "Role of Intimate Partner Violence."
22. Espín, "State of U.S. Latino/a Theology," 111.
23. González, "Who We Are," 79.
24. Pineda-Madrid, *Suffering and Salvation in Ciudad Juarez*.
25. Williams, *Sisters in the Wilderness*.
26. Gebara, *Out of the Depths*, 88.
27. Pineda-Madrid, *Suffering and Salvation in Ciudad Juarez*, 135.
28. Medina, *Mestizaje*, 121.
29. Medina, 123.
30. Medina, 124.
31. Medina, 126.
32. Medina, 126.
33. Isasi-Díaz, *La Lucha Continues*, 69.

34. Isasi-Díaz, 72.

35. Isasi-Díaz, *En La Lucha*, 129.

36. García-Rivera, *Community of the Beautiful*, 91–92.

37. García-Rivera, 92–93.

38. García-Rivera, 96.

39. García-Rivera, 79.

40. García-Rivera, 33.

41. García-Rivera, 104.

42. García-Rivera, 156.

43. García-Rivera, 137.

44. García-Rivera, 133.

45. García-Rivera, 157.

46. García-Rivera, 163.

47. Brown, *Religious Aesthetics*, 22.

48. García-Rivera, *Community of the Beautiful*, 167.

49. García-Rivera, 194–95.

50. García-Rivera, 92.

51. Goizueta, *Christ Our Companion*, 152.

52. García-Rivera, *Community of the Beautiful*, 39.

53. J. Smith, *Royce's Social Infinite*, 95.

54. Nussbaum, *Political Emotions*, 388.

55. Nussbaum, 388.

56. Kennedy, "Denver Production 'Gospel at Colonus.'"

57. Hollenbach, *Common Good and Christian Ethics*, 142.

58. Martha and the Vandellas, "Dancing in the Street."

5

The Aesthetic Dimension
of Solidarity

Plagued by apathy rooted in hopelessness, Padre Tomas resists Teresa, Kevin, and Juanito's pleas for him to defend the vulnerable church members from the injustices that ravage the community:

> TERESA: Padre Tomas, we have no place to stay and if you send me away, I may be killed. Help me!
> PADRE TOMAS: I am not a politician! [My] charge is your eternal soul.
> KEVIN: What about your soul, Padre Tomas?
> PADRE TOMAS: I have performed the seven sacraments, I am not a social activist.
> JUANITO: The people need help, Padre Tomas.
> PADRE TOMAS: Help them? Who will help me?
> (To Virgen) Please help me.[1]

Overwhelmed by their petitions, Padre Tomas cries out to Our Lady of Guadalupe. He turns his face toward Guadalupe, who stands in front of a foil backdrop encircled by Christmas lights at stage right, and pleads for her help.

Padre Tomas's conversion occurs within the context of his aesthetic encounter with Guadalupe, a relationship that unfolds over the course of the play. Guadalupe mediates this transformation, but Tomas's relationships are also mediated with the people gathered in his dilapidated and forgotten parish. Each member of the church participates in Guadalupe's story through imitation of various facets of Juan Diego's story. It is within this network of diachronic and synchronic encounters that Guadalupe and the church challenge Tomas to bear witness to the need for mercy and justice all around him. Becoming a witness to this suffering, Tomas forges a community of solidarity with his church, a relationship that calls him to pursue justice with and for them over and against the ecclesial and civic powers to which he has been obedient.

Interlacing *The Miracle at Tepeyac* with teachings about solidarity in Catholic social thought expresses the significance of aesthetic formation in the pursuit of solidarity in the life of democracy. Catholic theological ethicists have identified various dimensions of solidarity, including intellectual solidarity and practical solidarity. Even so, this ethical tradition has yet to articulate the aesthetic dimensions of solidarity that are essential to Catholic social thought and tradition. As established in chapter 4, Latine theological aesthetics provides crucial resources for specifying the aesthetics of solidarity. In this chapter I will explore accounts of intellectual and practical solidarity with a goal of outlining a constructive conception of aesthetic solidarity. I do not aim for aesthetic solidarity to supplant either intellectual solidarity or practical solidarity. Rather, I will show how these distinctive facets of solidarity can be interlaced to guide solidarity projects in the pluralistic context of twenty-first-century US democracy.

This final chapter begins with an overview of the intellectual and practical dimensions of solidarity in order to demonstrate the need for a distinctive account of aesthetic solidarity. After exposing this lacuna I will articulate a normative framework for aesthetic solidarity itself. I will begin this normative work by rejecting notions of virtual or consumptive solidarity—a false sense of community predicated on relationships of consumption and commodification rather than on equality and participation. I will then elaborate aesthetic solidarity in conversation with the political theology of Guadalupe and Juan Diego previously discussed. Finally I examine Guadalupe as a democratic symbol and argue for the potential of the aesthetic experience to forge communities of interpretation in a pluralistic society committed to the pursuit of a just solidarity.

SOLIDARITY IN CATHOLIC SOCIAL THOUGHT

"The most challenging virtue of our time may be solidarity."[2] Citing Pope Saint John Paul II, the US Conference of Catholic Bishops (USCCB) emphasizes the need for cultivating solidarity among the human family: "Loving our neighbor has global dimensions in a shrinking world. In our prayer, formation, service, and citizenship . . . we must break through the boundaries of neighborhood and nation to recognize the web of life that connects all of us in this age of globalization."[3] Indeed, the economic, political, and social dynamics of globalization have heightened the need for solidarity while simultaneously erecting new barriers to achieving it.

Identifying solidarity as a virtue situates it at the heart of a Catholic moral tradition that views formation—intellectual, moral, and aesthetic— as essential to the pursuit of the good life for individuals and communities alike. Nonetheless, as Meghan J. Clark has argued, the vague invocation of virtue obscures the true challenge of solidarity as a social practice. Greater specification of the virtue is necessary for articulating a solidarity rooted in authentic equality and meaningful participation in democratic processes by all members of society amid local, national, and global structures that systematically undermine these aims.[4] Responding to this need for additional conceptual clarity, ethicists have identified several distinctive facets of solidarity. Identifying these facets brings particular expressions of solidarity to the foreground of Catholic social thought, allowing for clearer delineation of each dimension. Disambiguating these facets allows for the systematic treatment necessary for identifying additional dimensions of solidarity in need of specification.

Intellectual Solidarity

Intellectual solidarity, as articulated by David Hollenbach, calls for discursive engagement with citizens within a pluralistic society who hold different visions of the good life, especially visions that differ from their own. Dialogue about these differences, he argues, is essential to the pursuit of a societal common good that seeks the flourishing of each particular person as well as society as a whole. At the heart of intellectual solidarity is the call to enter into dialogical relationship with those who do not share one's own conception of the good.

In a practical way this means that dialogue with those who do not share one's own religious, cultural, or philosophical presuppositions is necessary for the life of democracy. While this dialogue can include discussion of commonalities, it necessitates responding to public tensions generated by differing conceptions of the good. When pursued in the hope of cultivating solidarity, this dialogue across difference aims to cultivate justice, which Hollenbach defines as the minimal level of solidarity required for all of society's members to live with basic dignity (even as levels of solidarity beyond this basic minimum are desirable and should be pursued in public life).[5] Even if disagreements continue to exist, the pursuit of deep comprehension of another's conception of the good life, Hollenbach claims, is an act of solidarity in a pluralistic and democratic society.[6]

Intellectual solidarity is predicated on reciprocity, especially in the giving and receiving of arguments. "Reciprocity among citizens," he writes, "means that when one makes a proposal about important matters of common social life, one respects the freedom and equality of all those the proposal will affect."[7] Reciprocity assumes that an interlocutor is capable of articulating a position and listening attentively to the articulation of another position. It assumes that interlocutors are open to correction and development of their own positions. It invites the formation of a community committed to giving and receiving the best reasons for one's position. In this way intellectual solidarity is an act of reciprocity characterized by both critical and charitable dialogue.

Intellectual solidarity, Hollenbach explains, can be pursued in two distinctive modes: (1) the *conversational mode,* by which interlocutors pursue deeper understanding of their respective visions of the good life, and (2) the *argumentative mode,* by which participants present reasons in defense of their views over and against other views.[8] The conversational mode explores through dialogue each participant's vision of the good life, which can take on a more casual style. The argumentative mode, on the other hand, requires the presentation of reasons in favor of a particular position as well as making judgments about the adequacy of the reasons provided. Despite the distinction between them, both types of engagement require a deliberative democratic culture in which giving and receiving arguments and evidence are indispensable civic norms.

Rooted in traditions of deliberative democracy, intellectual solidarity is described by Hollenbach as an "orientation of mind" that is capable of regarding differences among people and traditions in a constructive way: "It is an orientation that leads one to view differences positively rather than with a mindset of suspicion and fear."[9] This orientation expects a citizen to probe challenging questions facing society without forgoing an affirmation of their opponent's fundamental human dignity. Hollenbach's articulation of intellectual solidarity demands the cultivation of intellectual, discursive, and relational habits that support the pursuit of dialogue across difference as committed to justice and the common good.

Writing in the early 2000s, Hollenbach asserts the need for a shared commitment to the norms of civility by those with divergent conceptions of the good life. Twenty years later civility has fallen on hard times among many participants in the life of US democracy. On the political right the erosion of civility is perhaps most visible in Donald Trump's election campaign and governing tactics. His campaign has worked to pack arenas awash in a sea of red hats, where civility and mercy are shunned in favor of cruelty, mockery, hatred, and even open violence toward his political opponents. In 2020, Trump's rallies continued in the midst of a global pandemic, against the urgings of public health officials and even as attendees fell ill after attending these events. At the same time the political left views calls for civility with increasing suspicion, but for a different reason. Whereas the far right has rejected civility in order to embrace hateful and exclusionary ideologies, rejection by some on the left is anchored in a critique of calls for civility that ask for toleration of the morally intolerable. In this context of social movements seeking to defend against assaults on the dignity of oppressed groups, calls for civility have been interpreted as attempts to quell the righteous anger and resistance of those seeking to call to account unjust systems and perpetrators. Civility, in conjunction with moderation, is associated with the defense of an unjust status quo that permits bona fide hate coalitions, such as White supremacists, to hold torchlit rallies that invoke lynching imagery that poses real threats to the safety and lives of their targets.

The violent riots of the Unite the Right rally in Charlottesville, Virginia, in August 2017 illustrate the problems of civility in our time. The erosion of civility was most evident in the actions of the rally's organizers and participants, all of whom employed lynching imagery and racist chants ("You will not replace us!"; "Jews will not replace us!"; "Blood and soil!") to terrorize racial, ethnic, and religious minorities in the city. Mirroring the uncivil political rhetoric of Donald Trump, these self-avowed Nazis and White nationalists openly defied the norms of civility that Hollenbach argues are essential to deliberative democracy that prioritizes the thriving of each of society's members.

While the actions of the White nationalists demonstrate the erosion of civility as an accepted norm, the response of administrators from both the city of Charlottesville and the University of Virginia demonstrate the problems of a shallow understanding and application of civility as a civic virtue. Despite participants' open and public threats and a reasonable fear of violence among minority groups in the city, Mayor Mike Signer called for civility in response to the rally. He urged the city's residents to ignore the gathering, to "not take the bait" by showing up as part of counterprotests, even as the White supremacists planned to march through the streets and openly brandished guns and other weapons.[10] The call for both the targeted groups and their community allies to ignore legitimate threats of violence—threats quickly and disastrously realized once the rally commenced—placed the lives of vulnerable populations in harm's way for the sake of a shallow notion of civility that amounts to little more than politeness.

In his response to the rally's aftermath, Donald Trump declared that there were "very fine people on both sides" of the Charlottesville conflict, implying a moral equivalence between White supremacists and the people they victimized.[11] Despite widespread criticism for this remark from liberal leaders, Trump's response is a reflection of the same empty notion of civility that was leveraged by Charlottesville's mayor during the Summer of Hate. Admonitions for this kind of civility ring hollow amid the sounds of racist chants and the wails of agony and the mangled bodies of counterprotesters bleeding and dying in the streets.

In some ways Hollenbach's conception of intellectual solidarity mirrors the insufficiency of liberal calls for civility and toleration in the face of injustice. Michael Jaycox, in his work on anger as a civic virtue, argues for the need for intellectual solidarity that can reckon with the necessity of social conflict—and even righteous anger—in the pursuit of solidarity. Jaycox argues for the necessity of *conflictual solidarity* that is capable of identifying and responding to injustice in an explicit manner: "It is necessary to adopt this specifically conflictual sense of solidarity because any social struggle must be able to negotiate the tensions involved in building political coalitions across the boundaries of oppressed and oppressor groups."[12] This kind of solidarity is essential for uncovering systematic injustices and not explaining them away as matters of political difference, but instead allowing for deconstruction of power structures that inhibit the cultivation of solidarity oriented toward justice. Offering a conception of conflictual solidarity as a corrective to this limitation of intellectual solidarity, Jaycox's conception foregrounds the argumentative dimensions of intellectual solidarity while also pushing for more explicit acknowledgment of concrete historical injustices in a way that goes beyond the abstract political liberal approach (discussed in chapter 2) that influences Hollenbach and other Catholic social ethicists.

Despite the shortcomings of civility discourse in our times, however, it remains a necessary virtue for the pursuit of solidarity in the twenty-first century. In the summer prior to the 2016 US presidential election, James F. Keenan identified civility—along with toleration, humility, justice, mercy, and solidarity—as a virtue for civil discourse.[13] Keenan offers a conception of civility that does not require the forgoing of justice claims for the sake of social mores. "Civility is not fundamentally about politeness but about proportionality," he writes. "It is not a virtue with fixity in its rules but rather about measured-ness in engagement."[14] That civility is not a private assessment of politeness or social acceptability allows Keenan to situate acts of protest within this virtue: "Protest in a variety of forms has had a legitimate expression in civil societies, even protest that was illegal, especially in societies where laws were known more for the censure of societies rather than for the promotion of the common good."[15] Keenan's specification of civility as a civic virtue allows for its effective retrieval in Catholic social thought. There is no place for civility as the mere performance of politeness nor as acquiescence to racially codified standards of public behavior. However, when specified via proportionality, the virtue of civility can justify—and even demand—anger and protest from those who pursue a vision of justice that prioritizes the flourishing of every member of society.

Further, the virtue of civility ought to be interpreted alongside the preferential option for the poor and the young, emanating from Latin American liberation theology, that insists on heeding the experiences, voices, perspectives, and arguments of the most vulnerable members of society. The norms of courtesy and respect commonly associated with civility should be directed toward the vulnerable, acknowledging and honoring dignity by attending to visions of the good life among "the least of these" (Mt 25:40 NRSV). Taken together, the virtue of civility and the preferential option for the poor leads to a rejection of the abuse of civility language as a codification of norms of White politeness. Civility as civic virtue requires solidarity with vulnerable communities and close and careful attendance to experiences of exploitation, marginalization, powerlessness, cultural imperialism, and violence. Reflecting on widespread skepticism of popular religious symbols such as Our Lady of Guadalupe in many sectors of US society (including the Church, the academy, and political life), Roberto Goizueta asks, "Can we truly be in solidarity with the poor while simultaneously deprecating or even rejecting their most basic assumptions about their own lives?"[16] Civility inflected by the preferential option requires acts of intellectual solidarity that take seriously the visions of the good life that are articulated by the vulnerable; engaging them is essential to any viable account of solidarity in the twenty-first century. Indeed, the preferential option for the poor and young is necessary for achieving the conditions of mutuality, equality, and participation that Clark outlines for solidarity. Goizueta's question thus gestures to the enduring significance of intellectual solidarity, albeit as it regards the minds of those most vulnerable in US society as partners in both conversation and argument.

Intellectual solidarity's prescription of dialogue among people who hold divergent views of the good life resonates with the community of interpretation articulated by Alejandro García-Rivera (see chapter 4). García-Rivera's pragmatic conception of interpretation underscores the relational character of intellectual solidarity: "Loyalty concerns *the will to interpret a mind other than one's own to another mind*. Such interpreting results in community, i.e., a community of interpretation."[17] If, as Hollenbach suggests, intellectual solidarity necessitates a mental orientation that views difference positively and seeks meaningful engagement with these differences toward generating and sustaining a truly democratic society, then García-Rivera reminds us that this orientation necessitates an act of the will by which one commits to rigorous intellectual practice. The will is crucial to ordering one's desires toward intellectual solidarity and the community of interpretation. Aesthetic experience, then, serves to orient the will toward this task by cultivating affection for the good resulting from deliberative democratic practices.

Moreover, the centrality of justice in this tradition of intellectual solidarity helps us to specify García-Rivera's understanding of the unifying aspects of aesthetics. García-Rivera elucidates the relational and aesthetic aspects of the act of interpretation, even if he does not offer a systematic ethical account of justice that undergirds aesthetic experience as a catalyst of just solidarity. Hollenbach's conception of justice demonstrates the potential for aesthetic encounters to create the conditions necessary for dialogical engagement about the societal common good. This potential is evident in the aesthetic examples employed herein: Guadalupe's symbol can foster dialogue—both conversational and argumentative—about the political, economic, and social institutions that form society's basic structures. Aesthetic practices and encounters can ignite conversation about justice for an entire society, and the resulting dialogical moments can help foster justice in society's basic structures. Dialogue preserves both minimal political coherence and participation in democratic society. In this way Hollenbach's definition of justice predicated on solidarity lays the foundation for aesthetic experience to be directed toward building a just solidarity and the common good.

Further, interpreting intellectual solidarity through the aesthetic lenses of Latine theological aesthetics helps foreground the aesthetic concerns implied in Hollenbach's work on the common good. These aesthetic inclinations emerge in Hollenbach's 2017 presidential address to the Catholic Theological Society of America in which he reflects on the common good in its relationship to the global rise of ethnonationalist movements that threaten to undermine solidarity. In response to the global prevalence of these movements, he asserts the need for an ethics of solidarity that renders the glory of God visible in history. Specifically he grapples with God's glory as revealed in the Cross and Resurrection, where Jesus Christ embodies solidarity with the human race and all of creation: "The unity of the community of faith is a sacrament of the divinizing union in which Christians come to share the glory of God's own life. This solidarity will make the glory of the kingdom incipiently visible in history."[18] This solidarity, of course, remains incomplete on this side of the *parousia*. Nonetheless, the revelation of the glory of God continues to unfold in history, expanding to acknowledge ever more fully God's glory as a source of solidarity.

Beyond solidarity among humans, Hollenbach avers, the glory of God reveals the necessity of solidarity between human creatures and the entire created order: "Christians are called to continue responding to God's grace in ways that advance the greater glory of God by promoting deeper human solidarity and greater integrity of creation. In this way, the fuller presence of God's reign, the greater glory of God, and the more complete common good of the human community and the earth will arise together."[19] This aesthetic development in Hollenbach's thought indicates intellectual solidarity's amenability to more fully incorporating material, embodied, and sensory aspects of both knowledge and relationship.

Invoking the glory of God as the basis of an ethics of solidarity in our turbulent world represents a crucial development in Hollenbach's thinking about the common good. He does not forgo the place of intellect, dialogue, or democratic deliberation in cultivating a good that is truly common; neither should we. Even so, he gestures to how God's revelation of Godself in history—and our embodied discernment of that revelation—directs our attention toward a more robust understanding of solidarity. In so doing he situates the imagination in the work of intellectual solidarity and allows us to bring into view our relationships with the created order and our attendant responsibilities. *Ad maiorem Dei gloriam.*

Practical Solidarity

Intellectual solidarity elucidates a vital facet of solidarity but it does not exhaust the meaning and significance of this concept. This section explores the practical dimension of solidarity that calls forth concrete actions toward the formation of communities that are characterized by mutuality, equality, and participation. Along with intellectual solidarity, this description makes way for specifying the aesthetic dimension of solidarity that emphasizes affective development by encouraging intellectual and practical pursuits of a community of solidarity.

Practical solidarity emphasizes the significance of actions within particular contexts in fostering a community committed to authentic solidarity. Efforts to outline the practical dimensions of solidarity benefit from reflection on the prominence of practical reason in contemporary Catholic moral theology. This emphasis develops via reflection on the role of practical reasoning as expressed by Thomas Aquinas in his *quaestiones* concerning natural law.

When identifying the first principle of natural law—that "good is to be pursued, and evil is to be avoided"—Aquinas asserts that truth and rectitude are the same for all people at all places and times.[20] Nevertheless, he distinguishes speculative reasoning from practical reasoning, where the former is concerned with universal principles while the latter is "busied with contingent matters."[21] This distinction matters for how moral reasoning influences human actions in particular contexts. Revisiting Aquinas's reflection on the matter helps to allay the incredulity of anyone who associates the natural law tradition with the assertion of universal truths only:

> As to the proper conclusions of the speculative reason, the truth is the same for all, but is not equally known to all: thus it is true for all that the three angles of a triangle are together equal to two right angles, although it is not known to all. *But as to the proper conclusions of the practical reason, neither is the truth or rectitude the same for all, nor, where it is the same, is it equally known by all.*[22]

In accord with Aquinas's reflection on natural law, Catholic moral theologians in the twenty-first century continue to emphasize the necessity of objective moral standards, especially as a bulwark against the grave injustices that threaten human life and flourishing: sexual abuse, human trafficking, and ecological degradation, for example. At the same time, many insist on attention to context in moral reasoning. Lisa Sowle Cahill, in affirming the necessity of universal (or transversal) truth claims in order to steer clear of relativistic morality that lacks the basis for affirmation of fundamental human rights, explains the contextual character of practical reasoning: "Knowledge of the natural law is always perspectival and partial, even when it is also true and accurate. Knowledge is never detached from the particular contexts, identities, and interests of knowing subjects."[23] Attention to context is a requirement for adequate moral reasoning. This has influenced Cahill's emphasis on attention to practices in Christian ethics, including in sexual ethics, family ethics, bioethics, and the ethics of global justice.

Practical reason has been crucial to the articulation of the broad practical dimension of solidarity in Catholic social thought. Ada María Isasi-Díaz emphasizes the place of lo cotidiano, the everyday, in moral discernment. Interpreted by the preferential option for the poor, attention to lo cotidiano highlights grassroots reflection on daily experiences by Latinas in their pursuit of liberation. Conceptually, lo cotidiano underscores a relationship between material reality and spirituality in a manner that does not capitulate to dualism or reduce materiality and spirituality to each other. From this angle she associates the practical actions taken in the context of history with the pursuit of spiritual transcendence through communion with the people of God.

Isasi-Díaz uses protest as an aperture for studying the relationship between spirituality and practice: "My own relationship with the divine finds expression walking picket lines more than in kneeling; in seeking ways to be

involved with the work of reconciliation more than in fasting and mortify-
ing the flesh; in striving to be passionately involved with other more than in
seeking to be attached from human love."[24] Walking the picket line in solidarity with her *compañeras en la lucha,* Isasi-Díaz highlights an indispensable
practical requirement of cultivating relationships characterized by equality,
mutuality, and participation: showing up.

In the months before the devastating events of August 11 and 12, 2017,
Charlottesville's local activists called on antiracist allies, including religious
activists, to join them in their counterprotest against the Unite the Right rally.
Some national religious leaders showed up, including Lisa Sharon Harper,
Cornel West, and Brian McLaren. But many others did not answer the fervent
calls for solidarity in the face of the White supremacy rising from the hills of
Charlottesville. A vivid tapestry of antiracist counterprotesters did respond
to the call to converge on Charlottesville, but both local and national religious
leadership was largely missing from the streets on August 12. While a small
number of lay Catholics participated in counterprotests, no Catholic clergy
linked arms with their fellow religious leaders that day. The lack of religious
antiracist counterprotesters on the ground made it more difficult to execute
the disciplined and strategic plan of nonviolent resistance being led by the
religious organizers of Congregate Cville.[25]

In the wake of the violence, local activists emphasized the necessity of
incarnational solidarity, or physically "showing up" in the struggle against
White supremacy.[26] Larycia Hawkins has called this *embodied* solidarity, which
underscores the need to specify the material and embodied aspects of practical
solidarity. "Embodied solidarity costs," she says. "But embodied solidarity is
worth that cost."[27] A solidarity of lo cotidiano calls for embodied presence in
community that opens us to the vulnerability of those who suffer. Of course
it is impossible to be physically present to all those who suffer. But the virtue of
solidarity calls for a practice of embodied presence to a suffering community
as formative habituation for the pursuit of solidarity on a global scale.

While lo cotidiano as a locus for moral reflection allows for greater
emphasis on practical reason, Isasi-Díaz cautions against simplifying the concept. Lo cotidiano, she contends, calls for a critique of the practices and habits in which we engage in everyday life:

> By *lo cotidiano* we do not refer to the a-critical production or repe-
> tition of all that we have been taught or to which we have become
> habituated. On the contrary, we understand by *lo cotidiano* that which
> is reproduced or repeated consciously by the majority of people in the
> world as part of their struggles for survival and liberation. This is why

this conscientized cotidiano carries with it subversive elements that can help us to question the reality in which we live.[28]

While John Rawls's liberalism veils its philosophical and political reflection from experience and history, Isasi-Díaz's call for a *conscientized cotidiano* insists on a reflection on history, culture, and experience that is both concrete and critical. This reflection on context employs practical reason toward comprehension of the social structures that cause and perpetuate injustice. It also highlights the necessity of attending to the place of our everyday practices in pursuing a just solidarity.

Isasi-Díaz's articulation of lo cotidiano is reflected in Catholic moral theology more broadly, especially concerning the social significance of local everyday practices. For example, Julie Hanlon Rubio describes the relationship between personal and social virtue, arguing that personal and familial practices—sexual intimacy, eating, tithing, church and community service—have broader implications that influence social goods.[29] She argues that local communities are an essential site for cultivating social solidarity, especially among groups that might be placed in opposition to one another within the broader US political landscape. In one example Rubio examines the potential for local everyday practices to respond to the needs of pregnant women within the broader political quagmire of abortion politics. She lifts up the work of local people and organizations developing practical strategies to support pregnant women, arguing that such local organizational work is crucial for developing a culture of life that "cooperates with the good."[30] Such actions show the potential of local people to negotiate the United States' hardened political dichotomy on abortion and demonstrate the generative potential of practical solidarity when attempting to forge communities of equality, mutuality, and participation across political, cultural, and religious differences.[31]

Addressing the possibility of cultivating solidarity on a global scale, Meghan J. Clark argues that solidarity necessitates habituation through the practice of human rights and a fostering of communities that are characterized by mutuality, equality, and participation. Criticizing alternative spring break and other short-term mission programs, Clark stresses that not all practical actions lead to solidarity: "Solidarity . . . requires genuine mutuality and reciprocity in the relationship. I can come in and help you, but if the relationship is not one of mutual participation, then it will not be one of solidarity."[32] The practical work of solidarity requires relationship that pursues equality. To illustrate her point she highlights the work of the Sudan National Helping Babies Breathe Initiative (HBB). Midwives and health officials work cross-culturally to support the development of best practices for reducing infant mortality. Rather than merely imparting practices on the Sudanese midwives, however, HBB relies on the exchange of knowledge among the initiative's participants, especially concerning best practices for care specific to various Sudanese contexts.[33]

The works of Cahill, Isasi-Díaz, Rubio, and Clark emphasize various dimensions of personal and social practices in the pursuit of social solidarity. The emphasis on practices poses a crucial question for this study: What is the role of *the aesthetic* in the practice of solidarity? This question brings to mind John Dewey's distinction between *art* as a process of making and the *aesthetic* as the experiential dimension of appreciating, perceiving, or enjoying what is created.[34] Drawing on his distinction, Maureen H. O'Connell elucidates the role of both the making and the beholding of art in the work of solidarity. Mural Arts Philadelphia, founded in 1984, draws community members together to create murals to adorn walls in neighborhoods victimized by White flight and urban industrialization. Professional muralists serve as the catalysts for the communal process of designing and painting the murals. Without regard to age, race, ethnicity, or religious affiliation, communities work together to create each mural. Most notably, however, the project leaders are able to involve incarcerated people as well as those who have been victimized through various forms of violence. In this way, O'Connell argues, Philadelphians cultivate solidarity through the communal praxis of creating murals: "Therefore, community murals illuminate the relationship between aesthetics and ethics through praxis; beauty and the good are no longer abstract concepts but rather lived practices that support justice and living in right relationship with others."[35] The community embodies justice as the restoration of right relationship as it seeks reconciliation through common practical action.

O'Connell's analysis of Mural Arts Philadelphia demonstrates the possibility of building communities of solidarity through what she calls the "Code of Creativity" in which engagement with the arts helps our society move beyond social impasses that maintain de facto segregation in urban contexts.[36] Beyond the practical act of working together on a common project, however, O'Connell suggests that *aesthetic engagement with the murals themselves* is crucial to cultivating solidarity. She describes the *aesthetic experience of beholding* the murals painted by members of the community: "Standing before these concrete canvases where meaningful social change has happened, where justice has been created and tacitly experienced, all citizens feel what Hollenbach names as 'sense of confidence, hope, energy and magnanimity'—states of the heart that can sustain them in the risky work of engaging impasse and knitting back together communities ripped apart by structural violence and poverty."[37] O'Connell's comment highlights an important distinction between practical solidarity and aesthetic solidarity. Practical solidarity is predicated on shared work, which is necessary and vital to building solidarity. Nonetheless, aesthetic experience itself—whether in the act of creation or in the act of perception—is essential to moral formation of people and communities for the work of justice and solidarity.

O'Connell thus magnifies the *aesthetic*—the beholding of art—as a distinct dimension of solidarity. Building on intellectual solidarity, O'Connell argues that aesthetic solidarity is necessary for effective engagement of differences within a pluralistic society, including religious differences. Aesthetic solidarity, she explains, is the "imaginative and nonverbal relationality that arises from collective commitments to perceive and cultivate the beauty of persons, communities, and the environment."[38] Attending to the imaginative aspects of human relationality, O'Connell defines aesthetic solidarity as "a series of generative practices through which people of different religious traditions and socioeconomic enclaves learn how to imagine together, to create together, and to build the kind of communities, city, and nation in which they want to live."[39] This definition of aesthetic solidarity allows O'Connell to articulate an aesthetics of the common good that helps us to perceive the value of human flourishing for all members of society but especially for those who are most vulnerable and marginalized. Resonant with Hollenbach's conception of justice as the minimal level of solidarity required for promoting human flourishing, O'Connell's common good aesthetics underscore the necessity of both justice and solidarity in cultivating an authentic common good that aims to promote the thriving of all people. "Creating common beauty," she writes, "becomes a way to identify the basic minimum conditions of life in community and to meet them in organic and relational ways."[40]

While O'Connell's analysis builds on articulations of both intellectual and practical solidarity, she directs our attention to the need for elaboration of the aesthetic dimensions of solidarity in Catholic social thought and, more broadly, in Christian social ethics. Building on O'Connell's call for attention to the aesthetic, it is necessary to further specify aesthetic solidarity by exploring its capacity to foster justice and an authentic common good in a pluralistic society. But first it is crucial to comment on the manipulation of aesthetic experience to form communities that are not committed to justice.

CONSUMPTIVE SOLIDARITY

If aesthetic solidarity is to become a viable framework for promoting human flourishing and the common good, then it is necessary to distinguish it from negative forms of aesthetic solidarity—images, narratives, and symbols that foster community but either fail to promote justice or seek to promote injustice. I have already identified one example of this type of negative solidarity: the Unite the Right rally in Charlottesville. The rally organizers and its participants, who represented a diverse range of White supremacist groups, employed signs and symbols associated with racial and religious violence to construct a community united by racial hatred. This White supremacist coalition employed an aesthetic experience to unite themselves in their inhumane pursuits. Their vicious tactics and goals are a stark illustration of the ramifications of aesthetic solidarity unhinged from a conception of justice to pursue a common good that is characterized by flourishing of all members of society and promotes equality, mutuality, and participation.

Beyond this blatant example of a community united around a hateful cause, aesthetic experience can function in a more insidious manner when forging a false sense of solidarity that mistakes the act of consumption with solidarity. In consumptive solidarity, communities form around consumer activities flavored by the practices of global capitalism rather than by the robust social solidarity necessary for sustaining a stable and participatory democratic life. Consumptive solidarity, akin to what Vincent Miller calls virtual solidarity, substitutes the ingestion of images, so to speak, for the kind of engagement that forms among communities of solidarity characterized by mutuality, equality, and participation.[41]

While current visual media have revolutionized how contemporary people encounter images, the changes they wrought have not necessarily been positive. One can become inured to the parade of suffering faces and mangled bodies displayed on the unending newsfeed. Facebook and Twitter feeds are inundated with images of human suffering and political advocacy that still fail to ignite moral conscience. Communities do form around the appreciation and interpretation of images, as García-Rivera suggests, but not necessarily around images that foster justice. The sheer volume of evocative images presents a new ethical issue: Can we truly encounter human suffering through images? Encounters with images shape society in powerful ways, but ethical principles for encountering images in this context are underdeveloped.

Laurie Cassidy demonstrates how images fail to foster a solidarity characterized by mutuality, equality, and participation. Her work engages tricky issues of power and agency involved with the project of illustrating suffering. For example, there are many instances of the commodification of suffering in photographs depicting human suffering. She employs for her case study Kevin Carter's 1993 Pulitzer Prize–winning photo of a Sudanese child crawling to a feeding station. The naked child is bowed over in weakness and incapable of moving. A vulture is perched nearby. There are no family or community members in the frame to imply that the child is protected or loved. While the photograph piqued public interest in the famine, Cassidy argues that the image did not promote solidarity. The image altered the child's suffering into a commodity, an object to be consumed. This commodification is characterized by the objectification of the one who suffers.[42] Though such photographs can invoke strong emotions of pity, they do not necessarily also contribute to a true sense of solidarity with the one who suffers or beckon others' participation in the work of restoring the sufferer's agency. Depictions of suffering risk further objectification of those who suffer without affirming or supporting their agency. These portrayals often fail to comprehend and communicate ethical issues at stake or suggest a viable ethical response.[43]

Cassidy's analysis points to a more insidious ethical problem: the substitution of acts of consumption for acts of solidarity. Resonant with Cassidy's critique, Miller illustrates the risks of commodification latent in the consumption of contemporary media. He describes the use of Black spirituals in popular music without compensation (or even without attribution) as a prime example of virtual solidarity, specifically Moby's sampling of Vera Hall's rendition of "Trouble So Hard" in his own song "Natural Blues."[44] Beyond the racial and cultural issues implicated in appropriative practices in the arts, Miller identifies the falsification of communities of solidarity as another issue associated with this act. Assuming, for the sake of argument, the best intentions of musicians and producers (that they intend to demonstrate solidarity with the struggles of Black people) and the best intentions of listeners (that they desire to be in solidarity with the political struggles of Black people), Miller argues that this act is, nonetheless, fundamentally one of consumption: "Such 'virtual' solidarity is hamstrung by the abstraction inherent in commodification. Moby's song tears Hall's music from the cultural matrix that produced it, reducing its laments to floating symbols of intensity, religiosity, and authenticity. At best, such music provides catharsis of the political sentiments of the audience; at worst, its abstraction reinforces the listeners' unreflective distance from similar injustices in their own lives."[45] Miller's criticism adds searing cogency to the arguments against appropriation of cultural and religious symbols; these consumer-driven acts erode solidarity characterized by mutuality, equality, and participation. "Whatever sentiments of solidarity we may attach to it," Miller writes, "the underlying act is consumption."[46]

Abstracted, disembodied, and disconnected from the realities of human suffering, virtual solidarity fails to foster concrete political solidarity. Virtual solidarity thus takes on the character of consumption, hindering its capacity to critique—and overcome—the pitfalls of consumer practices that erode mutuality, equality, and participation. Cheap and pliable, consumption is the kind of solidarity that trades in Facebook likes and Twitter shares rather than the kinds of exchanges that build relationships and affirm mutual personhood.[47]

Of course, one could argue that the consumption of images via social media can and does have positive effects. Social media is often at the heart of today's social movements, from the Coalition of Immokalee Workers to the Arab Spring to Black Lives Matter. Torrents of videos, images, and words across distance, culture, and context can sweep people up, however unsuspecting, into a common cause. On Memorial Day 2020, as people in the United States and around the world sat restless from quarantine and devastated from constant news of ever-climbing news of deaths from COVID-19, a video emerged of George Floyd being choked to death under the knee of Minneapolis police officer Derek Chauvin. The video quickly went viral, showing Floyd pleading for his mama as he gasped the final breaths of his life. Floyd was one more in a succession of Black people lynched by agents of the basic structure that alleges to serve and protect them. But it was also a spark in a tinderbox, a death that sent people around the world into the streets. Once a pariah of mainstream politics on both the left and right, #BlackLivesMatter quickly surged to the forefront of national and global political consciousness. From Minneapolis to Miami, from Denver to Mexico City, a deluge of masked protesters rolled into the streets like an ever-flowing stream. Local organizers used social media to coordinate enormous marches in the midst of the largest worldwide pandemic in more than a century. Corporate media homed in on looters and rioting, even as the "little stories" proved more compelling and powerful to those with ears to hear. Students organized rallies in cities and college towns around the country. Quarantined children drew Black Lives Matter signs to place in their windows. Small events cropped up in suburbs and small rural towns. While driving down a country road toward my home in Virginia I saw a handcrafted wooden sign nestled in the green foliage: Black Lives Matter.

Some have proclaimed that George Floyd's death will be a tipping point, one that changes race relations in the United States forever (presumably for the better). Writing just two months later, it is difficult for me to say whether these prognostications will come true. What can be said is that social media has also been responsible for concrete harm in the pursuit of justice for George Floyd and other Black people who have been killed by police. For example, many people of goodwill participated in the social media protest "Black Out Tuesday," which asked supporters to replace their social media profile pictures with black squares and the hashtag #blacklivesmatter while otherwise remaining silent. Presumably the goal of this action was to amplify the voices of Black organizers on social media. But the action saturated social media with blacked out profile pictures and diluted information being shared by Black Lives Matter activists. This misstep highlighted the necessity of social media practices that boost the voices of community organizers on the ground as opposed to campaigns of virtual solidarity that dilute these concrete efforts.

More pernicious than a bungled attempt at virtual solidarity, perhaps, is the constant stream of social media images showing the lynchings and gruesome deaths of Black people. These images reinforce social media patterns of White voyeurism and Black trauma. Like Carter's photo of the starving child, viral social media videos of Black murder are played and replayed out of context. They objectify the lynched Black body, making it yet another object for consumption by the White gaze. Social media affords many opportunities for transmission of information in our complex and globalized world, but these opportunities are not self-evidently good nor do they outweigh the major challenges of consumptive solidarity in our digital age.

The problems of consumptive solidarity are also evident in the consumption of Our Lady of Guadalupe in global capitalist culture. Guadalupe's image is often marshaled in support of capital-driven ends, like the selling of t-shirts, bags, and posters. These ends are usually pursued without regard for the interests of Guadalupanos—for whom Guadalupe is a significant religious, cultural, and political symbol—or the workers who produce these goods. Her image can easily be appropriated in a manner that perpetuates further marginalization of these overlapping communities.

Consumptive solidarity presents a considerable challenge to the project of aesthetic solidarity. But the danger of misuse does not render aesthetic experience useless for the work of solidarity.[48] Despite prominent traditions of iconoclasm within Christianity, a Catholic theological perspective that emphasizes the significance of both sacramental and embodied experience suggests that engagement with images, symbols, narratives, and other media ought not be dismissed in the elaboration of a Catholic social ethic of solidarity.[49]

As Pope Francis argues in *Lumen fidei,* seeing and other forms of aesthetic engagement are central to the life of Christian faith. Christian faith thus demands an outward gaze directed toward Christ: "In faith, Christ is not simply the one in whom we believe, the supreme manifestation of God's love; he is also the one with whom we are united precisely in order to believe. Faith does not merely gaze at Jesus, *but sees things as Jesus himself sees them, with his own eyes: it is a participation in his way of seeing.*"[50] Faith brings one's sight into union with Jesus' way of seeing. What happens to a Christian when she sees with Jesus? Pope Francis proclaims, "Faith's new way of seeing things is centered on Christ. Faith in Christ brings salvation because in him our lives become radically open to a love that precedes us, a love that transforms us from within, acting in us and through us."[51] In other words, faith demands solidarity and conversion. He builds on this point in his commentary on the parable of the good Samaritan in *Fratelli Tutti*: "If we extend our gaze to the history of our own lives and that of the entire world, all of us are, or have been, like each of the characters in the parable."[52] Extending the gaze of faith allows us to recognize power and vulnerability—both of ourselves and of others—as a basis for solidarity. From the perspective of Christian theology, then, aesthetic engagement should not be rejected merely on account of its abuses; it ought to be framed in terms of its capacity to change minds and hearts toward a just solidarity. This is aesthetic solidarity's objective.

AESTHETIC SOLIDARITY

Consumptive solidarity promotes relationships based on consumer habits rather than on a just solidarity. It attempts to evacuate human dignity through objectification. This consumption-driven-interaction does nothing to upset power imbalances that hinder equality and participation in the global economy; rectifying these imbalances is essential for addressing the sources of structural injustice today. Aesthetic solidarity—when understood as an imaginative and affective basis for relationships that are characterized by mutuality, equality, and participation necessary for fostering the common good—draws on aesthetic experience to help cultivate a just solidarity predicated on fundamental human dignity.

Aesthetic solidarity stands apart from the objectifying tendencies of consumptive solidarity by asserting that aesthetic experience can promote communal encounters that affirm human dignity both within communities and across broader society. Accordingly, aesthetic solidarity contains three integral components. First, it concerns the formation of a community through aesthetic engagement or encounter with a medium in a way that its perceptible form is crucial to the formation of imagination and affections. As this study has established, however, communities can unite around signs that promote justice or injustice. Therefore, second, in order for aesthetic solidarity to promote justice, the community united through aesthetic experience ought to be characterized by relationships of mutuality, equality, and participation that foster human dignity. Third, as one of its projects this community ought to seek a fostering of justice as the minimal level of solidarity required for human flourishing and the common good. Aesthetic solidarity thus defined operates on both the interpersonal and the social levels to promote justice.

The narrative of Juan Diego's encounter with Guadalupe illustrates all three components of this framework. As illustrated in chapter 1, aesthetic experience is central to interpreting the political dimensions of the relationship between Guadalupe and Juan Diego. Juan Diego's encounter with Guadalupe is imbued with flowers and song (*in xochi in cuicatl,*): the sound of birds singing, the fragrance of fresh roses, and the sight of Guadalupe's bright image. Guadalupe engages Juan Diego's senses in a way that conjure divine awareness and influence both his imagination and his emotions without forgoing her appeal to his intellect or respect for his autonomy or relational obligations. Juan Diego's aesthetic experience of Guadalupe creates the conditions necessary for a relationship of solidarity; this encounter signals to the power of aesthetics in imaginative and affective formation emphasized throughout this study.

Aesthetic experience also is the source of Juan Diego's realization of his full humanity. This realization enables Juan Diego and Guadalupe to enter into a relationship characterized by mutuality, equality, and participation. When Juan Diego first approaches Guadalupe, he views himself as one of the lowest members of society. His language and behavior indicate his lowly social position. Yet this aesthetic encounter with Guadalupe serves as a turning point in his self-understanding as a dignified human being. As discussed in chapter 1, Goizueta's analysis reveals the significance of flower and song in Juan Diego's encounter with Guadalupe: the aesthetic experience does not pacify him or reduce his vision to one of pacification. Instead, Juan Diego comes to understand his inherent dignity, that he is worthy of both self-respect and social respect. Resisting notions of passive reception that plague consumptive practices masquerading as solidarity, Goizueta asserts the intersubjective character of this encounter: "A community is defined by such intersubjective relationships. A byproduct of authentic community is, thus, the birth and development of free and unique human persons."[53] Authentic intersubjective community is thus a requirement of solidarity that affirm the dignity of human persons. This kind of relationship, promoted by aesthetic engagement, is central to justice.

Aesthetic solidarity also is directed toward the pursuit of justice that is an essential condition for an authentic common good. This element of the framework is illustrated in Juan Diego's interaction with colonial ecclesial authorities. Although his initial interactions with Bishop Zumárraga reinforce his lowly societal status, the falsehood of ecclesial superiority within the Church becomes evident through the humanizing and empowering aesthetic encounter that Juan Diego has with Guadalupe. This event sends a prophetic message to the colonial authorities: Juan Diego and the Indigenous members of society are not mere subjects to be ruled; they are fully human and worthy of respect. Despite Zumárraga's dramatic conversion, we know that the claim of full humanity of Indigenous subjects is continually rejected and resisted by social, economic, and political structures and actors in colonial society and to this very day. It is incorrect, then, to interpret this narrative as a historical account of the gradual enlightenment and conversion of the forces of empire and coloniza-tion. Nevertheless, Juan Diego's aesthetic experience is directed toward a larger social, political, and economic project: the full acknowledgment of Indigenous humanity and the pursuit of structures that assert and reassert this humanity. Practices such as Indigenous land acknowledgments by people, communities, and institutions that occupy such lands is a crucial, if still drastically insufficient, moment in the pursuit of justice and reconciliation.

Despite critiques of the insufficiency of the "aesthetic turn" in Latine theology to acknowledge and respond to issues of justice and ethics, I argue that Latine aesthetics resist the dynamics of consumptive ideology masquer-ading as solidarity. Starting from the perspective of Latine popular religious practices, Goizueta argues that solidarity with marginalized Latine people requires taking seriously the religious milieu from which their critiques of injustice arise.[54] He advocates for engagement in acts of concrete solidarity with the poor but also insists on the need for serious engagement with the religious and theological worldview that shapes the beliefs and experiences of poor people. This means attending to both the material situations that perpetuate marginalization and injustice as well as the narratives, songs, and other forms of expression emanating from these communities as a means of informing intellectual and practical solidarity. García-Rivera, with his atten-tion to the transcendentals, draws our attention to the place of beauty in the pursuit of truth and goodness. The community of the beautiful does not exist merely for its own sake. Beauty is engaged in an intricate dance with truth and goodness; it seeks to move the human heart via recognition and affirmation of the holy. Such witness has been essential throughout created history and seems especially essential today in light of the increasingly common use of the aesthetics of injustice (e.g., imagery of lynching and genocide to assert the supremacy of Whiteness) to undermine inherent human dignity.

The aesthetic turn in Latine theology warrants continued critical attention. Yet, read in the context of contemporary activism among Latine communities, the attention to the position of aesthetic experience in these movements must not be sacrificed in the pursuit of conceptual clarity. The next section explores how Latine art and activism cultivate solidarity in our times.

FLOR Y CANTO

In *The Miracle at Tepeyac* each character mirrors a particular dimension of Juan Diego's story. Juanito mirrors his lowly status in society. Teresa mirrors his profound vulnerability. Padre Tomas mirrors his longing for rescue and mercy. Kevin, a character situated as an outcast for his sexual identity and illness in the play, mirrors Juan Diego's recognition of beauty: "Roses are special. I like to plant them, care for them, watch them grow. This one is Spanish. I'm not sure what kind. Here, Juanito, why don't you put it on the altar someplace."[55] Enticed by the rose growing outside of the rectory, Kevin has an aesthetic experience of beauty in the midst of the deterioration of his health that eventually leads to his death. An outcast in both the church and society, Kevin's recognition of the rose expresses Guadalupe's care for the lowly, especially those despised by the institutions that are supposed to acknowledge their dignity and defend their lives.

Drawing our attention to *flor y canto*, Kevin directs our discourse on solidarity toward God's glory as manifest in the "new church." In so doing Kevin helps us recognize the necessity of aesthetic formation in the pursuit of social solidarity. At Kevin's prompting, I now bring to the foreground examples of how Latine communities have looked to Guadalupe's image to inspire their work for justice.

In New York City, Guadalupanos show how their devotion to Guadalupe inspires their work for immigration justice. Their aesthetic practices—from daily devotions to feast day processions to the international Guadalupe torch run—show their community as simultaneously prayerful and political in nature. These practices contribute to a realization of dignity among the devotees, a somebodiness that empowers them to advocate for justice in public life even though such advocacy comes with extreme risks in the current anti-immigrant climate of the United States. It is this realization that undergirds their view of themselves as worthy of respect and thus worthy of rights.[56] Solidarity anchored in aesthetic experience of Guadalupan devotion sends the community out in pursuit of justice in perhaps society's most basic structure—how it defines citizenship. At the same time, their aesthetic experience has helped them imagine a citizenship much more capacious than merely legal or juridical belonging. Alyshia Gálvez explains:

> A community is formed which demands rights for the collective, even while politicians' promises, activist coalitions, and public sympathy may be fickle and fleeting. Rather than ceding to the state all of the power to define those within its borders and waiting for an amnesty

to declare them citizens, residents, or some enfranchised status, these activists claim a different kind of citizenship for themselves and posit it as the prerequisite to the struggle for a juridical acknowledgment of their rights.[57]

Remarkably, Gálvez describes the Guadalupanos as political realists with an acute sense of the erratic nature of political will and political emotions. Nonetheless, the aesthetic formation of their practices supports their work, anchoring it in liturgies that sustain their collective energy for rights advocacy.

On Denver's Westside, Su Teatro and The SOURCE show us Guadalupe's potential to foster a community of solidarity in the context of racial difference and marginalization. The companies come together to express their stories of oppression and survival in each other's company, fostering relationships across racial, cultural, and religious differences with those who share many of their experiences. These relationships create opportunities for them to participate in each other's stories as well. Beyond their artistic relationship, however, these companies create a structure of solidarity that flourishes without relying on White generosity, comfort, or acceptance. This arrangement allows for the cultivation of solidarity that does not reinforce asymptotic Whiteness as its end. Rather, it seeks an organic, embodied solidarity between two communities with parallel histories that face a similar struggle against erasure from the city they call home. Su Teatro and The SOURCE welcome all audiences to their theater and share their respective works widely. That they are able to cultivate a space for fostering solidarity between their organizations in the presence of Guadalupe's banner, however, demonstrates the capacity for "lifting up the lowly" to be a multidimensional act of solidarity that dignifies and empowers.

North of Denver, the members of the Goat Hill Society continue their campaign to save Our Lady of Visitation from permanent closure. Currently they are allowed to hold two Masses per year, including one on Christmas Eve that coincides with the parish's founding. In 2018, more than a year after Archbishop Aquila ordered that the church be closed and merged with a larger parish down the road, the parishioners participated in the liturgy of *Las Posadas*, which remembers Mary and Joseph's search for shelter in Bethlehem.[58] Two young people portraying María y José led a group of fifty former Our Lady parishioners through the neighborhood. Two guitar players accompanied them; one wore a trucker hat with an image of Guadalupe embroidered on the front. María y José knocked on doors until, at last, someone let them in. After the procession the church members enjoyed bizcochitos and hot chocolate as they reminisced about their days worshiping together in their little pink church. "It hurts to see this building sit empty," said former church treasurer Fred Torres. "Generations of people devoted their time, their labor and their experience to build this church."[59] Comparing their experience to exile, the Goat Hill Society draws on Latine Catholicism's rich aesthetics to make their case for reclaiming their church. Like Juan Diego, they show up again and again, delivering their plea for justice to their archbishop. Inhabiting his appropriate role in the narrative, Archbishop Aquila views them with suspicion and denies their claim. But the Goat Hill Society believes its story to be true. They march behind Guadalupe's banner as a reminder to the bishop, and to themselves, that God "has brought down the powerful from their thrones, and lifted up the lowly" (Lk 1:52 NRSV).

CONCLUSION

Guadalupe was my grandmother. She was a humble woman without much formal education. Her faith guided her as she raised twelve children amid immense poverty in rural Nebraska. Born somewhere between *aqui y alla*, she lived all sixty-four years of her life largely invisible to those with power in the United States. Her life didn't matter much to those who write the Big Story.

Nevertheless, her life brimmed with little stories. Whether nurturing a child, a friendship, or a garden, she knew how to help things grow. In her habits of magnifying the Lord and lifting up the lowly, she emulated Guadalupe by illuminating God's pervasive beauty and good news to the poor. It was my grandmother's witness to beauty and justice that led to my own fascination with Guadalupe. Beginning with the presentation I made in seventh grade about my family's history and continuing in my academic research in theology and ethics, I have longed to know more about my grandmother's *tocaya* (namesake) and what her symbol means for the church and the world.

One aspiration of this work is to honor my grandmother by simply seeing Guadalupe. A theological, religious, or political aesthetics that cannot see Guadalupe—whether as an image of religious devotion or as a little girl in a cage weeping for her mamá at a migrant detention center—is inadequate for democracy in our century. The twenty-first century demands an aesthetics that can visualize Guadalupe in the multitude of her religious, cultural, and political dimensions.

To see Guadalupe requires new ways of thinking about the relationships between religion, race, culture, and democracy. It requires that we rearrange laws, structures, policies, and cultures so that we can bring Guadalupe into view. When we begin to see Guadalupe, we notice that she is everywhere.

And this recognition helps us make space not only for her but for her people too. And her people include anyone who is the least among us.

> She is everywhere.
> Dangling from my rearview mirror,
> she is a constant companion,
> journeying with me from place to place,
> a reminder to be patient with drivers
> and with my spouse sitting in the passenger seat.

> On a prayer card,
> she is a gift from my *madrina* on the day of my Baptism,
> a reminder that I belong to the Church,
> and that the Church belongs to me.

> On my rosary,
> she is a testament to my Catholic faith
> and my continual identification with México,
> even generations after separation.

> Standing adjacent to the altar,
> carefully observing her Son,
> God's mother reminds me
> to ponder, discern, affirm, and magnify.

> She is everywhere.
> She is my classmate,
> my checkout attendant,
> my tía,
> my nurse.

> Guadalupe is my grandma,
> who exuded grace, devotion, prudence, and fortitude
> as she raised twelve children
> amid unspeakable poverty.

> She is my daughter,
> the one I dream of,
> the one I pray for,
> even before she has been conceived.

She is my *comadre,*
holding me in her arms
while my son grasps my finger in his newborn hand,
clinging to life in the NICU.

She is a strong Brown/Black/Indigenous woman,
bringing hope to the downtrodden,
proclaiming justice to the oppressed.
She is me.

She is everywhere.
She is a community organizer,
walking humbly with the dispossessed,
gathering her people to struggle for justice
under her vibrant banner.

She is a revolutionary,
leading a people to self-determination,
embodying the complexity of *Latinidad*
and giving hope to a nation.

She is a theologian,
she is an artist,
constantly and creatively gesturing to her Son,
inviting us to discipleship in the life-giving Word.

She is a witness
to violence, poverty, corruption.
To conversion, transformation, rebirth.
To goodness, beauty, truth.

She is everywhere.
She is manipulated for the narrow self-interests of many.
She is misappropriated to defend exclusion and condemnation.
She is deployed as a weapon against willful women.
She is leveraged against otherness, distinguishing pure from profane.

She is everywhere.
She is rejected, despised, loathed.
"She distracts from the worship of her Son!"

"What does she have to do with the Gospel?"
She is misunderstood.

And still . . . she is everywhere.
Gas stations. Parking lots. Schoolyards. Street signs.
Bars. Bodies. Gardens. Fountains.
Bus stops. Train stations. Borders. Graves.
Bathrooms. Cathedrals. Monuments. Doors.

She is everywhere.
Pondered by pastors and theologians,
considered by CEOs and window washers.
"Is she Mary of Nazareth?"
"Is she the Holy Spirit?"

"Does she belong to the Church?"
"Does she belong to Mexico?"
"Does she belong to me?"
"Do I belong to her?"
She is everywhere – but what does this mean?

She is everywhere.
Preaching the good news in all places,
proclaiming to us that her Son is alive,
testifying that the Word is made flesh,
telling us of God's breaking into history,
witnessing to all people that God's love is real.

She is everywhere.
Speaking, guiding, prompting, praying.
Advocating, organizing, redefining, reconciling.
Calling, responding, giving, receiving.
Bleeding, healing, crying, rising.

She is everywhere.
Guiding her Son to his people,
Guiding her people to her Son.
Her people are His people.
I am His person.

She is everywhere.
Sitting with me in the silence of her sanctuary.
Speaking tender words of welcome and delight.
Standing next to her Son, inviting me to stand next to her.
Standing with her people, inviting me to stand up with them.

She is everywhere.
Looking at me, she knows my history.
Looking at me, she sees my future.
Looking at her, I know that He lives.
Looking at her, I know that He loves me.

—Written while on pilgrimage to the Basilica of Our Lady of Guadalupe

NOTES

1. Garcia, "Miracle at Tepeyac," 23.
2. USCCB, "Place at the Table," 10.
3. USCCB, 10.
4. Clark, *Vision of Catholic Social Thought*, 41.
5. Hollenbach, *Common Good and Christian Ethics*, 192.
6. Hollenbach, 137–38.
7. Hollenbach, 145.
8. Hollenbach, 144.
9. Hollenbach, 138.
10. Provence, "Lessons Learned?"
11. Thrush and Haberman, "Trump Gives White Supremacists an Unequivocal Boost."
12. Jaycox, "Civic Virtues of Social Anger," 135.
13. Keenan, "Virtues for Civil Society."
14. Keenan, "Virtues for Civil Society."
15. Keenan, "Virtues for Civil Society."
16. Goizueta, *Christ Our Companion*, 46.
17. García-Rivera, *Community of the Beautiful*, 133 (emphasis added).
18. Hollenbach, "Glory of God and the Global Common Good," 59.
19. Hollenbach, 59.
20. Aquinas, *Summa Theologica*, I–II, Q. 94, Art. 2, Resp.
21. Aquinas, I–II Q. 94, Art. 2, Resp.
22. Aquinas, I–II, Q. 94, Art. 4, Resp. (emphasis added).
23. Cahill, *Global Justice, Christology and Christian Ethics*, 265.
24. Isasi-Díaz, *La Lucha Continues*, 29.
25. I am indebted to Seth Wispelwey, a clergy organizer with Congregate Cville, for clarifying the events of those days for me in June 2019 and July 2020.
26. I am indebted to Jalane Schmidt's articulation of an incarnational solidarity during a conversation we had over tacos in the spring of 2019.

27. Hawkins, *Gospel and the Meaning of Embodied Solidarity.*

28. Isasi-Díaz, *La Lucha Continues*, 95.

29. Rubio, *Family Ethics*, 7.

30. Rubio, *Hope for Common Ground*, 159.

31. Rubio, 180.

32. M. Clark, *Vision of Catholic Social Thought*, 127.

33. M. Clark, 142.

34. Dewey, *Art as Experience*, 48–49.

35. O'Connell, *If These Walls Could Talk*, 17.

36. O'Connell, 113.

37. O'Connell, 123.

38. O'Connell, 257.

39. O'Connell, 259.

40. O'Connell, 214.

41. V. Miller, *Consuming Religion*, 76.

42. Cassidy, "Picturing Suffering," 105.

43. Tragically, Carter committed suicide within a few months of winning the Pulitzer Prize, leaving a note describing himself as haunted by the vivid memories of violence he photographed in Sudan. For a discussion of Carter's suicide in relation to the moral implications of photographs of human suffering, see Cassidy, "Picturing Suffering," 113.

44. V. Miller, *Consuming Religion*, 74.

45. V. Miller, 75–76.

46. V. Miller, 75.

47. Flores, "Beyond Consumptive Solidarity."

48. Viladesau, *Theological Aesthetics*, 189: "*Abuses non tollit usum.* The danger of misuse does not vitiate the proper use of art in the service of religion." Similarly, the abuse or falsification of aesthetic experience does not render it meaningless for the pursuit of solidarity.

49. De Gruchy, *Christianity, Art, and Transformation*; Carnes, *Image and Presence.* See DeGruchy's and Carnes's respective monographs for sophisticated discussions on the relationship between iconoclasm and religious art.

50. Pope Francis, *Lumen fidei*, no. 18 (emphasis added).

51. Francis, no. 20.

52. Pope Francis, *Fratelli Tutti*, no. 69.

53. Goizueta, *Caminemos Con Jesús*, 75.

54. Goizueta, *Christ Our Companion*, 46.

55. Garcia, "Miracle at Tepeyac," 22.

56. Gálvez, *Guadalupe in New York*, 16.

57. Gálvez, 173.

58. Slevin, "Members Fight to Re-open Small Denver Catholic Church."

59. Slevin, "Members Fight to Re-open Small Denver Catholic Church."

BIBLIOGRAPHY

Allen, Danielle S. *Talking to Strangers: Anxieties of Citizenship since Brown v. Board of Education.* Chicago: University of Chicago Press, 2004.

Alvarez, Julia. *In the Time of the Butterflies.* Chapel Hill, NC: Algonquin, 1994.

Anderson, Amanda. *Bleak Liberalism.* Chicago: University of Chicago Press, 2016.

Appiah, Kwame Anthony. "What's Wrong with Slavery?" In *Buying Freedom: The Ethics and Economics of Slave Redemption,* edited by Kwame Anthony Appiah and Martin Bunzl, 249–58. Princeton, NJ: Princeton University Press, 2007.

Aquinas, Thomas. *Summa Theologica.* Translated by Fathers of the English Dominican Province. Allen, TX: Christian Classics, 1991.

Aquino, Jorge A. "The Prophetic Horizon of Latino Theology." In *Rethinking Latino(a) Religion and Identity,* edited by Miguel A. De La Torre and Gastón Espinosa, 101–25. Cleveland, OH: Pilgrim, 2006.

Araiza, Lauren. *To March for Others: The Black Freedom Struggle and the United Farm Workers.* Philadelphia: University of Pennsylvania Press, 2014.

Arellano, Jeronimo. *Magical Realism and the History of Emotions in Latin America.* Lanham, MD: Bucknell University Press, 2015.

Ashton, John. "Chicano Opposition to Crusade Is Growing." *Rocky Mountain News,* October 16, 1977. Denver Public Library Western History Collection.

Auraria Higher Education Center website. https://www.ahec.edu, accessed July 5, 2019.

"Barack Obama's Speech on Race." *New York Times,* March 18, 2008. https://www.nytimes.com/2008/03/18/us/politics/18text-obama.html.

Benhabib, Seyla. *Another Cosmopolitanism.* Oxford, UK: Oxford University Press, 2006.

Bretherton, Luke. *Resurrecting Democracy: Faith, Citizenship, and the Politics of a Common Life.* Cambridge, UK: Cambridge University Press, 2015.

Brown, Frank Burch. *Religious Aesthetics: A Theological Study of Making and Meaning.* Princeton, NJ: Princeton University Press, 1989.

Cahill, Lisa Sowle. *Global Justice, Christology and Christian Ethics.* New York: Cambridge University Press, 2013.

———. "Justice for Women: Martha Nussbaum and Catholic Social Teaching." In *Transforming Unjust Structures: The Capability Approach,* edited by Severine Deneulin, Mathias Nebel, and Nicholas Sagovsky, 83–104. Dordrecht, The Netherlands: Springer, 2006.

———. *Theological Bioethics: Participation, Justice, and Change.* Washington, DC: Georgetown University Press, 2005.

Campbell, Ana. "Catholic Church Shutters Beloved Hispanic Parish in North Denver." *Westword,* February 6, 2018. https://www.westword.com/news/archdiocese-of-denver-shutters-our-lady-of-visitation-hispanic-parish-in-north-denver-9957380.

Carnes, Natalie. *Image and Presence: A Christological Reflection on Iconoclasm and Iconophilia.* Stanford, CA: Stanford University Press, 2018.

Carter, J. Kameron. *Race: A Theological Account*. Oxford: Oxford University Press, 2008.

Cassidy, Laurie. "Picturing Suffering: The Moral Dilemmas in Gazing at Photographs of Human Anguish." In *She Who Imagines: Feminist Theological Aesthetics*, edited by Laurie Cassidy and Maureen H. O'Connell, 103–23. Collegeville, MN: Liturgical Press, 2012.

Castañeda-Liles, María Del Socorro. *Our Lady of Everyday Life: La Virgen de Guadalupe and the Catholic Imagination of Mexican Women in America*. New York: Oxford University Press, 2018.

Cavanaugh, William T. *The Myth of Religious Violence: Secular Ideology and the Roots of Modern Conflict*. Oxford: Oxford University Press, 2009.

———. *Torture and Eucharist: Theology, Politics, and the Body of Christ. Challenges in Contemporary Theology*. Oxford: Blackwell, 1998.

Charlesworth, Hilary. "Martha Nussbaum's Feminist Internationalism." *Ethics* 111, no. 1 (2000): 64–78.

Charusheela, S. "Social Analysis and the Capabilities Approach: A Limit to Martha Nussbaum's Universalist Ethics." *Cambridge Journal of Economics* 2009, no. 33 (September 8, 2008): 1135–52. https://doi.org/10.1093/cje/ben027.

Clark, Eric. "The Order and Simplicity of Gentrification—A Political Challenge." In *The Gentrification Reader*, edited by Loretta Lees, Tom Slater, and Elvin Wyly, 24–29. London: Routledge, 2010.

Clark, Meghan J. *The Vision of Catholic Social Thought: The Virtue of Solidarity and the Praxis of Human Rights*. Minneapolis, MN: Fortress, 2014.

Coakley, Sarah. *God, Sexuality, and the Self: An Essay "On the Trinity."* Cambridge: Cambridge University Press, 2013.

Coday, Dennis. "Denver Catholics Fight to Restore Guadalupe Mural." *National Catholic Reporter*, October 14, 2010. https://www.ncronline.org/news/parish/denver-catholics-fight-restore -guadalupe-mural.

De Gruchy, John W. *Christianity, Art, and Transformation: Theological Aesthetics in the Struggle for Justice*. Cambridge: Cambridge University Press, 2001.

Derrida, Jacques. "Signature, Event, Context [1971]." In *Limited Inc*. Evanston, IL: Northwestern University Press, 1988.

Dewey, John. *Art as Experience*. New York: Perigee, 2005.

Dickens, Charles. *Hard Times: For These Times*. London: Bradbury & Evans, 1854.

Dillard, Sandra. "Police Search Denver Church." *Denver Post*, March 24, 1976. Denver Public Library Western History Collection.

Draper, Electa. "Faithful Again Demand Lady of Guadalupe Mural Be Uncovered." *Denver Post*, November 23, 2010. https://www.denverpost.com/2010/11/23/faithful-again-demand -lady-of-guadalupe-mural-be-uncovered/.

Dupré, Judith. "The Virgin Mary Becomes Pop Symbol." *Daily Beast*, December 11, 2014. http://www.thedailybeast.com/articles/2010/12/11/lady-of-guadalupe-virgin-marys -new-symbolism-for-gangs-and-commerce.html.

Elizondo, Virgilio. *Galilean Journey: The Mexican-American Promise*. Maryknoll, NY: Orbis, 1983.

Espín, Orlando O. "The State of U.S. Latino/a Theology." In *Hispanic Christian Thought at the Dawn of the Twenty-First Century: Apuntes in Honor of Justo L. Gonzalez*, edited by Alvin Padilla, Roberto S. Goizueta, and Eldin Villafane, 98–116. Nashville, TN: Abingdon, 2005.

Farley, Margaret A. *Just Love: A Framework for Christian Sexual Ethics*. New York: Continuum, 2006.

Flores, Nichole M. "Beyond Consumptive Solidarity: An Aesthetic Response to Human Trafficking." *Journal of Religious Ethics* 46, no. 2 (June 2018): 360–77.

———. "The Heart of the Neighborhood: Why Dioceses Need to Support Struggling Latino Parishes." *America: The Jesuit Review of Faith and Culture*, December 24, 2018.

———. "In Jefferson's Shadow: Can Catholic Theology Thrive at a Public University?" *America: The Jesuit Review of Faith and Culture*, May 29, 2017.

———. "Latina/o Families: Solidarity and the Common God." *Journal of the Society of Christian Ethics* 33, no. 2 (2013): 57–72.

———. "The Psalmist's Lament: What Does It Mean to Be 'Home' in a World without Roots and Relationships?" *America: The Jesuit Review of Faith and Culture*, January 20, 2020.

———. "Trinity and Justice: A Theological Response to the Sexual Assault of Migrant Women." *Journal of Religion and Society* 20, no. 1 (2018): 39–51.

Flores, Nichole M., and Charles T. Mathewes. "The First Citizen: Modesty Is Required for a President to Become a Moral Leader." *First Year 2017*, 2017. http://firstyear2017.org/essay/the-first-citizen.html.

Gadamer, Hans Georg. *Truth and Method*. Translated by Joel Weinsheimer and Donald G. Marshall. Rev. 2nd ed. New York: Bloomsbury Academic, 2013.

Gallegos, Magdalena, ed. *Auraria Remembered*. Denver, CO: Community College of Denver, 1991.

Galston, William. "Driven Up the Rawls." *New Republic*, April 7, 2009. https://newrepublic.com/article/64636/driven-the-rawls.

Gálvez, Alyshia. *Guadalupe in New York: Devotion and the Struggle for Citizenship Rights among Mexican Immigrants*. New York: New York University Press, 2010.

Garcia, Anthony J. "From Su Teatro Executive Artistic Director—Tony Garcia." Playbill, December 7, 2017.

———. "The Miracle at Tepeyac." 1995. Denver Public Library Western History Collection.

García-Rivera, Alejandro. *The Community of the Beautiful: A Theological Aesthetics*. Collegeville, MN: Liturgical Press, 1999.

———. *St. Martín de Porres: The "Little Stories" and the Semiotics of Culture*. Maryknoll, NY: Orbis, 1995.

Gebara, Ivone. *Out of the Depths: Women's Experience of Evil and Salvation*. Minneapolis, MN: Fortress, 2002.

Goizueta, Roberto S. *Caminemos Con Jesús: Toward a Hispanic/Latino Theology of Accompaniment*. Maryknoll, NY: Orbis, 1995.

———. *Christ Our Companion: Toward a Theological Aesthetics of Liberation*. Maryknoll, NY: Orbis, 2009.

González, Michelle. "Who We Are: A Latino/a Constructive Anthropology." In *In Our Own Voices: Latino/a Renditions of Theology*, edited by Benjamin Valentín, 64–84. Maryknoll, NY: Orbis, 2010.

González-Andrieu, Cecilia. *Bridge to Wonder: Art as a Gospel of Beauty*. Waco, TX: Baylor University Press, 2012.

———. "Our Lady's Final Appearance: The Legacy of 'La Virgen Del Tepeyac' at St. Juan Bautista Mission." *America: The Jesuit Review of Faith and Culture*, December 9, 2019.

Gregory, Eric. *Politics and the Order of Love: An Augustinian Ethic of Democratic Citizenship*. Chicago: University of Chicago Press, 2008.

Griego, Tina. "Church Wall Hiding Our Lady of Guadalupe Mural Brings Protest." *Denver Post*, July 2, 2010. https://www.denverpost.com/2010/07/02/griego-church-wall-hiding-our-lady-of-guadalupe-mural-brings-protest/.

Gutierrez, Sonia. "Denver's Latino Population Now Proportionally Represented on City Council." Emerge Colorado, June 6, 2019. https://co.emergeamerica.org/denvers-latino

-population-now-proportionally-represented-on-city-council/?fbclid=IwAR2eWAyAtRk M5CWnJhITBaynNNbR2YW8q7qOdXwPfUlMkzlBnH84eF-EKOQ.

Hanisch, Carol. "The Personal Is Political." Carolhanisch.org, http://www.carolhanisch.org /CHwritings/PIP.html.

Harris, Fredrick C. *Something Within: Religion in African-American Political Activism*. New York: Oxford University Press, 1999.

Hawkins, Larycia. *The Gospel and the Meaning of Embodied Solidarity*. TEDxWilmingtonSalon, Wilmington, Delaware, 2016. https://www.youtube.com/watch?time_continue=14&v= qn3lsZhWGy8&feature=emb_title.

Heyer, Kristin E. *Kinship across Borders: A Christian Ethic of Immigration*. Washington, DC: Georgetown University Press, 2012.

Hilkert, Mary Catherine. "Cry Beloved Image." In *The Embrace of God: Feminist Approaches to Theological Anthropology*, edited by Ann O'Hara Graff, 190–205. Maryknoll, NY: Orbis, 1995.

Hill, Jim, and Andrew Kenney. "Polis Announces Emergency Economic Advisory Council to Shepherd Colorado's Post-Coronavirus Recovery." Colorado Public Radio, March 20, 2020. https://www.cpr.org/2020/03/20/polis-announces-emergency-economic-advisory -council-to-shepherd-colorados-post-coronavirus-recovery/.

Hoffman, Shannon M. "Demonstrators Protest Ink! Coffee Sign Celebrating Gentrification." *Denver Post*, November 25, 2017. https://www.denverpost.com/2017/11/25/ink-coffee -gentrification-protest/.

Hogan, Linda. *Keeping Faith with Human Rights*. Washington, DC: Georgetown University Press, 2015.

Hollenbach, David. *The Common Good and Christian Ethics*. Cambridge: Cambridge University Press, 2002.

————. "The Glory of God and the Global Common Good: Solidarity in a Turbulent World." *CTSA Proceedings* 72 (2017): 51–60.

Hordern, Joshua. *Political Affections: Civic Participation and Moral Theology*. Oxford: Oxford University Press, 2013.

Isasi-Díaz, Ada María. *En La Lucha: Elaborating a Mujerista Theology*. Minneapolis, MN: Fortress, 2004.

————. *La Lucha Continues: Mujerista Theology*. Maryknoll, NY: Orbis, 2004.

————. "Mujerista Narratives: Creating a New Heaven and a New Earth." In *Liberating Eschatology: Essays in Honor of Letty M. Russell*, edited by Margaret A. Farley and Serene Jones, 227–43. Louisville, KY: Westminster John Knox, 1999.

Jaycox, Michael P. "The Civic Virtues of Social Anger: A Critically Reconstructed Normative Ethic for Public Life." *Journal of Society of Christian Ethics* 36, no. 1 (Spring/Summer 2016): 123–43.

Johnson, Richard S. "He Walks the Path of Christ." *Empire Magazine: Sunday Magazine of the Denver Post*, March 30, 1975. Denver Public Library Western History Collection.

Kao, Grace Y. *Grounding Human Rights in a Pluralist World*. Washington, DC: Georgetown University Press, 2011.

Kaveny, Cathleen. *Prophecy without Contempt: Religious Discourse in the Public Square*. Cambridge, MA: Harvard University Press, 2016.

Keenan, James F. "Virtues for Civil Society: Civility." *Commonweal*, June 26, 2016. https:// www.commonwealmagazine.org/virtues-civil-society-civility.

Kennedy, Lisa. "Denver Production 'Gospel at Colonus' Signals a Joyous Collaboration between Su Teatro and Source Theater Company." *Denver Post*, June 12, 2013. https://www.denverpost.com/2013/06/12/denver-production-gospel-at-colonus-signals-a -joyous-collaboration-between-su-teatro-and-source-theatre-company/.

Krieger, Dave. "Tooley and Pena's Goals for City Similar." *Rocky Mountain News*, June 13, 1983. Denver Public Library Western History Collection.

Kurlansky, Mark. *Ready for a Brand New Beat: How "Dancing in the Street" Became the Anthem for a Changing America*. New York: Riverhead, 2013.

Laborde, Cécile. *Liberalism's Religion*. Cambridge, MA: Harvard University Press, 2017.

LaCugna, Catherine Mowry. *God for Us: The Trinity in Christian Life*. New York: Harper-Collins, 1991.

Laso de la Vega, Luis. *The Story of Guadalupe: Luis Laso de La Vega's Hue tlamahuiçoltica of 1649*. Edited and translated by Lisa Sousa, Stafford M. Poole CM, and James Lockhart. Stanford, CA: Stanford University Press and UCLA Latin American Center Publications, University of California, Los Angeles, 1998.

León, Luís D. "César Chávez and Mexican American Civil Religion." In *Latino Religions and Civic Activism in the United States*, edited by Gastón Espinosa, Virgilio Elizondo, and Jesse Miranda, 53–64. New York: Oxford University Press, 2005.

Lepore, Jill. *These Truths: A History of the United States*. New York: W. W. Norton, 2019.

Levin, Sam. "Dick Morris Says Obama Won't Win Because His Supporters Aren't Going to Vote." *Westword*, September 12, 2012. https://www.westword.com/news/dick-morris -says-obama-wont-win-because-his-supporters-arent-going-to-vote-5853225.

Lipsky, Sherry, Raul Caetano, Craig A. Field, and Gregory L. Larkin. "The Role of Intimate Partner Violence, Race, and Ethnicity in Help-Seeking Behaviors." *Ethnicity and Health* 11, no. 1 (2006): 81–100.

Lloyd, Vincent, and David True. "What Political Theology Could Be." *Political Theology* 17, no. 6 (November 2016): 505–6.

Lugo, Luis. *Latinos and the 2012 Elections*. Interview by Erik Owens and Nichole Flores, November 1, 2012. http://www.bc.edu/content/dam/files/centers/boisi/pdf/f12/73%20Lugo %20Interview.pdf.

Marsh, Charles, Peter Slade, and Sarah Azaransky, eds. *Lived Theology: New Perspectives on Method, Style, and Pedagogy*. New York: Oxford University Press, 2017.

Massingale, Bryan N. "The Assumptions of White Privilege and What We Can Do about It." *National Catholic Reporter*, June 1, 2020. https://www.ncronline.org/news/opinion /assumptions-white-privilege-and-what-we-can-do-about-it.

———. "The Systematic Erasure of the Black/Dark-Skinned Body in Catholic Ethics." In *Catholic Theological Ethics, Past, Present, and Future: The Trento Conference*, edited by James F. Keenan, 116–24. Maryknoll, NY: Orbis, 2011.

———. "Vox Victimarum Dei: Malcolm X as Neglected 'Classic' for Catholic Theological Reflection." *CTSA Proceedings* 65 (2010): 63–88.

Mathewes, Charles T. *A Theology of Public Life*. Cambridge: Cambridge University Press, 2007.

Matovina, Timothy. *Theologies of Guadalupe: From the Era of Conquest to Pope Francis*. New York: Oxford University Press, 2019.

———. "Theologies of Guadalupe: From the Spanish Colonial Era to Pope John Paul II." *Theological Studies* 70, no. 1 (2009): 61–91.

Medina, Néstor. *Mestizaje: (Re)Mapping Race, Culture, and Faith in Latina/o Catholicism.* Maryknoll, NY: Orbis, 2009.

"A Mile High: Denver Buys Peña's Dream." *Time Magazine,* July 4, 1983. Denver Public Library Western History Collection.

Miller, Richard B. *Friends and Other Strangers: Studies in Religion, Ethics, and Culture.* New York: Columbia University Press, 2016.

Miller, Vincent J. *Consuming Religion: Christian Faith and Practice in a Consumer Religion.* London: Continuum, 2005.

Nagel, Thomas. *A Brief Inquiry into the Meaning of Sin and Faith: With "On My Religion."* Cambridge, MA: Harvard University Press, 2009.

Nanko-Fernandez, Carmen. *Theologizing in Espanglish: Context, Community, and Ministry.* Maryknoll, NY: Orbis, 2010.

Nash, Phil. "A Pena for Your Thoughts." *Westword,* April 21, 1983. Denver Public Library Western History Collection.

NRSV. New Revised Standard Version Bible.

Nussbaum, Martha C. *Anger and Forgiveness: Resentment, Generosity, Justice.* New York: Oxford University Press, 2016.

———. *Creating Capabilities: The Human Development Approach.* Cambridge, MA: Belknap, 2011.

———. *Frontiers of Justice: Disability, Nationality, Species Membership.* Cambridge, MA: Belknap, 2006.

———. *Poetic Justice: The Literary Imagination and Public Life.* Boston: Beacon, 2007.

———. *Political Emotions: Why Love Matters for Justice.* Cambridge, MA: Belknap, 2013.

———. *Upheavals of Thought: The Intelligence of Emotions.* New York: Cambridge University Press, 2001.

Nzegwu, Nkiru. "Recovering Igbo Traditions: A Case for Indigenous Women's Organizations in Development." In *Women, Culture, and Development,* edited by Martha C. Nussbaum and Jonathan Glover, 444–66. Oxford: Clarendon, 1995.

Obama, Barack H. "Remarks by the President in Eulogy for the Honorable Reverend Clementa Pinckney." White House, June 26, 2015. https://obamawhitehouse.archives.gov/the-press-office/2015/06/26/remarks-president-eulogy-honorable-reverend-clementa-pinckney.

O'Connell, Maureen H. *If These Walls Could Talk: Community Muralism and the Beauty of Justice.* Collegeville, MN: Liturgical Press, 2012.

Okey, Stephen. *A Theology of Conversation: An Introduction to David Tracy.* Collegeville, MN: Liturgical Press, 2018.

Peña, Federico. "Campaign poster." 1987. Denver Public Library Western History Collection, Peña Papers.

———. "Fundraiser Invitation." June 17, 1983. Denver Public Library Western History Collection, Peña Papers.

———. "Mile-High Achievements: Federico Peña Looks Back on Eight Years as Mayor of Denver" campaign poster. May 5, 1991. Denver Public Library Western History Collection, Peña Papers.

Pettegree, Andrew. *Brand Luther: 1517, Printing, and the Making of the Reformation.* New York: Penguin, 2016.

Phillips, Noelle. "Anti-Gentrification Activists Call on Politicians, Developers to Integrate Denver Neighborhoods Rather than Remake Them." *Denver Post,* January 13, 2018. https://

www.denverpost.com/2018/01/13/anti-gentrification-activists-call-on-politicians
-developers-to-integrate-neighborhoods-rather-than-remake-them/.

Pineda-Madrid, Nancy. Suffering and Salvation in Ciudad Juarez. Minneapolis, MN: Fortress, 2011.

"Poll: Many Say Tooley Tactics Backfired." *Rocky Mountain News*, June 22, 1983. Denver Public Library Western History Collection.

Poole, Stafford. *Our Lady of Guadalupe: The Origins and Sources of a Mexican National Symbol, 1531–1797.* Tucson, AZ: University of Arizona Press, 1995.

Pope Francis. *Fratelli Tutti*, 2020. http://www.vatican.va/content/francesco/en/encyclicals /documents/papa-francesco_20201003_enciclica-fratelli-tutti.html.

———. "Holy Mass at the Basilica of Our Lady of Guadalupe: Homily of His Holiness Pope Francis." February 13, 2016. http://www.vatican.va/content/francesco/en/homilies/2016 /documents/papa-francesco_20160213_omelia-messico-guadalupe.html.

———. *Laudato Si'*, 2015. http://w2.vatican.va/content/francesco/en/encyclicals/documents /papa-francesco_20150524_enciclica-laudato-si.html.

———. "Lumen Fidei," 2013. http://w2.vatican.va/content/francesco/en/encyclicals /documents/papa-francesco_20130629_enciclica-lumen-fidei.html.

Prince, Rob. "Goat Hill and Our Lady of Visitation Parish, Part Two: Remarks of Federico Pena—Former Denver Mayor at a Press Conference at Our Lady of Visitation Parish (Actually Outside of the Parish), Protesting the Archdiocese of Denver's Decision to Close the Parish." *View from the Left Bank: Rob Prince's Blog*, April 27, 2017. https:// robertjprince.net/2017/04/27/goat-hill-and-our-lady-of-visitation-parish-part-two -remarks-of-federico-pena-former-denver-mayor-at-a-press-conference-at-our-lady-of -visitation-parish-actually-outside-of-the-parish-protestin/.

Provence, Lisa. "Lessons Learned? Former Mayor Publishes His Take on Charlottesville's Darkest Days." *C-Ville Weekly*, March 11, 2020. https://www.c-ville.com/lessons-learned -former-mayor-publishes-his-take-on-charlottesvilles-darkest-days/.

Purcell, L. Sebastian. "Eudaimonia and Neltiliztli: Aristotle and the Aztecs on the Good Life." *Hispanic/Latino Issues in Philosophy* 16, no. 2 (2017): 10–21.

Quinn, Philip L. "Political Liberalisms and Their Exclusions of the Religious." *Proceedings and Addresses of the American Philosophical Association* 69, no. 2 (1995): 35–56.

Rawls, John. "On My Religion." In Nagel, *A Brief Inquiry into the Meaning of Sin and Faith: With "On My Religion."*

———. *Political Liberalism*. New York: Columbia University Press, 1993.

———. *A Theory of Justice*. Cambridge, MA: Belknap, 1971.

Rodriguez, Jeanette. *Our Lady of Guadalupe: Faith and Empowerment among Mexican-American Women*. Austin: University of Texas Press, 1994.

Rodríguez, Rubén Rosario. *Christian Martyrdom and Political Violence: A Comparative Theology with Judaism and Islam*. Cambridge: Cambridge University Press, 2017.

Rubio, Julie Hanlon. *Family Ethics: Practices for Christians*. Washington, DC: Georgetown University Press, 2010.

———. *Hope for Common Ground: Mediating the Personal and the Political in a Divided Church*. Washington, DC: Georgetown University Press, 2016.

Ruston, Roger. *Human Rights and the Image of God*. London: SCM, 2004.

Sánchez, David A. *From Patmos to the Barrio: Subverting Imperial Myths*. Minneapolis, MN: Fortress, 2008.

Schmidt, Jalane D. *Cachita's Streets: The Virgin of Charity, Race, and Revolution in Cuba*. Durham, NC: Duke University Press, 2015.

Siller Acuña, Clodomiro L. *Para Comprender El Mensaje de María de Guadalupe*. Buenos Aires: Editorial Guadalupe, 1987.

Singer, Daliah. "Su Teatro's New Play Recalls the Rise of Colorado's Chicano Movement." 5280.com, March 11, 2019. https://www.5280.com/2019/03/su-teatro-recalls-the-rise-of-colorados-chicano-movement-in-new-play/.

Slevin, Colleen. "Members Fight to Re-open Small Denver Catholic Church." *Denver Post*, December 25, 2018. https://www.denverpost.com/2018/12/25/denver-our-lady-of-visitation-church-reopening-christmas-vigil/.

Smith, John E. *Royce's Social Infinite: The Community of Interpretation*. New York: Liberal Arts Press, 1950.

Smith, Suzanne E. *Dancing in the Street: Motown and the Cultural Politics of Detroit*. Cambridge, MA: Harvard University Press, 1999.

Sobrino, Jon. *Christ the Liberator: A View from the Victims*. Translated by Paul Burns. Maryknoll, NY: Orbis, 2001.

Stout, Jeffrey. *Democracy and Tradition*. Princeton, NJ: Princeton University Press, 2004.

Su Teatro. "History." SuTeatro.org. Accessed July 1, 2019. http://suteatro.org/history.

Thrush, Glenn, and Maggie Haberman. "Trump Gives White Supremacists an Unequivocal Boost." *New York Times*, August 15, 2017. https://www.nytimes.com/2017/08/15/us/politics/trump-charlottesville-white-nationalists.html.

Tirres, Christopher D. *The Aesthetics and Ethics of Faith: A Dialogue between Liberationist and Pragmatic Thought*. New York: Oxford University Press, 2014.

Tjaden, Patricia, and Nancy Thoennes. "Extent, Nature, and Consequences of Intimate Partner Violence: Findings from the National Violence Against Women Survey." US Department of Justice, 2000. https://www.ncjrs.gov/pdffiles1/nij/181867.pdf.

Townes, Emilie M. *Womanist Ethics and the Cultural Production of Evil*. New York: Palgrave MacMillan, 2006.

Tracy, David. *The Analogical Imagination: Christian Theology and the Culture of Pluralism*. New York: Crossroad, 1981.

United States Conference of Catholic Bishops (USCCB). "A Place at the Table: A Catholic Recommitment to Overcome Poverty and to Respect the Dignity of All God's Children," November 13, 2002. https://www.usccb.org/resources/place-table.

University of Virginia. UVA Arts and Sciences. "General Education: The Engagements." https://gened.as.virginia.edu/engagements.

Valentín, Benjamin. *Mapping Public Theology: Beyond Culture, Identity, and Difference*. Harrisburg, PA: Trinity International, 2002.

Viladesau, Richard. *Theological Aesthetics: God in Imagination, Beauty, and Art*. Oxford: Oxford University Press, 2013.

Walker, Jimmy. "The Five Points/Wrapped Around My Soul" by The SOURCE Theater Company, Denver, Colorado, May 29, 2015.

Williams, Delores S. *Sisters in the Wilderness: The Challenge of Womanist God-Talk*. Maryknoll, NY: Orbis, 1993.

Wolfe, Alan. *The Future of Liberalism*. New York: Vintage, 2010.

Young, Iris Marion. *Justice and the Politics of Difference*. Princeton, NJ: Princeton University Press, 1990.

INDEX

liberal democracy/political liberalism, 3, 8,
44, 61, 66, 70, 87, 93–94, 119
liberation theology, 23–25, 32, 68, 111
Lincoln, Abraham, 88
literature, 14, 53, 77–79, 84, 92–96
little stories, 5–8, 51, 71, 139, 146
lo cotidiano, 9, 12, 93, 132–34
Lugo, Luis, 3
Luther, Martin, 61
lynching, 127, 139–43

Magnificat, 26–27, 34, 42, 106
marginalization/marginalized: assimilation
and, 98; community of the beautiful
and, 113–14; democratic participation
and, 14, 37, 89, 113–14; in Denver, 4–9;
family and, 108–9; Federico Peña campaign and 70; foregrounding and, 68;
identity and, 16; immigrant community
and, 28; justice and, 14, 77, 113–14;
liberal aesthetics and, 77; mestizaje and,
31–32; Miracle at Tepeyac play and, 1;
mothers and, 28; religion and, 64; throwaway culture and, 4–5
Marquez, Gabriel García, 95
marriage, 108
Martin, Eric, 13
Martin, Trayvon, 89
martyrdom/martyrs, 63–64, 98
Massingale, Bryan, 5
Matovina, Timothy, 24–26
McLaren, Brian, 133
McNichols, Bill, 51
Medina, Néstor, 111–12, 118–19
mestizaje, 31–32, 104, 111–12
Mexico City, Mexico, 1, 21, 23, 30, 59, 139
Miller, Vincent, 137–38
Miracle at Tepeyac (play): Archdiocese
conflict with, 19–22; Denver community
and, 1–2, 7, 75–76; description of, 1–2,
37–42, 75–76; family relations and, 108;
Juan Diego interpretation and, 144;
little stories and, 7; political emotions
of, 75–76, 88, 95; political theology and,
37–42; solidarity and, 124; Su Teatro
performance of, 19–22
Moby, 138

Morris, Dick, 51–52
Mother Emanuel AME Church (Charleston,
SC), 88
music, 10, 52, 92–97, 103–6, 119–20, 138

NAFTA (North American Free Trade
Agreement), 29
Nahuatl (language), 1, 22–23
Nanko-Fernández, Carmen, 15
Nash, Phil, 52
natural law, 131–32
Nebraska, 146
New York City, New York, 7, 24, 30, 59, 144
Nican Mopahua (text), 23, 32–33, 36
North American Free Trade Agreement
(NAFTA), 29
Northside neighborhood (Denver, Colo-
rado), 39–42, 48, 70
Nussbaum, Martha: Amanda Anderson
and, 53; as bleak liberal, 53; García-
Rivera and, 119; liberal aesthetics of,
10, 14, 72, 75–99; marginalized groups
and, 114; political emotions and, 75–99;
political stability and, 14, 75–99; Rawls
and, 10, 43
Nzegwu, Nkiru, 80–81

Obama, Barack, 47, 49, 52, 88
obverse collection (o-collection), 106, 116
O'Connell, Maureen H., 135–36
opera, 14, 95
oral tradition, 24
ordination, 60, 108
Our Lady of Guadalupe (Nuestra Señora):
Ciudad Juárez and, 110; Federico Peña
and, 48, 72; John Rawls and, 51, 59; in
Latine theological aesthetics, 106–7,
117–18; in Latine theology, 12; liberal
political philosophy and, 8–10; mestizaje
and, 111–12; in Miracle at Tepeyac, 1,
3, 7, 76, 95, 103, 120, 123, 144–45;
political theology of, 13, 15, 19–44,
124; solidarity and, 129, 140, 142–43,
144–50
Our Lady of Guadalupe Catholic Church
(Denver, Colorado), 13, 19–21, 39, 47,
70–71

St. Elizabeth of Hungary Catholic Church
(Denver, Colorado), 2
St. Martín de Porres, 5–6
Stout, Jeffrey, 58–59
Sudan National Helping Babies Breath
Initiative, 135
Su Teatro (Denver, Colorado): in Chicanx
community, 1–2, 7, 19–21, 40, 75–76,
103–6, 145; community of the beautiful
and, 118–21; historical account of, 13,
19–21; little stories and, 7; performance
of *Miracle at Tepeyac*, 1–2, 19–21, 40,
75–76; protest and, 75–76; solidarity and, 118–21; source for political
theology, 38; The SOURCE relationship
with, 103–6, 118–21

Tanco, Luis Becerra, 23
teologia en conjunto, 12–13
Teresa (fictional character), 37–38, 41,
75–76, 123, 144
The Five Points/Wrapped Around My Soul
(play), 13, 103–20
theological aesthetics, 3, 11, 14, 103–21, 130
The SOURCE theater company (Denver,
Colorado), 13, 103–6, 118–20, 145
Thomas Aquinas, 81, 131–32
throwaway culture, 4–5
tilma, 21–22, 32
Tirres, Christopher, 9–10
Tonatzin (Aztec goddess), 1
Tooley, Dale, 51–52
Torres, Fred, 146
Townes, Emilie, 51, 67–70, 90
Tracy, David, 21
Trump, Donald, 41, 126–28
Tubman, Harriet, 96

UFW (United Farm Workers), 6, 20,
23–24, 39, 59
United Farm Workers (UFW), 6, 20,
23–24, 39, 59
United States Conference of Catholic
Bishops (USCCB), 124
United States presidency, 88
Unite the Right Rally (Charlottesville,
Virginia), 11, 127, 133, 137

University of Colorado, Denver, 1–3
University of Virginia, 11, 55, 127
USCCB (United States Conference of
Catholic Bishops), 124
US-Mexico border, 30, 110, 144
utilitarianism, 84–85

Vatican, 72
Vigil, Don, 2
Virgin Mary, 27, 34
Virgin of Charity, 27

Walker, Jimmy, 103, 119
war on terror, 64
wars of religion, 61–62
Webb, Wellington E., 48
West, Cornel, 133
Westside neighborhood (Denver,
Colorado): Black community and, 116; in
Chicanx community, 5–8, 41, 75; gentrification in, 2; little stories and, 5–8; setting
for *Five Points* play, 118–20; setting for
Miracle at Tepeyac play, 41, 75; solidarity
with, 145
White Americans, 3–4, 7–8, 50–52, 60, 66,
89–90, 104, 109, 129, 135, 140
whiteness, 66, 104–6, 143, 146
white supremacy: aesthetics of, 137;
Charleston massacre and, 88; in
Charlottesville, 11–12, 127, 133, 137;
civility and, 127; incarnational solidarity
against, 133; oppression in Denver,
70; racial injustice and, 88, 137; role of
president and, 88; Unite the Right Rally
and, 11–12, 127, 133, 137; US political
culture and, 91, 99, 127; violence and,
11–12, 105, 133
Williams, Delores, 110
Wispelwey, Seth, 13
Wolfe, Allan, 52–53
Wright, Jeremiah, 49

Young, Iris Marion, 51, 65–68

Zimmerman, George, 89
Zumárraga, Bishop Juan de, 22, 33–34, 37,
41, 142–43

ABOUT THE AUTHOR

NICHOLE M. FLORES is an assistant professor of religious studies at the University of Virginia. She has authored essays in several prominent scholarly journals, including the *Journal of Religious Ethics*, the *Journal of the Society of Christian Ethics*, and *Modern Theology*. She is a contributing writer for *America* magazine. She has received grants from UVA's Institute for Humanities and Global Cultures and the Yale Center for Faith and Culture. She was the 2015 recipient of the Catherine Mowry LaCugna Award for best essay in academic theology by a junior scholar from the Catholic Theological Society of America. She earned a bachelor of arts from Smith College, master of divinity from Yale Divinity School, and doctorate in theological ethics from Boston College. Originally from Denver, Colorado, she now resides just outside of Charlottesville, Virginia, with her spouse and child.

Printed in the USA
CPSIA information can be obtained
at www.ICGtesting.com
JSHW081711261023
50893JS00011B/139

9 781647 120917